Praise for
Get a Great Job When You Do...

"Marky Stein's book is wonderful. She gives us a thorough analysis of the whole interviewing process . . . clear, kind, and full of good advice. . . Highly recommended."

ON LINE

—Barbara Sher, bestselling author,
Live the Life That You Love,
www.barbarasher.com

"Marky ...   d guide
to succ...   niques
that, if ...   etitors.
Her ex...   ary can
contain...

                                                             irector,
                                                             etwork;
                                                             Testing

". . . is...   nk you,
Marky, ...

                                                             eviewer,
                                                             Journal

"Mark...   the eye
of an ...   n inge-
nious ...   niquely
custor...   ner for
the se...

                                                             thor of
                                                             Guide:
                                                             System
                                                             b Now,
                                                             h.com

"Marky Stein shows readers how to develop their 'power proposition' and then weave that into a clear and winning résumé. Her down-to-earth approach, along with numerous tips and examples, turns the process of résumé writing into a confidence building experience, leading to the creation of the ultimate, 'fearless' résumé. Readers will find this book to be of real value in innumerable practical and motivational ways."

—Mark Guterman, principal,
MeaningfulCareers.com and author,
Common Sense for Uncommon Times

"Marky Stein's book is ALL about sales. How to hit the employers' 'hot buttons' and get their attention right off the bat, how to keep them 'hooked' all through the résumé and how to dramatically increase the probability of 'closing' with an invitation to an interview. She's definitely got the strategy job seekers need today to win the important meetings and coveted job offers they desire."

—Mitchell Goozé, CSP,
Customer Manufacturing Group, Inc.,
author of *Value Acceleration: Secrets To Building
An Unbeatable Competitive Advantage*

". . . promises to be the performance of your lifetime!"

—Sharon K. Thorpe, associate
director, Career Center, University
of North Carolina at Charlotte

"A great resources for all students and alumni. A viable tool in assessing interests, skills, and values."

—Veda Swift Jeffries, assistant
director Career Development Center,
Stanford University

". . . a clear workbook for a happier career. It might help you to find a better career, a rewarding job, and a fuller life."

—Lyle Troxell, host of Greek Speak,
KUSP Radio, an NPR Station,
http://greekspeak.org/

Get a Great Job When You Don't Have a Job

Get a Great Job When You Don't Have a Job

MARKY STEIN

New York   Chicago   San Francisco   Lisbon
London   Madrid   Mexico City   Milan   New Delhi
San Juan   Seoul   Singapore   Sydney   Toronto

This is a compilation of previously published McGraw-Hill books:

Marky Stein, *Fearless Résumés*, (0-07-148235-0) © 2010
Marky Stein, *Fearless Interviewing*, (0-07-140884-3) © 2003
Marky Stein, *Fearless Career Change*, (0-07-143912-9) © 2005

This publication is designed to provide accurate and authoritative information in regard to the subject matter covered. It is sold with the understanding that neither the author nor the publisher is engaged in rendering legal, accounting, futures/securities trading, or other professional service. If legal advice or other expert assistance is required, the service of a competent professional person should be sought

—From a Declaration of Principles jointly adopted by
a Committee of the American Bar Association
and a Committee of Publishers

McGraw-Hill books are available at special quantity discounts to use as premiums and sales promotions, or for use in corporate training programs. To contact a representative, please e-mail us at bulksales@mcgraw-hill.com.

To my first career counselor,
Astrid Berg, who told me,
"If it's in your heart, do it"

CONTENTS

ACKNOWLEDGMENTS

Thank you Rusty and Jill Stein for always being there.

I also wish to thank Phil, Karyn, Susan, and Diane Isaacs, Marty Bonsall, Gabrielle Antolovich, Patria Jacobs, Stu Levin, Monster.com, Dan Janal, Aileen Haynes, Bali Stein, Tony Frank, Amy Frost, Lynn Joseph, Kate Smith, Grace Engel, Gerd Salmonson, Kevin Donlin, Krishna Roman, Saundra Ridel and especially Melissa Greer, whose love and gentle guidance have shown me that for every challenge, there is a spiritual solution.

I appreciate all of the efforts that the publishers, editors, and marketing staff at McGraw-Hill have made to help my books be successful. Thanks to Mary Glenn, Ed Chupak, Daina Penikas, and Donya Dickerson. Your encouragement sustains me.

Special thanks to Wilma Marcus, Steven Beasley, Maggie Smith, Michael Mersman, Jack Chapman, Debbie Featherston, Carolyn Clark, Bill Shipley, and Mark Guterman for helping me discover a great well of ideas, courage, and creativiy.

Part One

Fearless
RÉSUMÉS

The Proven Method for Getting a Great Job Fast

CONTENTS

CHAPTER 1

Why Fearless Résumés?

> "One must have the adventurous daring to accept oneself as a bundle of possibilities and undertake the most interesting game in the world—making the most of one's best."
>
> —Harry Emerson Fosdick

Writing a résumé can really be scary! After all, unless all you have to do is fill out an application to get an interview, writing a résumé is just about the *only* way you have to get your foot in the door.

- Up until now, many doors may have been closed to you. You may not even have had the chance to go to an interview yet. You may be getting some interviews, but not the ones you really want. You may love your résumé or hate your résumé or not even have one, but those doors seem to be shut tighter and tighter. *Not for long.*

The guide you're holding is *not* a book about proper grammar or about making your résumé look "fancy" and expensive. Yes, those things may be nice, but we're going to take it just one step further.

A Strategic Approach to Writing Résumés

Fearless Résumés presents you with a *tested and unbeatable strategy*, proven time after time, to get people just like you the job offers you're dreaming of and working so hard to get.

Having personally tested the *Fearless Résumés* strategy on more than 15,000 clients since 1989, I'm here to take their successes and pass these job-seeking secrets on to you. You'll find this strategy for writing a résumé as simple, powerful, and effective as it was for those job seekers.

- I didn't say it would be easy, but I will tell you that writing your résumé will be far simpler than you ever imagined it could be.

Why?

Because I've boiled down what makes a résumé work to a few straightforward but extremely potent ideas that anyone, whether a student, at entry level, or an executive, can use.

In the few hours you spend reading this section and doing the concrete and practical exercises it contains, you're going to create a résumé that pries open those closely guarded doors and knocks them right down, allowing you to see and talk to the people you need to know in order to get the job or career that you've been striving so vigorously for.

A Brand New Approach to Résumé Writing

If you're at the bookstore, leafing through the many books on résumés that are for sale, you'll quickly see that *Fearless Résumés* is different from the others.

This is not just an ordinary résumé book, with hundreds of résumés for you to choose from and "customize" for yourself. In fact, this book takes an *utterly brand new and tested approach* to the often terrible task of crafting that all-important treatment.

As I said before, *Fearless Résumés* is going to teach you a carefully planned strategy, based upon what employers are *really* looking for, that will carry you through your job search, your interview, and finally to the offers you've been waiting for.

- It doesn't matter if writing a résumé or talking about yourself in an interview has been difficult or frustrating before.

You're going to learn a new and totally natural way to penetrate the employer's emotions, persuade his intelligence, and present yourself at your best. In the chapters that follow, you'll discover the secret of how employers, in fact, treat and look at your document.

You'll know the commonsense truth about what *really* motivates them, and it will make all the difference in what you say to them and how you say it in your Fearless Résumé.

In fact, it's been *proven* time and time again that using the secret you're about to learn will make employers pick up and pointedly concentrate on reading *your* Fearless Résumé at a moment's glance, while your competitors' résumés are swirling in the paper shredder.

I know you may have struggled with ordinary résumé writing before, and I know just how demoralizing and frustrating that can be. I know, too, that you may have spent hours and even days editing the résumé that you already have, but that just isn't delivering what you need or expect. You may feel puzzled about what to do and worried about whether you'll ever get the interviews or the job offers you want.

- You're not alone anymore in the task of creating this very important document that will influence the future of your work and your life. *Together*, you and I are going to wage an all-out war as an unstoppable team, and *we're going to win!*

How Can This Section Help You?

If you already have a résumé and you're getting lots of interviews with it, you may not need to read this section. Save your money and buy a few Starbucks coffees with it or take your best friend to lunch.

On the other hand, if your résumé *is* producing interviews for you, but you're having trouble in your interviews supporting what your résumé says about you, your résumé is probably not a good fit for you in the real world.

If that's the case, put a hold on that mocha chocolate nonfat extra foamy latte and invest in this book. You'll be very glad that you did.

- So, you may be worried that you really don't have a good existing résumé at all. You may also have a fear of writing your very *first* résumé or of crafting the document after being out of the job market for a while or changing your focus to a whole new industry.

You're going to learn how to tackle those problems and many more, but there may be a score of other worries you have about your résumé. Most people do. Let's look at some of them that will be answered for you as you progress through the pages of your new guide.

EXERCISE 1

Please check the box at the beginning of each paragraph on the list to figure out exactly how you feel about your own résumé needs.

Feel free to check more than one or to write your own version of your concerns at the end of this list.

☐ I have a résumé that was written by a professional or someone else, but that just doesn't seem to fit me. It looks well written, but I'm uncomfortable when I send it out and/or have to explain it at an interview.

☐ I have a résumé, and I've submitted it to many employers, including online, newspapers, and e-mail "blasts," but I'm *still* not getting any interviews. I feel frustrated!

☐ I have a great work history at good companies for over 25 years, and it's all documented on my résumé. Why isn't anyone calling me? Could I be the victim of age discrimination?

☐ I just graduated from school, and I don't have *any* "real" work experiences. Do odd jobs and internships count as work? I don't see how I can get hired if I've never been hired before. I don't have anything to write on a résumé. Can you help me?

☐ Several friends of mine, a recruiter, and a career counselor all told me that my résumé should be one page and *only* one page. I feel that I can't possibly condense all of my experience and other information onto one page without leaving out important accomplishments that I'm proud of. What should I do?

☐ I've had some bad luck with my employment history. It seems like I just start a job, and then in two or three months there's a layoff. I'm afraid that employers will think that I can't make a commitment, even though I would love to stay at a full-time permanent job for years if I had the chance. How can I solve this problem?

☐ I took some time out of my career to spend with my young family. I gave birth/helped my partner give birth to our infant son/daughter. I think that employers may be rejecting my résumé because of this gap in employment. My family is my top priority, but now it seems like I can't get back into the job market. I feel angry! I feel powerless about what to do.

☐ Last year I did some overseas travel and practiced my passion for photography at a community college. I didn't work for a year, and now it's harder than ever to get interviews. What can I do?

☐ I have reasons, such as health problems, an extended wedding and honeymoon, family illnesses, a painful divorce, or a disability, for gaps in employment. I don't want to lie, but is there any way to cover up these gaps?

☐ I feel that my résumé just looks dull. I haven't done anything that special in my life. I have nothing to brag about. I just did my job. But I can't get interviews. Is it because my résumé isn't good enough?

☐ I have all the experience in the world. I just don't have the degree that's needed for the jobs I'm applying for. I could run circles around half of those people with degrees, but I don't have a piece of paper to prove it. Am I really going to have to spend thousands of dollars and years of my life just to get a degree? Why can't I get hired when I have double the experience of these people with degrees?

☐ Every time I've gotten a job, either it's been through a friend or I just filled out a short application. Now I'm searching for a new job, and all those available require that I send a résumé. Help! I have no idea how to write a résumé.

☐ I got fired from a job—maybe even more than once. Can I just leave those jobs off my résumé in case they call the employers and find out that I was terminated? I'm really scared of a possible employer knowing about that/those incident(s).

☐ An employer or recruiter told me that I had a horrible résumé. Another one said it was great. It makes no sense to me. I'm confused. Which should I believe?

☐ I think I have a great résumé, but I've been looking for a job for over six months, and I know I have all the right qualifications. I just don't get interviews. I don't understand what I'm doing wrong. Any advice?

☐ This is my first time writing a résumé (*or*) I'm writing a brand new résumé for a new industry, location, or job change. I don't even know where to start.

☐ I've been on several interviews. They keep saying the same thing: I'm "overqualified." You'd think that was a *good* thing! What's wrong?

☐ Are there any other reasons that you find résumé writing scary? Write any other concerns you may have in the following spaces. *Let's solve them together!*

☐ _____
_____
_____
_____
_____
_____
_____.

☐ _____
_____
_____
_____
_____
_____
_____.

Did you find your own story in any of these questions? Well, if so, welcome! You're in the right place. If not, maybe you're reading this book for some other reason, and I'm glad you're here. We're about to go on a great adventure together.

This section, as I said, is not just a compilation of many different kinds of résumés. It is written with *you*, your concerns, and your career and livelihood in mind. It's not about the perfect model résumé. There is no such thing, and even career counselors still disagree about the best length, content, and format for a résumé. In fact, anyone who tells you that she'll write the perfect résumé for you or teach you how to write the perfect résumé is kidding herself.

- I can't promise you a flawless résumé. What I *can* promise is that you will start getting interviews.

What Can You Expect from This Section?

In the second chapter, "What Do Employers Really Want?" you're going to learn secrets about what *really* motivates employers when they pick up your résumé. By "tuning in" to both their conscious and their unconscious desires, you'll find out why it's important for you to "hook" your reader *instantly* and get him to take a look at the rest of your résumé.

In Chapter 3, you'll learn how to glue your employer to the page in less than seven seconds by using multiple hooks (words that emotionally attract employers).

I'll give plenty of examples of power propositions that have worked for real people, from those at entry level to managers to executives, in a wide range of positions and industries. Then, in Chapter 4, I'll walk you through the simple steps of drafting your own power proposition, something that is *guaranteed* to make you feel proud and unstoppable.

Your power proposition is going to be near the very top of your résumé (so that it will be the first thing seen by the reader). What about the rest of your résumé? It's important, too. Once you have the reader "hooked," you want to continue to rivet her attention on the rest of your skills, accomplishments, education, and work history.

The material in Chapters 5 and 6—identifying your skills, building a skills arsenal, and crafting what I call Q statements—will form the building blocks that make your résumé totally on target, irresistible to your reader, and absolutely unique.

Chapter 7 will show you how to organize these essential elements of your presentation into "blocks" of information; the contact block, the objective block, the summary block, the employment history block, the education and training block, and some optional blocks that will make it easy for the employer to see specific skills, awards, or achievements that make you right for the job.

In Chapter 8, I'll deliver the final ten tips that will eliminate most of the errors that people tend to make on résumés.

Finally, in Chapter 9, using the building blocks you've mastered in the first eight chapters, it will be *your* time to turn out your first Fearless Résumé! Some sample résumés are given in Chapter 10.

For now, I have faith in you and the absolute conviction that you will triumph in your job search. You've got me on your side, so let's start right now.

CHAPTER 2

What Do Employers Really Want?

> *"The truth of a thing is the feel of it, not the think of it."*
>
> —Stanley Kubrick

Do you know that it takes only three to seven seconds for a reader to determine whether your résumé goes in the "yes" pile or gets deleted or thrown in a paper shredder? Well, it's true.

Over 17 years as a career coach in almost constant contact with employers, recruiters, human resources representatives, and, of course, job seekers gives me an inside view of what *really* goes on when you submit your résumé to a company or small business.

What's Going On Behind the Scenes?

It has been estimated that when a job is advertised in a major metropolitan newspaper and on a few key Internet job sites, a human resources staffer or hiring manager may have as many as 350 résumés crowding his inbox or the corner of his desk *on a daily basis*. Do you think that such a person reads every one of those résumés from start to finish? The answer, you may be surprised to find out, is no.

It takes a very special résumé to grab your reader's attention and keep her reading all the way through when she may have already seen and thrown away 200 résumés before getting to yours. *That's just the kind of résumé you're going to have by the end of this Section.*

How, then, do we know how to write that special résumé? Did we learn it in school? Probably not. Did our parents show us how to do it? Maybe, but has the result worked for you? Have you ever read a book or seen a career counselor who could really tell you that magic formula that you could repeat, again and again, to achieve the same favorable results? If not, why not?

The fact is that too many people and the majority of books about résumés focus on the *résumé itself* rather than turning their target to deep down inside the *emotions* and the *mind* of the reader.

If you're going to get an interview by sending someone your résumé when there are almost 349 competitors a day up against you, you're going to need to know more than just how to write something neat and clean that lists your job history on it; you need inside, tested, and proven particulars about how to make that employer pick your résumé.

- The inside of the hiring process and the interior of employers' emotions are exactly those untapped, "secret" solutions to the problems of getting the interviews that I'm going to share with you right now.

To grab your reader in the first few seconds, to get her to read the whole page or two and then get her to take *action*, we're going to use the power of what I've named *résumé psychology*.

What Is Résumé Psychology?

Résumé psychology is the study and practice of using words in a prescribed document (your résumé) to get a reader to

1. Feel something
2. Think something
3. Do something

To express this chain of events as succinctly as possible, you can imagine the events taking place in this order and in a manner such as this:

Phase 1 (three to seven seconds): The reader will first *feel*, consciously or unconsciously, that you are going to help him.

Phase 2 (one to five minutes): He will then *think* that you are going to make money (or its equivalent) for his company.

Phase 3: Finally, he will be compelled to *do* something about it—that is, to discuss your résumé with his boss or just pick up the phone himself and call you.

Phase 1 *must* work if you are to get to Phase 2. Phase 3 *cannot* happen unless Phase 2 is complete. Therefore, your first task is to win the employer's emotions and get her to feel that you are on *her* side—that you are going to help her in some way.

Logic or Emotions?

One would hope that résumé readers would base their decisions on logic or rationality, carefully weighing the qualifications written on your résumé against the requirements of the position that you're applying for. We may imagine that this is true, but that is not how the human brain works. *An initial reaction is always emotional.*

- Once I show you how to influence the person's feelings (emotions), thinking (cognitions), and actions (behavior), you can bet that your phone will start ringing as expectant employers want to meet you.

Winning the Reader's Favor

To accomplish this, we're going take a peek inside the employer's brain before you even set pen to paper to craft your document. By mastering what the employer actually *sees* in the first seven seconds of laying eyes on your page and how it affects the *emotional* part of his brain, you're going to learn how to keep him reading down the page while other people's résumés are whirling in the paper shredder.

- Together, in this chapter, we're going to answer the question you may already be asking yourself: "What do employers *really* want, anyway?"

In this section, you're going to quickly learn what we now know about how human beings read and process information. We're going to use these powerful pieces of what psychology tells us about human perception to your advantage.

We're going to harness *résumé psychology* to put you on the fast track to winning an interview and getting a new job, and it all begins in a fraction of a second. Am I saying that someone's mind can make a snap decision about my résumé immediately? Yes!

Résumé psychology says that your résumé will be judged 80 percent on what the reader sees in the first few lines and about 20 percent on what appears in the rest of the résumé.

In fact, every single reader knows within just a few seconds whether you are likely to help her *meet her needs* or are likely to threaten her efforts.

The "Seven-Second" Zone

Psychologists say that we "know" in a split second (about 1/16 second, to be exact) whether *anything* that comes into our environment is going to help or threaten our instinct to survive.

This split-second test of whether something is good for us or bad for us is a top task of our brains and nervous systems because it governs our very survival. Say that it takes only 1/16 second (what psychologists call a "slice") for us to tell this. Whether it's an object, a car, a person, climate change, or even a piece of paper like your résumé, it will be evaluated by your brain at lightning speed.

Compared to 1/16 second, seven full seconds seems like an eon! Yet, that's all you have to snare the survival instinct of your reader and get her to salivate over the contents of your offering. If you miss that chance, you may never be able to recover it.

During this critical "seven-second zone," the brain is bombarded with impulses whose only purpose is to determine one thing: *is this (object, person, situation) going to pose danger to me or help me?*

You know yourself that a feeling of friendship, affection, intense dislike, or even "falling in love" can happen the moment you lay eyes on someone or something.

We're going to capitalize on those powerful feelings in the next chapter with something that I call a *power proposition*. Your power proposition, which the reader will see in that crucial seven-second zone, will rivet her to your résumé.

- With only the words in one powerful paragraph (about four to seven sentences), you will infuse the reader's nerve cells with energy and curiosity. In brief, you make the employer "fall in love" with you!

So just how are you going to strike up a "romance" with the employer that has the potential of blossoming into a long-term love affair (your new job)? Well, as with most romances and even great friendships, it's essential, as we've said, to make a good first impression.

On paper, you don't have your smile, your face, or the sparkle in your eye to let someone know that you're friendly and attractive. You don't even have the friendly, provocative, or interesting tone of voice to offer that you might have if you met someone face-to-face or on the telephone.

On your résumé, all you've got that can evoke positive feelings in the reader is the written word, and it's those words—especially the first few sentences that the reader encounters—that are going to make all the difference.

Your Power Proposition

What you'll soon come to know as a power proposition is a forceful, confident, and concise paragraph that contains one or more "hooks" that your reader will find irresistible.

  • These hooks, if you will, are words that express how well you can fulfill the employer's *financial, business, personal,* and *emotional* needs.

Think we can do all that in just a few lines? The answer is yes, and in the next chapter you'll see just how easy it really is.

Once you are clear about the statements you'll make in your power proposition, you'll also be clear about *how you can uniquely solve the problems faced by the employer and thereby satisfy one or more of her desires.*

Here is a list of the things that almost every employer either wants to have or wants to avoid. All of these things, at the bottom line, affect his ingrained sense of survival.

WHAT MOTIVATES YOUR READER?
  • Greater profits
  • Less waste of time, labor, money, and materials
  • A cleaner, better organized, and safer workplace
  • Better employee morale and commitment
  • Improved recruiting, hiring, and employee retention
  • Sturdier and more innovative technologies, machines, and instruments

- Recording and storing detailed and accurate information
- Keeping customers and clients happy
- Greater marketability and sales appeal for her products
- Better public perception of her company and its services and goods

The Key to Knowing about Survival Needs

When you, by your efforts at work, *increase* anything that the employer sees as valuable and *decrease* things that the employer sees as dangerous, you are fulfilling his primal needs for *safety, security,* and *well-being*.

- You show him that you can do this by writing a résumé that presents a variety of "tasty" hooks. Your power proposition contains the initial hooks.

A power proposition is easy to write, yet deceptively attractive. Once you know what's required to spark an attraction in the employer's brain, you'll have a lifelong tool that will help you not only with your résumé, but also with your interview and other parts of your job search.

How about moving on to constructing a paragraph that will rivet your reader's eyes to the page and, most important, fill her with a pleasant sense of anticipation?

CHAPTER 3

Rivet the Reader in the First Seven Seconds

> *"When love and skill work together, expect a masterpiece."*
>
> —John Ruskin

This chapter may be among the most important pieces of advice on résumés that you've ever seen. Read on and you'll find out why.

Multiple Uses of a Power Proposition

When you master making your power proposition come alive, you'll know how to capture the attention of your reader instantly. And there's more!

You're *also* going to be prepared for the interview question, "Tell me about yourself," as well as for other questions regarding your skills, strengths, and accomplishments. Not only will this special paragraph guide your résumé and aid you in interviewing, but you're going to be able to use *parts* of your power proposition to describe yourself to perfect strangers who may have job leads for you and to people you meet socially or in your job-hunting network.

- Your power proposition, because it is a rich mini-snapshot of yourself and what you can do, may indeed become one of the most critical tools in your job-seeking technique.

Let's get focused and learn how to harness the energy in the first few sentences of your résumé to get the employer on the hook. Are you ready?

Steps to Writing Your Power Proposition

In this chapter, we're going to prepare you to create your own personal power proposition.

First, I want you to look at several different power propositions so that you can observe how they fall into particular, predictable patterns, even though each is describing a very different position. In the next chapter, we'll write the paragraph in a predictable step-by-step process.

This process is moving toward a very worthy goal: a paragraph that will irresistibly influence your reader to take action. Here are 12 sample power propositions. Don't worry if the wording or the structure seems unfamiliar at first. This is "résumé talk."

We don't use the word *I* or *me*, and sometimes we simply use phrases rather than what one would consider "proper" English grammar.

All in all, it's not the punctuation that counts—it's the words that represent what we know from résumé psychology to be the very words the employer is looking for.

Once you read all of these power propositions and the additional ones from the sample résumés in Chapter 7, you're going to have a good feeling about expressing yourself in this way, and the style will be far more familiar to you.

Sample Power Propositions

Power Proposition 1

CUSTOMER SERVICE MANAGER

Over three years' experience as a customer service representative and manager serving small to medium-sized companies, specializing in retail sales, inventory control, and employee training. Designed and delivered trainings for up to 20 participants while working at Home Design Warehouse. Awarded for perfect cash drawers over 12 times in a five-year period. Voted Customer Service Manager of the Month in July 2006 and February 2008. A.A. in Business Administration from Silva Valley College. Certificate in Retail Management from University of New York extension program. Organized, friendly, and detail-oriented.

Now, has this candidate provided the bait for the hooks that will catch the reader's attention and lock it there until he has finished reading the whole résumé?

Of course she has. This little paragraph, her power proposition, answers not only the *minimum requirements* (and preferences) of the position that are spelled out in the job description, but indicates even more fertile talent than is expected.

Power Proposition 2

DIRECTOR OF STRATEGIC MARKETING

Over 10 years' director-level experience in strategic marketing, specializing in strategic planning, team leadership, and driving business development in the high-tech Fortune 100 sector. Executed multimillion-dollar deals of up to $4.5 million with global partners by developing long-term customer/partner relationships, directing multifunctional teams of up to 90 for projects with budgets of up to $75 million, and creating and developing company strategic framework and plans for expanding into new target markets. MSEE, Yale University; MBA with concentration in Marketing/Finance, Cornell University. Member of International Association of Marketing Professionals. Awarded the Trendsetter Award in 2007 for Innovation in Strategic Marketing from the American Marketing Association.

Power Proposition 3

COMPUTER NETWORK ADMINISTRATOR

Proficient computer network administrator in the manufacturing industry, specializing in UNIX and Linox platforms, troubleshooting and configuration of local area networks. Supervised the team of 16 technicians for a larger Fortune 500 company that reduced downtime for the manufacturer by 33 percent in the first year, thereby preventing almost 140 lost hours per week. Certified computer network IT administrator from Howard Vocational Technology School. Associate degree in Electronics from Hillsdale College.

Power Proposition 4

SALES AND MARKETING MANAGER

Over 8 years as senior sales and marketing manager in health care and biomedical devices fields, specializing in prospecting, presentations, and talent acquisition. In five years while at Dullard Insurance Inc., developed marketing collateral that was partially responsible for the 67% surge in state sales during the years 2003 to 2008. Received several diamond awards for sales and marketing while at Dullard, including recognition as Diamond Professional in the years 2005 and 2008. B.A. in journalism; M.B.A. from Chicago State University with an emphasis in international marketing.

Power Proposition 5

PRODUCTION SUPERVISOR

Over 5 years' experience as a production supervisor/assistant manager in the manufacturing and retail industries, specializing in team leadership, operations, quality control, and employee training. Selected career accomplishments: exceeded production objective by a 25% increase in efficiency and 50% reduction in injuries. B.S. in Industrial Technology; training in TQM.

Power Propostion 6

FILM PRODUCTION MANAGER

Over 6 years as a production manager and assistant director on more than 11 feature films, specializing in hiring, logistics, and budgeting films of up to $24 million.

Saved 22% of the planned budget on *Dinner with a Thief* (Sammy T. Productions) by instituting second unit shooting at a second location. Cut 7 days of shooting by tightening deadlines using Quick Story software, resulting in a total saving of $210,000 from an $18 million budget. Bachelor's degree in Media and Communications, Florida State University at Orlando.

What if I Have Little or No Experience on the Job?

Even if you have less than a year of experience or no experience at all, there are ways we can express your knowledge in a way that still hooks the employers:

Knowledge of the field of _____ gained from *volunteer/ internship/study* of _____, specializing in _____, _____, and _____.

So, if you're a recent college graduate, you may say something like that in the following power propositions.

Power Proposition 7

ENTRY-LEVEL COMPUTER ENGINEER

Knowledge of the field of computer engineering gained from 4 years of study and a B.S. in Computer Sciences, with classes in software engineering, Web design, and hardware troubleshooting. Got an A in Web design. Created a 90-page Web site using Flash design elements. Served as the president of the campus Computer Club. Dependable, detail-oriented, willing to learn.

Here's another for someone with a background as a volunteer.

Power Proposition 8

PRESCHOOL TEACHER

Six months' experience as a preschool aide gained from volunteer experience, specializing in play supervision, preparing meals, and reading to children. Handled groups of up to 15 children under the direction of the preschool director. Currently enrolled in a course of study leading to an A.A. degree in Early Childhood Education. Warm, fun, outgoing.

How about if you've had unpaid (or minimally paid) experience on the job for less than one year as an intern?

Power Proposition 9

ENTRY-LEVEL PHYSICAL THERAPIST ASSISTANT

Competence as a physical therapist assistant gained from earning a certificate in physical therapist assistant program at Hunter Community College, specializing in following treatment plans, kinesiology, and patient psychology. Completed an externship with excellent references at Simeone Sports Medicine and Chronic

Pain Clinic in Lexington, Vermont. Carried a patient load of 10 under the supervision of the physical therapy director. Trustworthy, knowledgeable, great patient rapport. Graduated in the top 10 percent of the class at Hunter Community College.

What if you built your own home from scratch and made it energy-efficient or "green," but did not get paid for it?

What if you rigged your home with solar surfaces and wind turbines so well that you did not need conventional electricity at all? All that skill, effort, and knowledge does not have to be reserved for your personal life. If you wanted a job in sustainable energy, solar energy, or (the latest term) "green" technology, you could certainly say that you were *proficient* in the areas of construction, plumbing, tiling, building solar panels, installing special insulation, and a host of other skills that you gained while building a home for yourself. You could then use your proficiency in your power proposition.

Power Propostion 10

SUSTAINABLE ENERGY CONSULTANT

Proficiency in building green technology homes gained from building a 13,000-square-foot home in California that is independent of the traditional energy grid. Saved approximately $2,100 per month on electricity costs alone and an additional $300 from saved water usage.

Landscaped the home with 12 varieties of low-maintenance native plants and planted and maintained a vegetable and herb garden that is 20 square feet. Certificate in Sustainable Energy Planning from University of California Extension Program.

Power Proposition 11

ENTRY-LEVEL VIDEO CAMERA OPERATOR (STUDENT)

Competent video camera operator specializing in multicamera shoots, lighting, and editing. As an intern, worked on 1 hour and 55 minute documentary film about global warming and was hired again by the same company for a stipend to do lighting for a studio shoot on gifted children. Student film, *Capture of the Giants*, was voted "most popular student film" in 2006 at Xavier University. A.A. in theater arts, B.A. in film and television arts, Xavier University.

Power Proposition 12

ENTRY-LEVEL OFFICE MANAGER

Knowledge of office management in the medical field, specializing in customer care database creation, filing, billing, and coding gained from successful completion of a Certificate in Medical Office Management. Expert in Microsoft Office suite, including Microsoft Office Access. Earned an A-plus in medical terminology courses at Keller Community College, Orlando, Florida. Advanced Certificate in Office Management from Keller Community College.

Some other useful phrases to start off the first sentence of your power proposition are

Externship in (medical assisting)

Internship as a(n) (associate editor)

Apprenticeship as a(n) (electrician)

Okay, you've just seen several power propositions. Are you impressed?

Did you ever get a strange feeling that some of the people who wrote these were bragging?

That's not an uncommon response for someone who's writing a résumé. Bragging is exaggeration mixed with deceit. All of the power propositions you just read are simply facts. How can you brag when you're just telling the truth?

Is a shopkeeper bragging when he displays his finest merchandise in the store window?

Of course not. He, like you, is putting his most attractive wares out front for you to see in hopes that you'll come into the store, look more closely, and then buy something. It's the same with your power proposition. You're putting your best foot forward right away to attract the employer with the hope that she will read your résumé and call you for an interview.

Now that you've accepted that you're going to *have* to say some really good things about yourself, let's get to the next chapter and I'll walk you through writing each part of your own power proposition, step by step.

CHAPTER 4

Your Power Proposition

> "The best bet is to bet on yourself."
>
> —Arnold Glasgow

I'm sure that in reading the paragraphs in the last chapter, you noticed that all of them are constructed in the same or a very similar way. There is structure to a power proposition—a beginning, a middle, and an end.

- That's what makes a power proposition so easy to write. Every sentence and every part has a specific purpose.

Parts of a Power Proposition

This section gives a power proposition that's divided into nine parts, with some of the information left blank. Before each blank space, there is a number in parentheses.

We're going to talk about what kind of data goes after each number. Before you know it, you're going to have a power proposition of your own!

Writing your power proposition is just as easy as filling in the three to nine blank spaces.

- A power proposition has three *mandatory* ("must have") statements and four *optional* sentences.

I'll explain exactly how each part works so that you'll know how to fill in the blanks with tempting hooks that *grab* the reader in the first seven seconds.

Model Power Proposition

You don't need to write anything in the blank spaces now. After you take a peek at this model, I'll explain to you how to do it for yourself.

First Sentence

Write your level/years of experience, job title, industry(ies), and special skills.

Over (1) _____ years as a(n) (2) _____ in the
_____ [optional] industry(ies), specializing in

(4) _____ , _____ ,
and _____ .

Second Sentence

Write an accomplishment here: (5)

_____

_____

_____ .

You may choose to write another accomplishment here,
but this is optional:

_____

_____

_____ .

Third and Further Sentences

Use one to four of the following:

Your degree(s) and/or certifications. (6)

_____

_____ .

Your awards and/or special recognitions. (7)

_____

_____ .

Memberships in professional organizations. (8)

_____

_____ .

Personal characteristics. (9)

_____

_____ .

What Does Each Part Mean?

Each sentence in your power proposition communicates something very important to the employer and has a potential hook (or many hooks) to grab his attention within the first seven seconds. Let's take each sentence and section one by one, and soon you'll have a completed paragraph.

Sentence 1, Blank 1: Level or Years of Experience

The first sentence indicates the number of years or level of experience you have doing a certain type of job.

- Remember from the previous chapter that if you have less than one year of experience, unpaid experience, or no paid working experience at all, you can start off with words like *competent, knowledgeable, proficient, volunteer, intern(ship), residency, externship, apprenticeship,* or *classroom study.*

For those with paid experience in the workplace, the first sentence would begin with the number of years of experience you've accumulated in your field. Listing anywhere from one to ten years is fine. Ten years of experience is enough to show that you are at the highest level of your job.

Listing more than 10 to 15 years of experience, however temping it is to show your professionalism, may consciously or unconsciously cause the reader to reject your résumé because of an unfortunate epidemic in some societies called *ageism.*

AGEISM

What is ageism? People are *wrongly* convinced that a more mature person may not stay long, may be unhealthy on the job, might get bored, could have trouble being supervised by a younger manager, or may demand higher pay.

Even though studies have proved these beliefs to be dead wrong, many employers persist in harboring these inexcusable and damaging myths. Until we as a society do the work of ridding ourselves of this very wrong form of discrimination based on age, it is wise not to risk an employer's concluding that he does not want to interview you because of his conscious or unconscious belief in ageism. The *only* reason to list something more than ten years ago is if it is absolutely necessary to support your job target.

So let's keep your years of experience down to 10, or 15 at the most.

In Chapter 10, "Sample Résumés," I'll show you how to represent important positions that you may have held 16 or more years ago.

Sentence 1, Blank 2: My Job Title or Titles

Enter the job titles you've had over the span of your experience. For example, you could say any one of these things and still be expressing your expertise to the employer:

- Director of operations
- Upper management position in operations
- Executive position in operations
- X years' experience as an operations professional

Sentence 1, Blank 3: The Industry or Industries I've Worked In

The blank after the number (3) in the model represents the industry or industries you've worked in. You may look at the end of this chapter for a list of industries you might like to use in this spot.

- Listing an industry is optional and can simply be used to *clarify* or *strengthen* a job title. This is optional, but it is commonly used if you're staying in the same industry but going for a different job title in that industry.

EXERCISE 2

Please write the information for the first three blanks in the first sentence of your power proposition here:

1. _____

2. _____

3. _____

Wow, congratulations! In less than the blink of an eye, you've already told an employer your level of experience, a job title, and an industry! Unlike with traditional résumés, the employer will not have to go to all the trouble of scrolling down through the dates of your job history to determine how many years you've been at it.

You *already* have at least one and potentially three hooks into her.

Sentence 1, Three Blanks Marked 4: My Skills, Strengths, and Specialties

The second part of the first sentence deals with your specialties.

- What are some of the things you do well and some of the things you like doing that pertain to your job target?

Do you have a job description in front of you? If so, use it. It will probably contain five to ten skills or areas of knowledge that the employer is looking for.

If any of your skills exactly *match* the job description, pick out the three that you most enjoy doing or are best at and write them in the specialty section. This is great bait for a hungry employer.

If you'd like some more ideas for skill words, refer to the lists of skills in Chapter 5. You'll be pleasantly surprised to find that you have many more skills than you've ever imagined. Every one of these skills is a potential hook for the right employer.

- Now you have your first sentence, and just look at how much information you've transmitted to the employer in such a short reading/time span!

Sentence 2 (and 3—optional)

The next two sentences contain descriptions of past accomplishments that you are proud of and/or that relate to the job you're applying for. What is the difference between a skill and an accomplishment?

Well, a skill is a word or phrase indicating something that you *can* do, like management, assembly, diagnosis, or writing reports. Accomplishments are specific ways in which you *used* your skills in world.

WRITING AN ACCOMPLISHMENT

For example, in the following sentences, the skill is underlined and the rest of the sentence describes an accomplishment.

> <u>Managed</u> the finance department for a large grocery chain.
>
> <u>Assembled</u> semiconductors for use in a defense company.
>
> <u>Diagnosed</u> and <u>treated</u> over six patients per day in a private clinic.
>
> <u>Wrote reports</u> on the earthquake preparedness of government buildings.

So, for the next exercise, I'm going to ask you to *pencil* in at least one accomplishment. If you can think of two, that's great, but the second one is optional for this exercise.

We're going to use these accomplishments as placeholders for now, because in the next chapter, you're going to learn a proven way to make your accomplishments *really* shine.

EXERCISE 3

Please write one or two accomplishments in the following spaces:

Accomplishment:

_____

_____

_____

_____.

Accomplishment:

_____

_____

_____

_____.

CHANGING AN ACCOMPLISHMENT TO A Q STATEMENT

We're going to use the accomplishments you just listed as a foundation to construct statements that are at the very heart of your work history.

They are called *Q statements*, and they usually include numbers, percentages, and/or *very specific* information that appeals to virtually *every* employer's survival instinct.

We'll come back after the next chapter and turn your penciled-in accomplishments into Q statements that will reflect not only what you did, but the results that you produced.

Right now, I hope you've created at least one accomplishment and penciled it in. Great! We're almost finished with your unique power proposition, something that is essential for your Fearless Résumé.

- You'll find that your proposition also has an unmistakable "ring" to it when you actually *say* it in an interview, or even to someone who may have a job lead for you in an informal setting.

At this point, don't worry if you're thinking to yourself, "I just did my job. I really don't have anything that special to say." Most people think that at first.

As you discover more, you'll feel firsthand that once you learn how to turn skills into accomplishments and accomplishments into Q statements, as thousands of people have, your résumé and your interviewing skills are going to hit the sky, and your confidence, both on paper and in person, is going to soar.

Now, there are a few more optional sentences in your power proposition. We'll discuss those next.

Further Sentences

In the last sentences, you can add short phrases or sentences relating to one or all of the following:

1. Your education, training, certificates, or licenses, or education that you are still enrolled in. For example,

   Masters in Business Administration with an emphasis in Finance

Currently enrolled in a course of study leading to a Bachelor's Degree in Information Sciences

2. Awards, excellent grade point averages, or recognitions. For example,

Awarded Salesperson of the Year in 2007

Graduated with a 3.85 grade point average from Millman City College

3. Professional or student associations, organizations, or clubs that pertain to the position for which you're applying. For example,

Society for Human Resource Management

Event Planning Association of America

Now, I can't wait for you to see your whole power proposition on paper. You can make it very simple for now and add other parts that you want later. Remember, you don't have to fill in all of the blanks.

EXERCISE 4
First Draft of My Own Power Proposition

Over _____ years as a(n) _____ in the

_____ industry, specializing in

_____,

_____, and

_____. [Accomplishment(s)]:

_____

_____

_____.

_____

_____

_____. [Education, awards, personal traits, etc.]

_____

_____

_____

_____

_____

_____.

Your Finished Power Proposition

You may have drafted this version of your proposition in a way that's very similar to the way it's written here, *or* you may have already chosen your own wording that you feel comfortable with. As a test, please read the sentence *as if you were an employer*.

How long did it take you to read it? Three seconds? Ten seconds? What's important for you to understand is that in well under ten seconds, you have *already* told the employer a lot about you.

Traditional résumés may have taken two pages—about two minutes *past* our employer's initial attention span—to say what you've said in less than ten seconds.

In fact, it is customary (though not always) for educational qualifications to be left until the very end of the résumé. We don't want to take the risk that the employer won't read all that way, so we're going to put your education into your power proposition if it seems relevant, and it almost always does.

- You've already won your employer over. Congratulations! She won't have seen anyone give her so much useful information—in fact, the *exact* information she's looking for—in so little time.

In the next chapters, we're going to identify some of the skills that form the foundation of Q statements. Then, we're going to put a "spin" on those penciled-in accomplishments that you just wrote: we're going to turn them into Q statements. Now let's use them to deal the final blow.

List of Industries

Taken from http://www.sec.gov/info/edgar/siccodes.htm.

100	9	AGRICULTURAL PRODUCTION—CROPS
200	5	AGRICULTURAL PROD—LIVESTOCK & ANIMAL SPECIALTIES
700	9	AGRICULTURAL SERVICES
800	5	FORESTRY
900	9	FISHING, HUNTING AND TRAPPING
1000	4	METAL MINING
1040	4	GOLD AND SILVER ORES
1090	4	MISCELLANEOUS METAL ORES
1220	4	BITUMINOUS COAL & LIGNITE MINING
1221	4	BITUMINOUS COAL & LIGNITE SURFACE MINING
1311	4	CRUDE PETROLEUM & NATURAL GAS
1381	4	DRILLING OIL & GAS WELLS
1382	4	OIL & GAS FIELD EXPLORATION SERVICES
1389	4	OIL & GAS FIELD SERVICES, NEC
1400	4	MINING & QUARRYING OF NONMETALLIC MINERALS (NO FUELS)
1520	6	GENERAL BLDG CONTRACTORS— RESIDENTIAL BLDGS
1531	6	OPERATIVE BUILDERS
1540	6	GENERAL BLDG CONTRACTORS— NONRESIDENTIAL BLDGS
1600	6	HEAVY CONSTRUCTION OTHER THAN BLDG CONST—CONTRACTORS
1623	6	WATER, SEWER, PIPELINE, COMM & POWER LINE CONSTRUCTION

1700	6	CONSTRUCTION—SPECIAL TRADE CONTRACTORS
1731	6	ELECTRICAL WORK
2000	4	FOOD AND KINDRED PRODUCTS
2011	5	MEAT PACKING PLANTS
2013	5	SAUSAGES & OTHER PREPARED MEAT PRODUCTS
2015	5	POULTRY SLAUGHTERING AND PROCESSING
2020	4	DAIRY PRODUCTS
2024	4	ICE CREAM & FROZEN DESSERTS
2030	4	CANNED, FROZEN & PRESERVD FRUIT, VEG & FOOD SPECIALTIES
2033	4	CANNED FRUITS, VEG, PRESERVES, JAMS & JELLIES
2040	4	GRAIN MILL PRODUCTS
2050	4	BAKERY PRODUCTS
2052	4	COOKIES & CRACKERS
2060	4	SUGAR & CONFECTIONERY PRODUCTS
2070	4	FATS & OILS
2080	9	BEVERAGES
2082	9	MALT BEVERAGES
2086	9	BOTTLED & CANNED SOFT DRINKS & CARBONATED WATERS
2090	4	MISCELLANEOUS FOOD PREPARATIONS & KINDRED PRODUCTS
2092	4	PREPARED FRESH OR FROZEN FISH & SEAFOODS
2100	5	TOBACCO PRODUCTS
2111	5	CIGARETTES

2200	2	TEXTILE MILL PRODUCTS
2211	2	BROADWOVEN FABRIC MILLS, COTTON
2221	2	BROADWOVEN FABRIC MILLS, MAN MADE FIBER & SILK
2250	2	KNITTING MILLS
2253	9	KNIT OUTERWEAR MILLS
2273	2	CARPETS & RUGS
2300	9	APPAREL & OTHER FINISHD PRODS OF FABRICS & SIMILAR MATL
2320	9	MEN'S & BOYS' FURNISHGS, WORK CLOTHG, & ALLIED GARMENTS
2330	9	WOMEN'S, MISSES', AND JUNIORS' OUTERWEAR
2340	9	WOMEN'S, MISSES', CHILDREN'S & INFANTS' UNDERGARMENTS
2390	9	MISCELLANEOUS FABRICATED TEXTILE PRODUCTS
2400	6	LUMBER & WOOD PRODUCTS (NO FURNITURE)
2421	6	SAWMILLS & PLANTING MILLS, GENERAL
2430	6	MILLWOOD, VENEER, PLYWOOD, & STRUCTURAL WOOD MEMBERS
2451	6	MOBILE HOMES
2452	6	PREFABRICATED WOOD BLDGS & COMPONENTS
2510	6	HOUSEHOLD FURNITURE
2511	6	WOOD HOUSEHOLD FURNITURE (NO UPHOLSTERED)
2520	6	OFFICE FURNITURE
2522	6	OFFICE FURNITURE (NO WOOD)

2531	6	PUBLIC BLDG & RELATED FURNITURE
2540	6	PARTITIONS, SHELVG, LOCKERS, & OFFICE & STORE FIXTURES
2590	6	MISCELLANEOUS FURNITURE & FIXTURES
2600	9	PAPERS & ALLIED PRODUCTS
2611	9	PULP MILLS
2621	9	PAPER MILLS
2631	9	PAPERBOARD MILLS
2650	9	PAPERBOARD CONTAINERS & BOXES
2670	9	CONVERTED PAPER & PAPERBOARD PRODS (NO CONTAINERS/BOXES)
2673	6	PLASTICS, FOIL & COATED PAPER BAGS
2711	5	NEWSPAPERS: PUBLISHING OR PUBLISHING & PRINTING
2721	5	PERIODICALS: PUBLISHING OR PUBLISHING & PRINTING
2731	5	BOOKS: PUBLISHING OR PUBLISHING & PRINTING
2732	5	BOOK PRINTING
2741	5	MISCELLANEOUS PUBLISHING
2750	5	COMMERCIAL PRINTING
2761	5	MANIFOLD BUSINESS FORMS
2771	5	GREETING CARDS
2780	5	BLANKBOOKS, LOOSELEAF BINDERS, & BOOKBINDG & RELATD WORK
2790	5	SERVICE INDUSTRIES FOR THE PRINTING TRADE
2800	6	CHEMICALS & ALLIED PRODUCTS
2810	6	INDUSTRIAL INORGANIC CHEMICALS

2820	6	PLASTIC MATERIAL, SYNTH RESIN/RUBBER, CELLULOS (NO GLASS)
2821	6	PLASTIC MATERIALS, SYNTH RESINS & NONVULCAN ELASTOMERS
2833	1	MEDICINAL CHEMICALS & BOTANICAL PRODUCTS
2834	1	PHARMACEUTICAL PREPARATIONS
2835	1	IN VITRO & IN VIVO DIAGNOSTIC SUBSTANCES
2836	1	BIOLOGICAL PRODUCTS (NO DIAGNOSTIC SUBSTANCES)
2840	6	SOAP, DETERGENTS, CLEANG PREPARATIONS, PERFUMES, COSMETICS
2842	6	SPECIALTY CLEANING, POLISHING AND SANITATION PREPARATIONS
2844	6	PERFUMES, COSMETICS, & OTHER TOILET PREPARATIONS
2851	6	PAINTS, VARNISHES, LACQUERS, ENAMELS & ALLIED PRODS
2860	6	INDUSTRIAL ORGANIC CHEMICALS
2870	5	AGRICULTURAL CHEMICALS
2890	6	MISCELLANEOUS CHEMICAL PRODUCTS
2891	6	ADHESIVES & SEALANTS
2911	4	PETROLEUM REFINING
2950	6	ASPHALT PAVING & ROOFING MATERIALS
2990	6	MISCELLANEOUS PRODUCTS OF PETROLEUM & COAL
3011	6	TIRES & INNER TUBES
3021	6	RUBBER & PLASTICS FOOTWEAR
3050	6	GASKETS, PACKG & SEALG DEVICES & RUBBER & PLASTICS HOSE

3060	6	FABRICATED RUBBER PRODUCTS, NEC
3080	6	MISCELLANEOUS PLASTICS PRODUCTS
3081	6	UNSUPPORTED PLASTICS FILM & SHEET
3086	6	PLASTICS FOAM PRODUCTS
3089	6	PLASTICS PRODUCTS, NEC
3100	9	LEATHER & LEATHER PRODUCTS
3140	9	FOOTWEAR (NO RUBBER)
3211	6	FLAT GLASS
3220	6	GLASS & GLASSWARE, PRESSED OR BLOWN
3221	6	GLASS CONTAINERS
3231	6	GLASS PRODUCTS, MADE OF PURCHASED GLASS
3241	6	CEMENT, HYDRAULIC
3250	6	STRUCTURAL CLAY PRODUCTS
3260	6	POTTERY & RELATED PRODUCTS
3270	6	CONCRETE, GYPSUM & PLASTER PRODUCTS
3272	6	CONCRETE PRODUCTS, EXCEPT BLOCK & BRICK
3281	6	CUT STONE & STONE PRODUCTS
3290	6	ABRASIVE, ASBESTOS & MISC NONMETALLIC MINERAL PRODS
3310	6	STEEL WORKS, BLAST FURNACES & ROLLING & FINISHING MILLS
3312	6	STEEL WORKS, BLAST FURNACES & ROLLING MILLS (COKE OVENS)
3317	6	STEEL PIPE & TUBES
3320	6	IRON & STEEL FOUNDRIES
3330	4	PRIMARY SMELTING & REFINING OF NONFERROUS METALS

3334	4	PRIMARY PRODUCTION OF ALUMINUM
3341	6	SECONDARY SMELTING & REFINING OF NONFERROUS METALS
3350	6	ROLLING, DRAWING, & EXTRUDING OF NONFERROUS METALS
3357	6	DRAWING & INSULATING OF NONFERROUS WIRE
3360	6	NONFERROUS FOUNDRIES (CASTINGS)
3390	6	MISCELLANEOUS PRIMARY METAL PRODUCTS
3411	6	METAL CANS
3412	6	METAL SHIPPING BARRELS, DRUMS, KEGS & PAILS
3420	6	CUTLERY, HANDTOOLS & GENERAL HARDWARE
3430	6	HEATING EQUIP, EXCEPT ELEC & WARM AIR; & PLUMBING FIXTURES
3433	6	HEATING EQUIPMENT, EXCEPT ELECTRIC & WARM AIR FURNACES
3440	6	FABRICATED STRUCTURAL METAL PRODUCTS
3442	6	METAL DOORS, SASH, FRAMES, MOLDINGS & TRIM
3443	6	FABRICATED PLATE WORK (BOILER SHOPS)
3444	6	SHEET METAL WORK
3448	6	PREFABRICATED METAL BUILDINGS & COMPONENTS
3451	6	SCREW MACHINE PRODUCTS
3452	6	BOLTS, NUTS, SCREWS, RIVETS & WASHERS
3460	6	METAL FORGINGS & STAMPINGS
3470	6	COATING, ENGRAVING & ALLIED SERVICES
3480	6	ORDNANCE & ACCESSORIES (NO VEHICLES/GUIDED MISSILES)

3490	6	MISCELLANEOUS FABRICATED METAL PRODUCTS
3510	10	ENGINES & TURBINES
3523	10	FARM MACHINERY & EQUIPMENT
3524	10	LAWN & GARDEN TRACTORS & HOME LAWN & GARDEN EQUIP
3530	10	CONSTRUCTION, MINING & MATERIALS HANDLING MACHINERY & EQUIP
3531	10	CONSTRUCTION MACHINERY & EQUIP
3532	10	MINING MACHINERY & EQUIP (NO OIL & GAS FIELD MACH & EQUIP)
3533	4	OIL & GAS FIELD MACHINERY & EQUIPMENT
3537	10	INDUSTRIAL TRUCKS, TRACTORS, TRAILERS & STACKERS
3540	10	METALWORKG MACHINERY & EQUIPMENT
3541	10	MACHINE TOOLS, METAL CUTTING TYPES
3550	10	SPECIAL INDUSTRY MACHINERY (NO METALWORKING MACHINERY)
3555	10	PRINTING TRADES MACHINERY & EQUIPMENT
3559	10	SPECIAL INDUSTRY MACHINERY, NEC
3560	10	GENERAL INDUSTRIAL MACHINERY & EQUIPMENT
3561	10	PUMPS & PUMPING EQUIPMENT
3562	6	BALL & ROLLER BEARINGS
3564	6	INDUSTRIAL & COMMERCIAL FANS & BLOWERS & AIR PURIFING EQUIP
3567	6	INDUSTRIAL PROCESS FURNACES & OVENS
3569	6	GENERAL INDUSTRIAL MACHINERY & EQUIPMENT, NEC

3570	3	COMPUTER & OFFICE EQUIPMENT
3571	3	ELECTRONIC COMPUTERS
3572	3	COMPUTER STORAGE DEVICES
3575	3	COMPUTER TERMINALS
3576	3	COMPUTER COMMUNICATIONS EQUIPMENT
3577	3	COMPUTER PERIPHERAL EQUIPMENT, NEC
3578	3	CALCULATING & ACCOUNTING MACHINES (NO ELECTRONIC COMPUTERS)
3579	3	OFFICE MACHINES, NEC
3580	6	REFRIGERATION & SERVICE INDUSTRY MACHINERY
3585	6	AIR-COND & WARM AIR HEATG EQUIP & COMM & INDL REFRIG EQUIP
3590	6	MISC INDUSTRIAL & COMMERCIAL MACHINERY & EQUIPMENT
3600	10	ELECTRONIC & OTHER ELECTRICAL EQUIPMENT (NO COMPUTER EQUIP)
3612	10	POWER, DISTRIBUTION & SPECIALTY TRANSFORMERS
3613	10	SWITCHGEAR & SWITCHBOARD APPARATUS
3620	10	ELECTRICAL INDUSTRIAL APPARATUS
3621	10	MOTORS & GENERATORS
3630	11	HOUSEHOLD APPLIANCES
3634	11	ELECTRIC HOUSEWARES & FANS
3640	11	ELECTRIC LIGHTING & WIRING EQUIPMENT
3651	11	HOUSEHOLD AUDIO & VIDEO EQUIPMENT
3652	11	PHONOGRAPH RECORDS & PRERECORDED AUDIO TAPES & DISKS
3661	11	TELEPHONE & TELEGRAPH APPARATUS

3663	11	RADIO & TV BROADCASTING & COMMUNICATIONS EQUIPMENT
3669	11	COMMUNICATIONS EQUIPMENT, NEC
3670	10	ELECTRONIC COMPONENTS & ACCESSORIES
3672	3	PRINTED CIRCUIT BOARDS
3674	10	SEMICONDUCTORS & RELATED DEVICES
3677	10	ELECTRONIC COILS, TRANSFORMERS & OTHER INDUCTORS
3678	10	ELECTRONIC CONNECTORS
3679	10	ELECTRONIC COMPONENTS, NEC
3690	10	MISCELLANEOUS ELECTRICAL MACHINERY, EQUIPMENT & SUPPLIES
3695	11	MAGNETIC & OPTICAL RECORDING MEDIA
3711	5	MOTOR VEHICLES & PASSENGER CAR BODIES
3713	5	TRUCK & BUS BODIES
3714	5	MOTOR VEHICLE PARTS & ACCESSORIES
3715	5	TRUCK TRAILERS
3716	5	MOTOR HOMES
3720	5	AIRCRAFT & PARTS
3721	5	AIRCRAFT
3724	5	AIRCRAFT ENGINES & ENGINE PARTS
3728	5	AIRCRAFT PARTS & AUXILIARY EQUIPMENT, NEC
3730	5	SHIP & BOAT BUILDING & REPAIRING
3743	5	RAILROAD EQUIPMENT
3751	5	MOTORCYCLES, BICYCLES & PARTS
3760	5	GUIDED MISSILES & SPACE VEHICLES & PARTS

3790	5	MISCELLANEOUS TRANSPORTATION EQUIPMENT
3812	5	SEARCH, DETECTION, NAVAGATION, GUIDANCE, AERONAUTICAL SYS
3821	10	LABORATORY APPARATUS & FURNITURE
3822	10	AUTO CONTROLS FOR REGULATING RESIDENTIAL & COMML ENVIRONMENTS
3823	10	INDUSTRIAL INSTRUMENTS FOR MEASUREMENT, DISPLAY, AND CONTROL
3824	10	TOTALIZING FLUID METERS & COUNTING DEVICES
3825	10	INSTRUMENTS FOR MEAS & TESTING OF ELECTRICITY & ELEC SIGNALS
3826	10	LABORATORY ANALYTICAL INSTRUMENTS
3827	10	OPTICAL INSTRUMENTS & LENSES
3829	10	MEASURING & CONTROLLING DEVICES, NEC
3841	10	SURGICAL & MEDICAL INSTRUMENTS & APPARATUS
3842	10	ORTHOPEDIC, PROSTHETIC & SURGICAL APPLIANCES & SUPPLIES
3843	10	DENTAL EQUIPMENT & SUPPLIES
3844	10	X-RAY APPARATUS & TUBES & RELATED IRRADIATION APPARATUS
3845	10	ELECTROMEDICAL & ELECTROTHERAPEUTIC APPARATUS
3851	10	OPHTHALMIC GOODS
3861	10	PHOTOGRAPHIC EQUIPMENT & SUPPLIES
3873	2	WATCHES, CLOCKS, CLOCKWORK OPERATED DEVICES/PARTS
3910	2	JEWELRY, SILVERWARE & PLATED WARE

3911	2	JEWELRY, PRECIOUS METAL
3931	5	MUSICAL INSTRUMENTS
3942	5	DOLLS & STUFFED TOYS
3944	5	GAMES, TOYS & CHILDREN'S VEHICLES (NO DOLLS & BICYCLES)
3949	5	SPORTING & ATHLETIC GOODS, NEC
3950	9	PENS, PENCILS & OTHER ARTISTS' MATERIALS
3960	6	COSTUME JEWELRY & NOVELTIES
3990	6	MISCELLANEOUS MANUFACTURING INDUSTRIES
4011	5	RAILROADS, LINE-HAUL OPERATING
4013	5	RAILROAD SWITCHING & TERMINAL ESTABLISHMENTS
4100	5	LOCAL & SUBURBAN TRANSIT & INTERURBAN HWY PASSENGER TRANS
4210	5	TRUCKING & COURIER SERVICES (NO AIR)
4213	5	TRUCKING (NO LOCAL)
4220	5	PUBLIC WAREHOUSING & STORAGE
4231	5	TERMINAL MAINTENANCE FACILITIES FOR MOTOR FREIGHT TRANSPORT
4400	5	WATER TRANSPORTATION
4412	5	DEEP SEA FOREIGN TRANSPORTATION OF FREIGHT
4512	5	AIR TRANSPORTATION, SCHEDULED
4513	5	AIR COURIER SERVICES
4522	5	AIR TRANSPORTATION, NONSCHEDULED
4581	5	AIRPORTS, FLYING FIELDS & AIRPORT TERMINAL SERVICES
4610	4	PIPELINES (NO NATURAL GAS)

4700	5	TRANSPORTATION SERVICES
4731	5	ARRANGEMENT OF TRANSPORTATION OF FREIGHT & CARGO
4812	11	RADIOTELEPHONE COMMUNICATIONS
4813	11	TELEPHONE COMMUNICATIONS (NO RADIOTELEPHONE)
4822	11	TELEGRAPH & OTHER MESSAGE COMMUNICATIONS
4832	11	RADIO BROADCASTING STATIONS
4833	11	TELEVISION BROADCASTING STATIONS
4841	11	CABLE & OTHER PAY TELEVISION SERVICES
4899	11	COMMUNICATIONS SERVICES, NEC
4900	2	ELECTRIC, GAS & SANITARY SERVICES
4911	2	ELECTRIC SERVICES
4922	2	NATURAL GAS TRANSMISSION
4923	2	NATURAL GAS TRANSMISSION & DISTRIBUTION
4924	2	NATURAL GAS DISTRIBUTION
4931	2	ELECTRIC & OTHER SERVICES COMBINED
4932	2	GAS & OTHER SERVICES COMBINED
4941	2	WATER SUPPLY
4950	6	SANITARY SERVICES
4953	6	REFUSE SYSTEMS
4955	6	HAZARDOUS WASTE MANAGEMENT
4961	2	STEAM & AIR-CONDITIONING SUPPLY
4991	2	COGENERATION SERVICES & SMALL POWER PRODUCERS
5000	2	WHOLESALE—DURABLE GOODS

5010	5	WHOLESALE—MOTOR VEHICLES & MOTOR VEHICLE PARTS & SUPPLIES
5013	5	WHOLESALE—MOTOR VEHICLE SUPPLIES & NEW PARTS
5020	2	WHOLESALE—FURNITURE & HOME FURNISHINGS
5030	6	WHOLESALE—LUMBER & OTHER CONSTRUCTION MATERIALS
5031	6	WHOLESALE—LUMBER, PLYWOOD, MILLWORK & WOOD PANELS
5040	2	WHOLESALE—PROFESSIONAL & COMMERCIAL EQUIPMENT & SUPPLIES
5045	3	WHOLESALE—COMPUTERS & PERIPHERAL EQUIPMENT & SOFTWARE
5047	9	WHOLESALE—MEDICAL, DENTAL & HOSPITAL EQUIPMENT & SUPPLIES
5050	5	WHOLESALE—METALS & MINERALS (NO PETROLEUM)
5051	5	WHOLESALE—METALS SERVICE CENTERS & OFFICES
5063	10	WHOLESALE—ELECTRICAL APPARATUS & EQUIPMENT, WIRING SUPPLIES
5064	10	WHOLESALE—ELECTRICAL APPLIANCES, TV & RADIO SETS
5065	10	WHOLESALE—ELECTRONIC PARTS & EQUIPMENT, NEC
5070	6	WHOLESALE—HARDWARE & PLUMBING & HEATING EQUIPMENT & SUPPLIES
5072	6	WHOLESALE—HARDWARE
5080	6	WHOLESALE—MACHINERY, EQUIPMENT & SUPPLIES
5082	6	WHOLESALE—CONSTRUCTION & MINING (NO PETRO) MACHINERY & EQUIP

5084	6	WHOLESALE—INDUSTRIAL MACHINERY & EQUIPMENT
5090	2	WHOLESALE—MISC DURABLE GOODS
5094	2	WHOLESALE—JEWELRY, WATCHES, PRECIOUS STONES & METALS
5099	2	WHOLESALE—DURABLE GOODS, NEC
5110	9	WHOLESALE—PAPER & PAPER PRODUCTS
5122	9	WHOLESALE—DRUGS, PROPRIETARIES & DRUGGISTS' SUNDRIES
5130	9	WHOLESALE—APPAREL, PIECE GOODS & NOTIONS
5140	2	WHOLESALE—GROCERIES & RELATED PRODUCTS
5141	2	WHOLESALE—GROCERIES, GENERAL LINE
5150	5	WHOLESALE—FARM PRODUCT RAW MATERIALS
5160	6	WHOLESALE—CHEMICALS & ALLIED PRODUCTS
5171	4	WHOLESALE—PETROLEUM BULK STATIONS & TERMINALS
5172	4	WHOLESALE—PETROLEUM & PETROLEUM PRODUCTS (NO BULK STATIONS)
5180	9	WHOLESALE—BEER, WINE & DISTILLED ALCOHOLIC BEVERAGES
5190	2	WHOLESALE—MISCELLANEOUS NONDURABLE GOODS
5200	6	RETAIL—BUILDING MATERIALS, HARDWARE, GARDEN SUPPLY
5211	6	RETAIL—LUMBER & OTHER BUILDING MATERIALS DEALERS
5271	2	RETAIL—MOBILE HOME DEALERS
5311	2	RETAIL—DEPARTMENT STORES

5331	2	RETAIL—VARIETY STORES
5399	2	RETAIL—MISC GENERAL MERCHANDISE STORES
5400	2	RETAIL—FOOD STORES
5411	2	RETAIL—GROCERY STORES
5412	2	RETAIL—CONVENIENCE STORES
5500	2	RETAIL—AUTO DEALERS & GASOLINE STATIONS
5531	2	RETAIL—AUTO & HOME SUPPLY STORES
5600	9	RETAIL—APPAREL & ACCESSORY STORES
5621	9	RETAIL—WOMEN'S CLOTHING STORES
5651	9	RETAIL—FAMILY CLOTHING STORES
5661	9	RETAIL—SHOE STORES
5700	2	RETAIL—HOME FURNITURE, FURNISHINGS & EQUIPMENT STORES
5712	2	RETAIL—FURNITURE STORES
5731	2	RETAIL—RADIO, TV & CONSUMER ELECTRONICS STORES
5734	2	RETAIL—COMPUTER & COMPUTER SOFTWARE STORES
5735	2	RETAIL—RECORD & PRERECORDED TAPE STORES
5810	5	RETAIL—EATING & DRINKING PLACES
5812	5	RETAIL—EATING PLACES
5900	2	RETAIL—MISCELLANEOUS RETAIL
5912	1	RETAIL—DRUG STORES AND PROPRIETARY STORES
5940	2	RETAIL—MISCELLANEOUS SHOPPING GOODS STORES
5944	2	RETAIL—JEWELRY STORES

5945	2	RETAIL—HOBBY, TOY & GAME SHOPS
5960	2	RETAIL—NONSTORE RETAILERS
5961	2	RETAIL—CATALOG & MAIL-ORDER HOUSES
5990	2	RETAIL—RETAIL STORES, NEC
6021	7	NATIONAL COMMERCIAL BANKS
6022	7	STATE COMMERCIAL BANKS
6029	7	COMMERCIAL BANKS, NEC
6035	7	SAVINGS INSTITUTION, FEDERALLY CHARTERED
6036	7	SAVINGS INSTITUTIONS, NOT FEDERALLY CHARTERED
6099	7	FUNCTIONS RELATED TO DEPOSITORY BANKING, NEC
6111	7	FEDERAL & FEDERALLY SPONSORED CREDIT AGENCIES
6141	7	PERSONAL CREDIT INSTITUTIONS
6153	7	SHORT-TERM BUSINESS CREDIT INSTITUTIONS
6159	7	MISCELLANEOUS BUSINESS CREDIT INSTITUTIONS
6162	7	MORTGAGE BANKERS & LOAN CORRESPONDENTS
6163	7	LOAN BROKERS
6172	7	FINANCE LESSORS
6189	5	ASSET-BACKED SECURITIES
6199	7	FINANCE SERVICES
6200	8	SECURITY & COMMODITY BROKERS, DEALERS, EXCHANGES & SERVICES
6211	8	SECURITY BROKERS, DEALERS & FLOTATION COMPANIES

6221	8	COMMODITY CONTRACTS BROKERS & DEALERS
6282	6	INVESTMENT ADVICE
6311	1	LIFE INSURANCE
6321	1	ACCIDENT & HEALTH INSURANCE
6324	1	HOSPITAL & MEDICAL SERVICE PLANS
6331	1	FIRE, MARINE & CASUALTY INSURANCE
6351	1	SURETY INSURANCE
6361	1	TITLE INSURANCE
6399	1	INSURANCE CARRIERS, NEC
6411	1	INSURANCE AGENTS, BROKERS & SERVICE
6500	8	REAL ESTATE
6510	8	REAL ESTATE OPERATORS (NO DEVELOPERS) & LESSORS
6512	8	OPERATORS OF NONRESIDENTIAL BUILDINGS
6513	8	OPERATORS OF APARTMENT BUILDINGS
6519	8	LESSORS OF REAL PROPERTY, NEC
6531	8	REAL ESTATE AGENTS & MANAGERS (FOR OTHERS)
6532	8	REAL ESTATE DEALERS (FOR THEIR OWN ACCOUNT)
6552	8	LAND SUBDIVIDERS & DEVELOPERS (NO CEMETERIES)
6770	9	BLANK CHECKS
6792	4	OIL ROYALTY TRADERS
6794	3	PATENT OWNERS & LESSORS
6795	4	MINERAL ROYALTY TRADERS
6798	8	REAL ESTATE INVESTMENT TRUSTS

6799	8	INVESTORS, NEC
7000	8	HOTELS, ROOMING HOUSES, CAMPS & OTHER LODGING PLACES
7011	8	HOTELS & MOTELS
7200	11	SERVICES—PERSONAL SERVICES
7310	11	SERVICES—ADVERTISING
7311	11	SERVICES—ADVERTISING AGENCIES
7320	11	SERVICES—CONSUMER CREDIT REPORTING, COLLECTION AGENCIES
7330	11	SERVICES—MAILING, REPRODUCTION, COMMERCIAL ART & PHOTOGRAPHY
7331	11	SERVICES—DIRECT MAIL ADVERTISING SERVICES
7340	8	SERVICES—TO DWELLINGS & OTHER BUILDINGS
7350	6	SERVICES—MISCELLANEOUS EQUIPMENT RENTAL & LEASING
7359	6	SERVICES—EQUIPMENT RENTAL & LEASING, NEC
7361	8	SERVICES—EMPLOYMENT AGENCIES
7363	11	SERVICES—HELP SUPPLY SERVICES
7370	3	SERVICES—COMPUTER PROGRAMMING, DATA PROCESSING, ETC.
7371	3	SERVICES—COMPUTER PROGRAMMING SERVICES
7372	3	SERVICES—PREPACKAGED SOFTWARE
7373	3	SERVICES—COMPUTER INTEGRATED SYSTEMS DESIGN
7374	3	SERVICES—COMPUTER PROCESSING & DATA PREPARATION

7377	3	SERVICES—COMPUTER RENTAL & LEASING
7380	11	SERVICES—MISCELLANEOUS BUSINESS SERVICES
7381	11	SERVICES—DETECTIVE, GUARD & ARMORED CAR SERVICES
7384	11	SERVICES—PHOTOFINISHING LABORATORIES
7385	11	SERVICES—TELEPHONE INTERCONNECT SYSTEMS
7389	2 & 3	SERVICES—BUSINESS SERVICES, NEC
7500	5	SERVICES—AUTOMOTIVE REPAIR, SERVICES & PARKING
7510	5	SERVICES—AUTO RENTAL & LEASING (NO DRIVERS)
7600	11	SERVICES—MISCELLANEOUS REPAIR SERVICES
7812	5	SERVICES—MOTION PICTURE & VIDEO TAPE PRODUCTION
7819	5	SERVICES—ALLIED TO MOTION PICTURE PRODUCTION
7822	5	SERVICES—MOTION PICTURE & VIDEO TAPE DISTRIBUTION
7829	5	SERVICES—ALLIED TO MOTION PICTURE DISTRIBUTION
7830	5	SERVICES—MOTION PICTURE THEATERS
7841	5	SERVICES—VIDEO TAPE RENTAL
7900	5	SERVICES—AMUSEMENT & RECREATION SERVICES
7948	5	SERVICES—RACING, INCLUDING TRACK OPERATION
7990	5	SERVICES—MISCELLANEOUS AMUSEMENT & RECREATION

7997	5	SERVICES—MEMBERSHIP SPORTS & RECREATION CLUBS
8000	9	SERVICES—HEALTH SERVICES
8011	1	SERVICES—OFFICES & CLINICS OF DOCTORS OF MEDICINE
8050	11	SERVICES—NURSING & PERSONAL CARE FACILITIES
8051	11	SERVICES—SKILLED NURSING CARE FACILITIES
8060	1	SERVICES—HOSPITALS
8062	1	SERVICES—GENERAL MEDICAL & SURGICAL HOSPITALS, NEC
8071	9	SERVICES—MEDICAL LABORATORIES
8082	9	SERVICES—HOME HEALTH CARE SERVICES
8090	9	SERVICES—MISC HEALTH & ALLIED SERVICES, NEC
8093	1	SERVICES—SPECIALTY OUTPATIENT FACILITIES, NEC
8111	11	SERVICES—LEGAL SERVICES
8200	11	SERVICES—EDUCATIONAL SERVICES
8300	9	SERVICES—SOCIAL SERVICES
8351	9	SERVICES—CHILD DAY CARE SERVICES
8600	5	SERVICES—MEMBERSHIP ORGANIZATIONS
8700	6	SERVICES—ENGINEERING, ACCOUNTING, RESEARCH, MANAGEMENT
8711	6	SERVICES—ENGINEERING SERVICES
8731	1	SERVICES—COMMERCIAL PHYSICAL & BIOLOGICAL RESEARCH
8734	9	SERVICES—TESTING LABORATORIES

8741	8	SERVICES—MANAGEMENT SERVICES
8742	8	SERVICES—MANAGEMENT CONSULTING SERVICES
8744	6	SERVICES—FACILITIES SUPPORT MANAGEMENT SERVICES
8880	99	AMERICAN DEPOSITARY RECEIPTS
8888	99	FOREIGN GOVERNMENTS
8900	11	SERVICES—SERVICES, NEC
9721	99	INTERNATIONAL AFFAIRS
9995	9	NONOPERATING ESTABLISHMENTS

CHAPTER 5

Skills That Sell

"*Knowing others is wisdom; knowing yourself is enlightenment.*"

—Lao-Tzu

Knowing your skills builds a rock-solid foundation for your Q statements. It will also be an extremely valuable lesson to you for interviewing.

If you know *as few as six* of your skills as well as you know your own home address, both your interview and your résumé are likely to be smashing successes. Once you can describe your skills (how you used them and what the result was) on your résumé and in your interview, you are literally unstoppable as a job seeker.

This is exactly what Q statements do. Consider this study:

When more than 4,000 employers were interviewed about why they did *not* select certain candidates, the first thing they said was that the candidates could not clearly describe their skills.

Now stop and read that last sentence again. It doesn't say that the candidates who were not chosen did not *have* the right skills for the job. It says that, in the employer's eyes, they *could not clearly describe their skills*. The employers in that survey also responded that, in their opinion, 85 percent of the job seekers they saw could not or would not describe their skills in a clear and specific manner.

You *will* be able to do this. And you certainly don't have to be a writer or a scholar to do so. All you have to know, you're going to learn in the next two chapters. If you know what the words *who, what, when, where, how,* and *why* and the question *what happened?* mean, you will very shortly become an expert at clearly describing your skills.

- Can you believe that simply by completing this and the next chapter, you will be part of the top 15 percent of job seekers? Well it's true. And the sad part is that everyone doesn't take the time or have the knowledge that *you* are going to learn in just a few pages. Are you ready?

Three Categories of Skills

There are three types of skills that we will be talking about in this chapter, and all of them are very important for both your résumé and your interview.

These three essential skill categories are

1. General skills
2. Job-specific skills
3. Personal traits or characteristics

- Identifying your skills in each of these three categories is the first in crafting Q statements clearly and convincingly on your résumé.

General Skills

First, let's take a look at general skills and see why they can be so important to you, whether you're planning to stay in the same occupation or are thinking about making a move into an entirely new profession.

Here are some examples of general skills to remind you of some of the actions you may have performed in the past while on the job, volunteering, going to school, or in other situations. Please go through the list and check off the skills that you know how to perform and even the ones that you feel you *could* perform with just a little bit of practice.

- In other words, you don't have to be an expert at a skill to check it off on this list. You may have used the skill only once, but if you have even a bit of knowledge about how to use it, check it off.

After all, every time you switch to a new job, you have to brush up on or even spend a bit of time relearning certain skills. Be generous with yourself as you do this assessment. Don't cheat yourself out of a skill just because you feel you can't do it perfectly. Even experts aren't perfect.

EXERCISE 5
General Skills Inventory

☐ Acting   ☐ Advertising
☐ Adding   ☐ Advising
☐ Administering   ☐ Analyzing

- ☐ Announcing
- ☐ Arranging
- ☐ Assessing
- ☐ Assisting
- ☐ Attaching
- ☐ Attending
- ☐ Auditing
- ☐ Balancing
- ☐ Budgeting
- ☐ Building chemical compounds
- ☐ Building cooperation
- ☐ Building rapport
- ☐ Building relationships
- ☐ Building structures
- ☐ Buying
- ☐ Calculating
- ☐ Caring
- ☐ Celebrating
- ☐ Charting
- ☐ Chiseling
- ☐ Choosing
- ☐ Classifying clients
- ☐ Cleaning
- ☐ Clearing
- ☐ Climbing
- ☐ Closing
- ☐ Coaching
- ☐ Cold calling
- ☐ Collecting
- ☐ Communicating feelings
- ☐ Communicating ideas
- ☐ Communicating instructions or commands
- ☐ Communicating in writing
- ☐ Communicating nonverbally
- ☐ Communicating verbally
- ☐ Competing
- ☐ Compiling
- ☐ Completing
- ☐ Composing
- ☐ Conceptualizing
- ☐ Consulting
- ☐ Convening
- ☐ Cooperating
- ☐ Coordinating
- ☐ Correcting
- ☐ Corresponding
- ☐ Counseling
- ☐ Crafting
- ☐ Creating
- ☐ Customer relations
- ☐ Dancing
- ☐ Data processing
- ☐ Decision making
- ☐ Decorating
- ☐ Decreasing
- ☐ Defining
- ☐ Delegating
- ☐ Designing

☐ Developing
☐ Diagnosing
☐ Directing
☐ Diving
☐ Drafting
☐ Drawing
☐ Dressing
☐ Driving
☐ Editing
☐ Educating
☐ Elevating
☐ Eliminating
☐ E-mail
☐ Empathizing
☐ Enforcing
☐ Engineering
☐ Entertaining
☐ Enumerating
☐ Evaluating
☐ Fighting
☐ Filing
☐ Financial
☐ Financing
☐ Finding
☐ Finishing
☐ Fixing
☐ Flying
☐ Forecasting
☐ Framing
☐ Fund-raising
☐ Gardening

☐ Gesturing
☐ Gifting
☐ Giving
☐ Grafting
☐ Graphing
☐ Greeting
☐ Growing
☐ Guarding
☐ Handling
☐ Healing
☐ Helping
☐ Hiring
☐ Illustrating
☐ Imaging
☐ Imagining
☐ Imbuing
☐ Implementing
☐ Increasing
☐ Influencing
☐ Initiating into a tank
☐ Injecting
☐ Innovating
☐ Integrating
☐ Intervening
☐ Inventing
☐ Investing
☐ Judging
☐ Launching
☐ Leading
☐ Lecturing
☐ Lifting

☐ Lighting
☐ Listening
☐ Litigating
☐ Locating
☐ Lowering
☐ Maintaining
☐ Managing
☐ Marketing
☐ Massaging
☐ Mediating
☐ Mentoring
☐ Mitigating
☐ Molding
☐ Monitoring
☐ Mounting
☐ Multiplying
☐ Networking
☐ New rising
☐ Nullifying
☐ Numbering
☐ Nursing
☐ Nurturing
☐ Observing
☐ Operating
☐ Orchestrating
☐ Organizing
☐ Orienting
☐ Overseeing
☐ Painting
☐ Performing
☐ Persuading
☐ Piloting

☐ Planning
☐ Playing
☐ Polishing
☐ Prescribing
☐ Presenting
☐ Preserving
☐ Preventing
☐ Probing
☐ Producing
☐ Program managing
☐ Programming
☐ Programming computers
☐ Project managing
☐ Promoting
☐ Prospecting
☐ Public speaking
☐ Publishing
☐ Qualifying
☐ Quality assurance
☐ Quantifying
☐ Raising
☐ Rebuilding
☐ Reconciling
☐ Reconstructing
☐ Recording
☐ Redirecting
☐ Redoing
☐ Refurbishing
☐ Renovating
☐ Repairing
☐ Reporting
☐ Researching

☐ Responding
☐ Retracting
☐ Returning
☐ Revamping
☐ Reversing
☐ Sales
☐ Sanding
☐ Sanitizing
☐ Saving
☐ Scaling
☐ Sealing
☐ Searching
☐ Selecting
☐ Selling
☐ Servicing
☐ Serving
☐ Sewing
☐ Signaling
☐ Signing
☐ Sizing
☐ Speaking
☐ Stocking
☐ Stripping
☐ Structuring
☐ Supervising
☐ Supporting
☐ Surveying
☐ Synchronizing
☐ Synergizing
☐ Taking
☐ Talking
☐ Teaching

☐ Team building
☐ Teasing
☐ Telecommunicating
☐ Telemarketing
☐ Telephoning
☐ Tending
☐ Terminating
☐ Tipping
☐ Titling
☐ Tooling
☐ Training
☐ Translating
☐ Transporting
☐ Treading
☐ Treating
☐ Tripling
☐ Troubleshooting
☐ Ultrasound
☐ Understanding
☐ Unplugging
☐ Using
☐ Using equipment
☐ Using the Internet
☐ Using resources
☐ Watching
☐ Weaving
☐ Welding
☐ Winning
☐ Wiring
☐ Wrangling
☐ Writing
☐ X-ray

Write other general skills or action words that are not on this list, but that fit you or your past jobs:

_____

_____

_____

_____

_____

_____

_____

_____

_____

At this point, you should be feeling pretty good. I will bet you right now that you actually have more skills than you suspected you had.

You may also be thinking, "Okay, good organizational skills, communication abilities, and supervisory accomplishments are all parts of my profile, but that's not *all* there is to what I know how to do."

You're absolutely right!

Job-Specific Skills

All we've talked about so far are very general skills that could be used in a number of jobs. But when you think about it, in your *particular* area of expertise, you use very specific skills that are not used in other professions.

We call these abilities job-specific skills, or those abilities that you need if you are to succeed in your particular job at your particular company in your particular industry.

Scan the following information for some examples of job-specific skills for different occupations. You may not see your occupation listed, but you'll get an idea of the difference between job-specific skills and the general skills you've already identified.

- Your job-specific skills are usually listed on your résumé, but remember to describe exactly *what you did* with those skills, as we will in the next chapter with Q statements.

Please take a look now at the following lists of some job-specific skills. These are abilities in which proficiency is necessary in selected occupations.

For example, people in accounting, bookkeeping, or finance may have the following job-specific skills:

- Accounts payable
- Accounts receivable
- Payroll
- Tax filings

A football player would have

- An understanding of football strategy
- The ability to stay in shape off-season
- The ability to play the position to which he is assigned
- Knowledge of how to get motivated before the game

A computer programmer's job-specific skills would include knowledge of

- Computer languages
- Computer platforms
- Computer programs
- Computer networking

A surgeon would have expert knowledge of

- Human anatomy and physiology
- How to make a diagnosis and prognosis
- Necessary sterilization procedures
- The ability to perform surgery

Marketing specialists have job-specific skills like

- Press release writing
- Trade show coordinating
- Forecasting
- Branding

Psychotherapists would have special skills in

- Diagnosing a client's mental health
- Nonverbal behavior
- Cognitive behavioral therapy
- Brief therapy

A financial planner may possess

- Special licenses, like a Series 7 or a Series 35
- Knowledge of stocks, bonds, insurance, and mutual funds
- Information concerning advising clients on how to save money
- Knowledge of retirement planning

An environmental planner would have job-specific skills such as

- Knowledge of geology
- Master of biology and chemistry
- Knowledge of city and county zoning laws
- Information on the causes of and solutions for pollution

A publisher would be required to have

- Exceptional literacy
- Expertise in the publishing process, from pitching to marketing
- Knowledge of how to evaluate books for publication
- Insight into trends in bookselling

Job-specific skills of a semiconductor assembler would be

- Knowledge of the component parts of a wafer
- Information on clean room technology
- Knowledge of safety procedures
- Superior fine motor control

An office manager would know how to

- Order office supplies and keep the whole office running within a budget
- Operate Microsoft Office or other computer programs
- Answer the phone, take messages, and route calls professionally
- Operate modern office equipment

Your job or career was very likely not mentioned in this section. Still, I think you've caught on quickly to the differences between general and job-specific skills and can now identify some job-specific skills of your own.

EXERCISE 6
Job-Specific Skills Inventory

Please write 10 to 20 job-specific skills that you've acquired. Don't forget to include *both* the skills you've used in your work life *and* those you've used in other settings, such as the following:

- Running a household
- Being a student
- Contributing to your church, temple, or faith
- Being in a club
- Playing on a sports team
- Serving in the military

- Volunteering
- Being an intern
- Serving a jail sentence
- Traveling

Please write your job-specific skills here.

_____

_____

_____

_____

_____

_____

_____

_____

_____

Keep in mind that we are always learning and hopefully accepting new responsibilities, and thus even things that you may take for granted, such as doing your laundry, balancing your checkbook, replacing a flat tire, or investing in the stock market as a hobby, are all part of who you are and what you can do.

Just think of all the things you do in a day, a week, a year, or a decade! You could probably write a book about it, but don't worry. We're just going to stick to a one- or two-page résumé for now.

Personal Characteristics

Personal characteristics are not like the other skills you've just identified. Personal characteristics are not something that you *do*; they instead represent something that you *are*.

- Personal characteristics are special qualities that make up parts of your personality. Your personality greatly affects how you do your job and how well suited you would be for a certain job or company.

It's possible that you already know a typical personal profile for your industry or occupation. In that case, by all means list the qualities that make up that profile. But let's take it a bit further and include those characteristics that make you, and only you, a unique contributor to the workplace.

EXERCISE 7
Personal Characteristics Inventory

The following is a list (inventory) of many personal traits. My guess is that you possess quite a few of these qualities and that they will make a positive impact on both your résumé and your interview. Please place a check by those personal characteristics that apply to you.

Remember, there's nothing to be gained from being modest. If you asked any good friend or coworker, she would probably agree that you do indeed possess these qualities. *Be sure to give yourself credit for your own best traits.*

- ☐ Accepting
- ☐ Accurate
- ☐ Achievement oriented
- ☐ Action oriented
- ☐ Aggressive
- ☐ Ambitious
- ☐ Analytical
- ☐ Artistic
- ☐ Assertive
- ☐ Aware
- ☐ Balanced
- ☐ Brilliant
- ☐ Businesslike
- ☐ Calm
- ☐ Caring
- ☐ Cautious

☐ Challenging	☐ Fair
☐ Charismatic	☐ Fit
☐ Committed	☐ Friendly
☐ Communicative	☐ Frugal
☐ Compassionate	☐ Generous
☐ Competitive	☐ Gentle
☐ Concerned	☐ Genuine
☐ Confident	☐ Gifted
☐ Conservative	☐ Hardworking
☐ Courageous	☐ Healthy
☐ Creative	☐ Helpful
☐ Dedicated	☐ High self-esteem
☐ Dependable	☐ Honest
☐ Detail oriented	☐ Humorous
☐ Determined	☐ Independent
☐ Diligent	☐ Innovative
☐ Diplomatic	☐ Insightful
☐ Direct	☐ Inspirational
☐ Driven	☐ Intellectual
☐ Dynamic	☐ Intelligent
☐ Easygoing	☐ Introverted
☐ Economical	☐ Intuitive
☐ Effective	☐ Inventive
☐ Efficient	☐ Kind
☐ Emotionally strong	☐ Knowledgeable
☐ Energetic	☐ Likable
☐ Entertaining	☐ Lively
☐ Enthusiastic	☐ Logical
☐ Entrepreneurial	☐ Loved
☐ Ethical	☐ Loyal
☐ Exemplary	☐ Mature
☐ Expressive	☐ Methodical

- ☐ Meticulous
- ☐ Modest
- ☐ Moral
- ☐ Motivating
- ☐ Nice
- ☐ Nurturing
- ☐ Obedient
- ☐ Observant
- ☐ Optimistic
- ☐ Orderly
- ☐ Outgoing
- ☐ Patient
- ☐ Perfectionist
- ☐ Persuasive
- ☐ Physically strong
- ☐ Powerful
- ☐ Precise
- ☐ Private
- ☐ Proactive
- ☐ Productive
- ☐ Punctual
- ☐ Purposeful
- ☐ Rational
- ☐ Relaxed
- ☐ Reserved
- ☐ Resilient
- ☐ Resourceful
- ☐ Respected
- ☐ Respectful
- ☐ Responsible
- ☐ Responsive
- ☐ Results oriented
- ☐ Scientific
- ☐ Self-controlled
- ☐ Self-motivated
- ☐ Sincere
- ☐ Sociable
- ☐ Spontaneous
- ☐ Supportive
- ☐ Systematic
- ☐ Tactful
- ☐ Task oriented
- ☐ Team oriented
- ☐ Team player
- ☐ Tenacious
- ☐ Thorough
- ☐ Thoughtful
- ☐ Thrifty
- ☐ Tidy
- ☐ Tolerant
- ☐ Trustworthy
- ☐ Uninhibited
- ☐ Unique
- ☐ Unselfish
- ☐ Unstoppable
- ☐ Unusual
- ☐ Visionary
- ☐ Vivacious
- ☐ Warm
- ☐ Well groomed
- ☐ Well liked
- ☐ Well spoken
- ☐ Winner

Please write any other positive words that come to mind when describing yourself. Don't forget the compliments that *others* have given you.

_____

_____

_____

_____

_____

_____

_____

_____

Excellent! Now that you've taken the time to really concentrate on the special skills and personal characteristics that you possess, let's note them down for future reference so that you can refer to them at a glance when writing your résumé or when preparing for an interview. Choosing the skills that you like most and that are most relevant for your future, I'd like you to assemble what I call your skills arsenal. You may not use every single one of these skills on the first résumé you write, but I can guarantee that your selections will come in handy any time you wish to compose or revise your Fearless Résumé.

Modify Your Power Proposition

Note: If you think that some of the words you include in the next exercise are more suited to the specialties section of your power proposition than the ones you selected when you first wrote it, then by all means go back and change your power proposition so that it has your most up-to-date reflection of your specialties (skills) and your personal characteristics.

General Skills Arsenal

Please select and write your top ten general skills.

1. _____
2. _____
3. _____
4. _____
5. _____
6. _____
7. _____
8. _____
9. _____
10. _____

Job-Specific Skills Arsenal

Good work! Now think about your 6 to 10 most used job-specific skills and note them here, keeping in mind that you may be using many of them to describe skills on your Fearless Résumé that pertain to a job or new career goal. Please select at least 6 to 10.

1. _____
2. _____
3. _____
4. _____
5. _____
6. _____
7. _____
8. _____
9. _____
10. _____

Personal Characteristics Arsenal

You've now completed a fantastic list of what some human resources people call your "hard" skills. Now, let's look at the very important aspect that is also important in the workplace—your personal characteristics—sometimes called your "soft" skills. Use the previous exercise in this chapter to select three to six of the personal characteristics that you know you have and that you think would be useful for the next job you apply for, and note them here.

1. _____

2. _____

3. _____

4. _____

5. _____

6. _____

- I'm impressed! Never again will you have to fumble or guess about what your strengths and abilities really are. They're right here on paper, and you should take a moment to feel *very* proud of them.

Your Unique Blend of Skills

I am not trying to be nice when I say that you—yes, you!—are absolutely unique, and therefore *profoundly* special. I defy you to search the world for a person with your *exact* blend of general skills, job-specific skills, and personal traits. Whether you believe in a supreme being, are a staunch geneticist, or are a bit of both, I will tell you that there is *no one* like you. Your Fearless Résumé will make that evident.

CHAPTER 6

Make Your Job History Sizzle

"The road to happiness lies in two simple principles—find what interests you and that you can do and put your whole soul into it."

—John D. Rockefeller III

Can you picture yourself saddled with the task of reading up to 1,500 résumés for *one* job opening? Well, you can be sure that *someone* is in the middle of doing just that right now. Let's say that you are the hiring manager. Imagine that you've reached résumé 809 out of the 1,500 you're responsible for reviewing. You've got to admit that, up to now, you've gathered a couple of "maybes," but no one résumé has really struck an *emotional* chord with you.

Suddenly, holding number 809 in your hand, you get a feeling in your gut the second you lay eyes on it, and you are eager to read more. This (Fearless) résumé conjures up vivid and clear images in your mind of the writer doing detailed, engaging, or even colorful tasks.

Even better, these tasks have consequences. They could help you as a manager! They could help the company!

Would you keep reading that résumé? Would it put you in a different mood? Do you think you might be relieved, hopeful, and happy?

Do you think that, if the descriptions of this person and her skills were closely enough matched to both the job requirements and your own personal preferences, you might even want to *meet* this person?

If you were a hiring manager, you bet you would. Hiring managers aren't robots, you know. The person reading your résumé is a real person, just like you. Just as you don't want the drudgery of reading a lot of dull documents, neither does he.

That's where Q statements come in. Q statements are more than just phrases about your job duties. Instead, they are dynamic and often measurable sentences that give rich sensory information.

- Because a Q statement is so specific and detailed, it causes readers to form pictures in their minds of you doing tasks and reaching goals that spell out "*hire*."

What Is a Q Statement?

A Q statement is a phrase or sentence that actively and vividly describes something that you have accomplished.

Most often, Q statements include

1. A *skill* or *skills* that you used to accomplish this.
2. Some description of either *how, what, when, where,* or *why* you achieved this accomplishment.
3. A *measurement* of some sort, such as a number of people, an amount of money, a percentage, or a number on a scale.
4. The *result* of what you did—for example, how you helped your company, clients, customers, or patients.

Here's a formula for writing a Q statement:

Skill + what you did (including the quantity—usually a number) + the result of what you did

Turning Skills into Q Statements

Let's take the skill *supervised* (which you may have already checked on your general skills exercise in the last chapter) and make it into a Q statement using this formula.

"Supervised [skill] a group of *10 people* on a sales training project lasting *60 days* [what you did, plus numbers to measure what you did], which resulted in the group *exceeding the sales quota for the year by 28 percent* [the result of what you did].

Here are some more Q statements:

✓ Answered [skill] 250 customer service calls per day [what you did, plus a number to measure what you did], resulting in an average of 97 new customers per week, making the company over $6,000 in new customer registration fees per month [the result of what you did].

✓ Configured [skill] two new servers on a wireless networking system [what you did, plus a number to measure what you did] that decreased downtime by 24 percent, saving the company over $12,800 per month [the result of what you did].

You can see that the following Q statements also include a skill word, what the person did, some form of numerical measurement, and a clear result.

- ✓ Planned a fund-raising event involving 350 people paying $1,000 apiece that generated a net profit of over $30,000.
- ✓ Targeted a new market for vending machines that resulted in approximately 1,900 new vending machine locations and a gross profit of $47,890 per month.
- ✓ Sold over 15 new corporate training accounts per quarter, earning the company over $770,000 in new accounts revenue per year.
- ✓ Handled over 300 customer calls per day and routed them to over 85 employees.
- ✓ Instituted and implemented a manufacturing process that increased profits by 47 percent in the fourth quarter.
- ✓ Maintained an average caseload of 55 multicultural clients, only 3 percent of whom required hospitalization.
- ✓ Engineered a prototype that tolerated 18 percent more stress than its precursor.
- ✓ Oversaw landscape design of projects costing up to $450,000.
- ✓ Reduced overhead by 37 percent while increasing profitability by 17 percent per year.

Getting the Employer to Visualize

In every Q statement, there is a little "story" that may include all or just some of the elements of

Who

What

When

Where

How

Why

How much

As in any good story, you want your readers to both be able to clearly picture, in their minds, what you're talking about *and* have an emotional reaction to what you're saying. Let's look at some comparisons between Q statements and phrases that indicate "regular" job duties.

Comparison of Q Statements and Job Duties

PAIR 1. SKILL WORD: LED

Job duty: Led a successful team.

Q statement: Led a team of 12 computer software engineers to develop a new program that resulted in $1.6 million in profits after the first year of its launch.

PAIR 2. SKILL WORD: (TO) RUN

Job duty: Ran an office.

Q statement: Ran and kept detailed records for a busy dental office seeing more than 45 patients per day.

PAIR 3. SKILL WORD: COACH

Job duty: Coached a sports team.

Q statement: Coached a basketball team, using mind-body visualization techniques, that went from number 32 in the state to number 1 in a period of one year.

Did the *first* statement (job duty) in each of the pairs cause you to have a strong sense of what the writer did or how she might contribute to your company? How about the second account (Q statement)?

If you were reading one résumé that was full of statements of job duties and another résumé that was replete with Q statements, which of the two people would you want to interview? Remember, both the first and second statements represent the same skill. Which is more believable? Which is more compelling? Why?

- I think I can guess that you'd agree that Q statements sizzle, while job duty statements are stale.

The magic of a Q statement is not only that it causes your reader to have a more vivid reaction. There's something much more exciting about a Q statement.

When your reader can clearly "see" or "feel" what you did in one of your past jobs, as you describe it with a quantified statement, she also unconsciously imagines you achieving something similar at *her* company!

Don't Force It

Don't worry. You don't have to force the employer to create images in his mind, and you don't have to be a writer, either. If you just supply *detailed* information, which sometimes can be done by using numbers, measurements, amounts, and percentages along with places, people, ideas, and things, the employer's brain will respond automatically.

Using Your Skills as a Starting Point

Since the first word in a Q statement is almost always a skill, you can use some of the general skills and job-specific skills you selected in the last chapter to form some Q statements of your own. In the following statements, simply look at how the skill word fits into the Q statement. Just a bit later in the chapter, you'll find out how to quantify parts of your statement and/or show a quantified result of what you did.

Examples of Skill-Based Q Statements

SKILL: DRIVING

Statement: *Drove* over 350 miles per week through the Central Coast, delivering over 1 ton of cargo.

SKILL: LEADING

Statement: *Led* a team that produced a piston that was over 12 percent more effective than the previous version.

SKILL: SELLING

Statement: *Sold* an average of two real estate properties per month, totaling an average of $30,000 a month in commission.

SKILL: WINNING

Statement: *Won* an award in 2006 for decreasing materials costs from 871 per inch to 686 per inch.

SKILLS: INITIATING AND DEVELOPING

Statement: *Initiated* and *developed* a retraining program for the Hallerite County Police Department that improved public perception of police officers from 2.9 to 4.8 on a scale of 1 to 5.

SKILL: DESIGNED

Statement: *Designed* a new production process that decreased production time by four days a month, resulting in a savings of $430,000 quarterly.

You'll notice that the results and descriptions contained in a quantified statement almost always include some measurement, like a number, an amount of money, a percentage, or a number on a scale.

What we know about employers is that when you can show that you can increase certain things and/or decrease other things, you either directly or indirectly help the employer to *make a profit*.

- What could possibly be a more irresistible hook for an employer than making money?

How to Hook the Employer with a Q Statement

In general, you can be sure that when you directly or indirectly *increase* something that an employer wants, like one of the things listed here, you provide a tangible hook that makes him want to read more and ultimately can lead to an interview. Some things that you might show that you *increased* are

✓ Employee morale
✓ Prestige
✓ Safety
✓ Speed of production (saving time)
✓ Profits
✓ New products
✓ New services
✓ Good public perception
✓ Efficiency or integrity of operations
✓ Government compliance
✓ Branding
✓ Customers/clients
✓ Return on investment
✓ Overtaking competitors
✓ Expansion into new markets
✓ Locations
✓ Financial stability

The same thing is true in the other direction. When you *decrease* something that an employer doesn't want, it often can mean saving the employer money or the firm's reputation. Things that you can create hooks with your Q statements by *decreasing* are

✓ Waste
✓ Accidents
✓ Bad publicity
✓ Unlawful activities
✓ Inefficiency
✓ Downtime
✓ Overhead
✓ Expenses
✓ Workplace harassment
✓ Time it takes to complete a project or process

✓ Poor-quality products
✓ Returns
✓ Excessive maintenance
✓ Tardiness
✓ Sick days
✓ Lawsuits
✓ Disorganization
✓ Unacceptable health and safety practices
✓ (Usually) paying overtime
✓ Unattractive or dirty workplace
✓ Malfunction of equipment

Creating some Q statements right now will propel your résumé into the highest ranking and imbue your interview with the sound of earned success. Remember, you do not have to know *exact* numbers, percentages, or lengths of time.

- Sometimes it's just too hard to recall an exact number, so the best thing to do is to *estimate* your measurements and quanities to the best of your ability.

If you happen to have forgotten the exact details of some of your numbers—say that you indicated on your résumé that you earned $152,000 in sales, but the fact was that you really earned $149,934—no one, unless you're applying at an accounting firm, will call you a liar.

Most of us, of course, don't want to misrepresent ourselves; in fact, most of my clients actually *underestimate* their numbers on their résumés.

Please don't underestimate yourself. You must find a balance that's fair and honest. Few people can recall amounts to the point of perfection. When you are quantifying your accomplishments, just do your best to state your best guess, within reason, as to what you did or what results you achieved. One test for this is to ask, "Would I feel comfortable saying this figure out loud?" If you would, and you spare yourself the harsh judgment of perfectionism, your numbers are probably fine. If not, go back and adjust them a bit.

Now, please create at least five to ten Q statements for yourself. You may adjust them or use different ones when you actually compose your résumé, but there's nothing like getting into the habit of creating Q statements for your skills. It will make you believable, powerful, and, most of all, confident.

1. _____

_____

_____

2. _____

_____

_____

3. _____

_____

_____

4. _____

_____

_____

5. _____

_____

_____

6. _____

_____

_____

7. _____

_____

_____

8. _____

_____

_____

9. _____

_____

_____

10. _____

_____

_____

Good! In the next chapter, you'll see how well your Q statements fit into the body of your résumé in a section called "Employment History."

CHAPTER 7

Organize Your Data for Maximum Impact

"It is only when doing my work that I truly feel alive."

—Federico Fellini

Your Fearless Résumé, as a whole, can be seen as the answers to five simple questions that the employer wants to ask about you. They are

1. Who are you?
2. What do you want?
3. Tell me about yourself.
4. What can you do, and where and how have you done it? What was the result of your actions?
5. Where and how were you trained or educated?

That's it. Whether you're a carpenter, a nurse, or the vice president of a company, these five questions remain basically the same.

Résumé Blocks

Interestingly, in answering these five questions, there are also five mandatory sections of a Fearless Résumé (we'll refer to them as *blocks*). Here are the basic blocks of the résumé. They correspond exactly to the order of the questions just given.

1. The contact block (Who are you?)
2. The objective block (What do you want?)
3. The summary block (Tell me about yourself— your power proposition)
4. The employment history block (What can you do? Where have you done it? What were the results?— your Q statements)
5. The education and training block (Where were you educated?)

Résumés almost always start with block 1 (the contact block) and descend in order down the page to block 5 (the education and training block). That's it. It makes sense, doesn't it?

Order of Résumé Sections

The following is a working diagram of the order of each part of your Fearless Résumé, plus a guideline about the question each section answers.

Contact Block

Question: *Who are you?*

Answer: *Your name, address, phone number(s), and e-mail address*

Example:

Tom Collins
347 24th Avenue
Twin Peaks, WA 2733X
(555) 222-6767 Home
(555) 223-9375 Cell
tcollins@bestinternet.com

Objective Block

Question: *What do you want?*

Answer: *Your job objective (title of the job you're targeting)*

Example: A position as a senior accountant.

Summary Block

Question: *Tell me about yourself.*

Answer: *Your power proposition*

Summary: Over 5 years as an accountant in the health-care industry. Specialties include bookkeeping, accounts receivable, and payroll. Reduced accounts receivable time by an average of 6 days per month using QuickContact software, thereby saving the company over $3,200 in mailing costs. A.A. in Business; B.A. in Finance with an emphasis in Accounting.

Relevant (or "Technical") Skills Block [Optional]

Microsoft Office Suite	Bookkeeping	QuickBooks
Accounts payable	Accounts receivable	Payroll

Employment History Block

Question: *What can you do, and where have you done it? What were the results of your actions?*

Answer: *Your job title, the company(s) you worked for, the city and state, and the dates you were employed there (in that order)*

Plus two to six bulleted Q statements per job

Example:

Senior Accountant
Procorp Health Systems, Twin Peaks, WA   **1999–present**
(Use no less than two and no more than six Q statements)

- ✓ Q statement
- ✓ Q statement
- ✓ Q statement
- ✓ Q statement
- ✓ Q statement
- ✓ Q statement

Junior Accountant
Smindia Hospital, Smindia, WA   **1998–1999**

- ✓ Q statement
- ✓ Q statement
- ✓ Q statement
- ✓ Q statement

The following is the format if you have more than one job title at different times at the same company.

Jetlands Department Store
Bellingham, WA   **1995–1998**
Accountant I (1996–1998)

- ✓ Q statement
- ✓ Q statement

Customer Service Representative (1995–1996)

- ✓ Q statement
- ✓ Q statement

Education Block

Question: *Where were you educated or trained?*

Answer: *List your degrees, licenses, certificates, and any relevant education or training that is in progress.*

Example: Currently enrolled in a course of study leading to a Master of Business Administration with an emphasis in Finance at University of Seattle

B.A. Finance, University of Seattle

A.A. Accounting, Bellingham City College

Publications Block [Optional]

"The Impact of Government Provided Health Care on Acute Care Facilities Management," *Student Journal of Health Care Finance*, September 2006.

Awards Block [Optional]

Employee of the Year Award, Procorp Health Systems, 2001

Professional Affiliations Block [Optional]

Western U.S. Accounting Society

MBA Study Association of UOS

Here's another sample résumé with basic blocks that answers all five questions:

[Who are you?]

Lisa Y. Nguyen

26XX Hillsbury Court, FL 1XXXX

Home phone: (254) XXX-XX23

Mobile phone: (254) XXX-XX54

lisa_yvette_nguyen@hts.net

[What do you want?]

OBJECTIVE

A position as a production manager in the film industry.

[Tell me about yourself]
PROFESSIONAL SUMMARY

[This section would contain Lisa's power proposition. You will notice that we don't actually write the words power proposition on the résumé itself. Instead, we identify this section on the résumé itself as "summary." Other words that are occasionally used instead of summary *are* professional summary, highlights of qualifications, summary of qualifications, *and* professional expertise, *and you may feel free to use those terms on your résumé if you wish.]*

[What have you done, and with what result?]
WORK HISTORY

[Your job title, the name of the company, its city and state, and the years that you worked there. We'll talk later about why you do not need to write the months that you worked, only the years. Your most recent job always goes first.]

Production Manager
Sammy T. Productions, Tampa, FL   2005–2009

[Underneath your title, years, and company, you'll write two to six Q statements.]

- Managed a crew of 3 assistant directors, 4 production assistants, and production.
- Hired a technical and artistic crew of 349.
- Adhered to all Screen Actors Guild and IATSE union rules, including those for children.
- Negotiated and saved 18% of a $16 million budget.
- Scheduled a 27-day shooting schedule with 206 separate scenes.
- Collected records and analyzed personnel, equipment, and expendables usage throughout production to ensure staying on budget.

[Continue in the same manner, going back only 10 to 15 years.]

1st Assistant Director
Archway Film Visions, Orlando, FL   2003–2004

- Coordinated all action on set and ensured timely production of scenes, saving up to 30 minutes daily.
- Managed the actions of 2 other assistant directors and 1 set production assistant.
- Directed 8 second unit scenes and 14 special effects scenes.
- Assisted production manager in scheduling over 117 scenes.

2nd Assistant Director
Metro Net Pictures, Miami, FL   2002–2003

- Ensured that all 11 actors were dressed, made up, and ready for shooting scenes.
- Kept detailed daily records of talent, scenes shot, and adherence to union rules.

Set Production Assistant
GDC Television in conjunction with
Let Her Rip Productions, Orlando, FL   2001

- Followed the orders of the first and second assistant directors.
- In charge of 2 other production assistants for maintaining crowd control on exterior shots.

[Where were you educated or trained?]
EDUCATION
A.A. in Mass Communications, John Blue Community College, Miami, FL

These two résumés show the formula for organizing your Fearless Résumé. You don't have to include the optional blocks unless they apply to you. You do have a great deal of latitude and choice in formatting your résumé, but do stick to this basic template and you're sure to succeed.

The Conversational Approach to Résumé Writing

If you ever feel "stuck" on your résumé and want to get back on track, take a look at the question being asked for the section you're working on. You may even imagine a real person asking the question. Your mind will automatically respond.

This lively question-and-answer approach keeps your imagination fresh as to what the employer wants. *A fearless résumé is therefore about "you and me" rather than just "me, me, me."*

- Rather than being a monologue, as most résumés are, a Fearless Résumé is in fact a *conversation* in which we predict and then answer the questions that the employer naturally has on her mind.

This gets the reader involved and makes your résumé vital and refreshing. It's the responsive and precise way that you will learn to answer these queries that will turn your Fearless Résumé into the roadway to your interview!

Sound good? Okay. I'd bet you'd like to see a Fearless Résumé in action. Let's have a look at a sample résumé and see how the answers to the basic five questions fit on the page.

The questions on the résumés, which appeared earlier in this chapter, are there for you to see and learn from, but you don't actually write the questions on the résumé itself. The sections written in italics are also just guidelines. The italicized sentences should not be written on your real résumé.

Next, I am going to show you some of the optional blocks mentioned earlier. If you have a need for these blocks, use them. If not, they can be left out.

- You'll see plenty of résumés with just the basic blocks *and* some with optional blocks in Chapter 10.

Optional Blocks

For review, optional blocks that *can* be included on your résumé but are not mandatory are

1. Relevant skills (sometimes called "technical skills" or "professional skills")
2. Professional affiliations
3. Publications and patents
4. Awards

Would you like to see some more Fearless Résumés, or are you ready to put pen to paper already?

Either way, you're on your way to producing a fantastic piece of writing. Further examples of Fearless Résumés are provided for you in the last chapter, if you'd like to take a peek at them before you write your own.

CHAPTER 8

Tips for a Terrific Résumé

> "Confidence . . . is directness and courage in meeting the facts of life."
>
> —John Dewey

Okay, you've hit the mark. There are only a few more details to remember. Again, congratulations for caring enough about yourself, your time, and your chosen occupation to learn the state-of-the-art Fearless Résumé.

Yours is a document that will give you an unbeatable start in your job search and a true edge on your competition; it is a marketable, sellable, provable depiction of yourself and your skills that will never, ever bore the reader.

In fact, in the first ten seconds, your document will stop your reader in her tracks and instill within her the *emotional* desire to hire you. In the rest of your petition, she will discover the logical clarity behind this and the survival instinct that leads her to want to have you on her team.

Now it's time for you to compose your own Fearless Résumé, using a template (partly blank form) that I've used with over 15,000 people, from entry-level to executive and from age 18 to 75.

Before you set pen to paper or sit down at your computer, however, let me review some quick tips that will ensure your credibility and make your Fearless Résumé flow seamlessly.

Tips for Your Contact Block

Don't use a nickname. *Do* use your full name. A middle initial or middle name is optional.

For example, write "Bud Smith" rather than "Bud 'the Stud' Smith" or "Bud 'Buddy' Smith."

Of course, this example is quite farfetched, but you wouldn't believe how many silly nicknames I've seen or heard about on résumés!

Basically, using this kind of nickname is a turnoff and will serve only to diminish the importance of your document. Once you get the job, if you would like your coworkers or your boss to refer to you by your nickname, that's fine. Just don't make him try to swallow the nickname before he gets to know you in person or before you get the job.

The same goes for e-mail addresses.

Some of the far-out ones I've seen are rocketman4563@thataway.com and ladyloveyou9835@netscore.net.

E-mail addresses with catchy or clever elements like that are fun to use with your friends and family, but they really are not dignified enough for a résumé.

Try not to use the e-mail address of the company that you currently work for.

If you use the e-mail address of the company you are still working for, watch out. An e-mail address like guy.henry@company1stillworkfor.net will raise understandable suspicions that you are using your own desk, your own time, and your company's time and resources to conduct your own personal business. This is something that is strictly frowned upon. Even if your former company allows you to use their resouces, it is wise to refrain from using your old e-mail address because you never know how the prospective employer will react.

- If the prospective employer sees that you've taken up the habit of wasting your present employer's time, why should he expect that you wouldn't do the same if you were hired to work for his company?

Do use an *11 or 12 point Times New Roman or Arial regular (not bold or italic) font.* Don't use any fancy graphics, typefaces, large-sized letters, or layout. This kind of style, however artistic it may look, is really more confusing to the potential employer and makes the résumé harder to read.

Take the time to get an e-mail address that is *both* personalized to you and professional.

If you're going for a more professional impression, try getting an e-mail account with Yahoo!, hotmail, gmail, Comcast, AOL, or some other free e-mail provider, and pick something that resembles your own name, such as janicegold@freee-mail-provider.com.

Do use a regular street address. Don't use a P.O. box, if at all possible. Although the use of a post office box may serve to protect your privacy, employers often view it with suspicion.

Do use a professional-sounding answering machine or voice mail system with a clear and dignified message. Finally, just a tip: for whatever phone number(s)— home, office, mobile, or toll free—you are listing in the name block on your résumé, be sure that they are equipped with a *professional-sounding message* (without dogs barking, kids yelling, traffic sounds, music, or other distractions).

The simplest message to leave would be something in your own voice (not a mechanical or prerecorded voice if possible) that says:

> "Hello. You've reached Bob Winston at 243-777-7877. Thank you for calling. Please leave a complete message after the tone, including your phone number and the best time to reach you."

Again, *after* you get the job, you can put a more personal or fun touch on your message, but for now, keep it simple and to the point. Try to get an answering machine or voice mail system that allows you to check messages remotely if you are not near your phone so that you'll stay on top of your messages and be able to return calls promptly. Employers absolutely love to get a quick response. It shows that you're efficient and enthusiastic about the job.

You might also consider a call forwarding system, so that if the employer calls your home phone, for example, the call will be automatically forwarded to your cell phone so that you can answer it immediately.

Call forwarding is also available on most cell phones. Call your local phone company or cell phone provider to arrange for one of these easy and inexpensive systems while you're job hunting.

Tips for Your Objective Block

When you're submitting a résumé as a direct response to a printed or Internet ad, *always* use the job title that is used in the job posting. For the reader, who, you remember, may have 350 résumés on his desk or in his inbox, it is annoying to say the least to have to wonder what job you're applying for. As much as you may like to think that the person will read your résumé and find the best "fit" for you in his company, that is *not* his job, and it is extremely rare for a busy recruiter or hiring manager to afford you that favor. Even when you post your résumé on a job board or Web site, hoping that many readers for many companies will view it, you must *still* include some sort of job title. So, in the case of a résumé submission to *one* company for a particular job, if your Fearless Résumé has the title Financial Advisor and the job offered is for a Financial Consultant, you *must* take the little bit of extra time to go back into your résumé and change the job title for this company. It is both a courtesy to the company and an indication that you're serious about applying for *that* particular job in that particular company. Hiring managers like to know that you've put thought into singling out their company because you specifically want to work there. Having no objective or using the wrong words in your objective when you're applying directly for an advertised position indicates that you were careless and did not really *choose* that company at all.

Word Choice

A résumé is a *living* document.

You don't get to write it once and then use the same thing forever. You may change it many times in one job search and several times during your working life.

It is wise to have the words—*all* the words—conform to the verbiage in the job description as much as possible.

So, if the job description mentions Information Technology several times, and the first draft of your résumé refers to the same thing as Computer Science, then by all means change your résumé.

- Some researchers have shown that the more closely the expressions in your résumé mirror the wording in the job description, the better your chances of getting interviewed.

This rule does not apply when you're talking about official degrees and certificates. Do not change the name of an official degree.

Dates

If you've been using months *and* years when presenting your work history, try this little trick (which is completely acceptable on modern résumés, by the way). Do *not* use the months on your résumé at all. Let's look at a sample of a hypothetical job for which you note *both* the months and the years that you worked there and compare it to including *only* the years that you were at the position.

Example of months and years:

Job Title, Company,	December 2006–
City, State	January 2007

How long does it look like you were at that company? You're right—about one month. A very short stay at a particular company raises suspicion in the eyes of the employer. Were you "job hopping"—just looking around casually and leaving if the job didn't work out for you?

- Did you quit prematurely? Were you fired? Could you not adjust to your responsibilities or to the personalities of those you were working with? Did you quarrel with your boss or your supervisor?

What happened, and why did you stay for only a month? Are you afraid of commitment? Are you unable to keep your word? All of these fears and more enter the employer's mind when he sees one, two, or a pattern of short stays at positions.

Although, in my own opinion, you have a right to leave a job for almost any reason whenever you wish, most employers don't see it that way, and it makes sense from their perspective. As you already read, when you put together all the time it takes to do the advertising, paperwork, interviewing, and training of a new hire, it can cost the employer well over $10,000 and sometimes much more.

When a company is making an investment like that, it wants you to stay *at least* long enough for it to get a return on its investment—that is, profitable productivity from your efforts.

I don't have any judgment if you have a "choppy" work history. There are a host of reasons, including family issues, marital separation or discord, medical problems, disability, emotional upset, financial challenges, addiction, harassment on the job, trouble with the law, layoffs, company closures or reorganization, travel or study opportunities, or just simply changing your mind, that may make the work history on your résumé not look as smooth as you would like it to be. The point is, most people, whether you know it or not, have some gaps in their employment history.

The very idea that people should have a perfectly smooth and untainted record of service from the time they graduate from high school or college until the time they retire is unfair and absurd. It's not often that real life works that way.

Still, most companies frown upon obvious gaps in your employment history, and they may pass your résumé by or ask about these gaps at the interview if you don't do something about them on your résumé. Fortunately, there are ways to tackle this problem and still maintain your integrity without having to lie. Three of them are

1. Listing only years on your résumé
2. Omitting certain jobs, if possible
3. Indicating on the résumé what you were doing and/or that you are willing to discuss a gap of more than one year at the interview

Listing Only Years on Your Résumé

Let's look at each of these solutions one by one. Remember the example of the person's résumé that indicated that she had worked for only one month at a company? Here it is again:

Job Title, Company,   December 2006–
City, State   January 2007

Now, what if we omit the months and use only the years of employment?

Job Title, Company,   2006–2007
City, State

Much better, isn't it? It's even possible that the person was at that job from January 2006 to December 2007—almost *two* years.

- On a job application, you must write the year, the month, and sometimes even the day that your employment began and ended. Fortunately, this is not necessary on a résumé unless the employer specifically requests it, which is very rare.

Omitting a Job from Your Résumé

Let's look at an example of omitting a job from your employment history.

October 2005–December 2008

June 2005–August 2005

June 2001–May 2005

Take a look at what happens when we omit the middle job, then delete the months and use only years:

2005–2008

2001–2005

Unless the short job in the summer of 2005 (in the middle) is *absolutely essential* to the job you're seeking, I recommend that you leave it out. We've already listed some of the many reasons that jobs can end. If your shorter job ended for any of those reasons, it's within your rights and definitely to your advantage to put it behind you.

Explain at Interview

If you have a gap of two years or more between positions, it's better to say on your résumé that you're willing to explain the gap than it is to ignore it. This is very simply done.

2008–present

Will explain at interview.   2004–2008

2000–2004

Dates for More than One Job at a Company

There is another way to make your dates look smooth and make your tenure at a company where you've had *more* than one job title seem longer.

Mary Lou Smith
222 XXX Drive
Honolulu, HI XXXXX
(808) 344-XXXX

Objective: XXXXX

Summary: XXXXX

Employment History
JJL Inc., Honolulu, HI   **1999–2008**

  Human Resources Director (2003–2008)
  Human Resources Manager (2001–2003)
  Human Resources Representative (1999–2001)

Education: XXXX

- When you've had more than one position, list your cumulative (largest) span of years in bold type and the time you spent at each particular job title in parentheses in a regular typeface.

Dates on Your Education

Your reader may be prejudiced on the grounds that you are either too young or too old if you list the dates of your education, so please leave those dates blank. Do list education in progress.

Blocks You Should Not Use

Hobbies

Notice that we do *not* include a hobbies block. Listing hobbies is an old-fashioned custom that is outmoded today. You may think that using it makes you look like a well-rounded person (which, to some degree, it does), but in a modern résumé, including hobbies and other personal information is unnecessary and detracts from the image of the professional "you" that your résumé is going to portray. It's best not to mention your hobbies, even if you think they make you unique.

Mentioning your hobbies can sometimes backfire on you if the employer disapproves of certain activities or believes that the time you spend pursuing your outside interests might detract from your time or focus on the job.

Don't let the temptation to test the open-mindedness of the reader ruin your chances to make a living. Perhaps when you've been hired and your employer and colleagues know you better, you can have fun sharing more of your personal side by talking about or even inviting others to participate in some of your hobbies.

References

You also do not need to write your references' names and phone numbers on your document. Likewise, including a phrase like "References Available upon Request," which is a very common mistake, is actually redundant and does not belong on your Fearless Résumé. The employer knows that he can request your references if necessary.

When You've Finished Writing

Be sure to use spell check *and* have someone else *read* (not judge) your résumé to correct any errors that may be lurking there. As I said, it's almost impossible for *everyone* to agree that any résumé is perfect, but let's make sure we get your Fearless Résumé as close to the highest goal as possible. After all, your Fearless Résumé is about you, and it's time to show the world *just how incredible you are.*

Now, let's move ahead where you'll find a template for writing your *own* Fearless Résumé to make sure it's the best it can be.

Your Name
Your Street Address
City, State, Zip Code
Home phone:
Cell phone:
E-mail address:

Objective: A position as a(n) _____.

Summary: (power proposition)

Over _____ years (or *knowledge of, proficient in,* or *competent in*) as a(n) _____ in the _____ industry, specializing in _____, _____, and _____.

Write a Q statement here. _____.

[Optional] Write another Q statement here. _____ _____.

[Optional] Write one or two degrees and/or one or two certifications or licenses here (write current progress in education if applicable). _____ _____.

And/or [optional] write one or two awards here. _____ _____.

And/or [optional] write one or two professional affiliations here. _____.

And/or write three applicable personal characteristics here. _____, _____, and _____.

[Optional] Relevant Skills. To make a skills box using Microsoft Office, go to the top of the screen to "Table." Click on it and find a drop-down menu. Click on "Draw Table" and find a pop-up toolbar. Go to the small picture of a table that says "Insert Table" when you place your cursor over it. Click on the icon and see a pop-up box called "Insert Table." Choose the number of columns (horizontal) and rows (vertical) that you would like to have in your table, then press "OK." List 6 to 12 skills.

SKILL	SKILL	SKILL
SKILL	SKILL	SKILL

Employment History (put last job first)
Job Title
Company Name, City, State   **2003–Present**

- Write two to six Q statements with a simple round bullet (under "Format" in MS Word). Even if you already used a Q statement in your power proposition, write it here under the job in which it was accomplished.

- XXX _____

_____

_____.

- XXX _____

_____

_____.

- XXX _____

_____

_____.

- XXX _____

_____

_____.

- XXX _____

_____

_____.

- XXX _____

_____

_____.

(Continue to do this for previous positions going back no more than 10 to 15 years. For very old jobs, you may need only two bullets. If a job is more than 10 years ago, you may put zero bullets if you wish.)

Job Title
Company Name, City, State   2003

- XXX _____

  _____

  _____.

- XXX _____

  _____

  _____.

- XXX _____

  _____

  _____.

- XXX _____

  _____

  _____.

Your first initial, last name, p. 2

Job Title
Company Name, City, State   1997–2002

- XXX _____

  _____

  _____.

- XXX _____

  _____

  _____.

Job Title
Company Name, City, State   1995–1997

Education. Even though you may have stated this in your power proposition, you need to write it here too.

Put highest education first

Publications and Patents

Awards

_____ Achievement Award

Awarded for _____

Recognized for _____

Received bonus for _____

Best _____ Award

Professional Affiliations

Member in good standing of _____

Member of _____

Honorary member of _____

Charter member of _____

Student member of _____

Affiliate member of _____

Professional member of _____

Union member, Local #_____

Note: There is no need to write "Hobbies" or "References Available upon Request."

CHAPTER 9

Your Moment of Triumph

"Courage is the most important of all virtues,
because without it we can't practice any other virtue
with consistency."

—Maya Angelou

This is your big moment. You know your skills; you can quantify your accomplishments; and, most of all, you know how to emotionally capture and keep your readers' attention. I'm truly proud of you! Now, it's *your* turn to write your own Fearless Résumé.

So that you won't have to flip through the entire section to find all the great work you've done, the page numbers of the essential parts are provided here so that you can refer to them as you construct your document.

My power proposition	p. 20
My general skills	p. 67
My job-specific skills	p. 72
My personal characteristics	p. 76
My Q statements	p. 84

Your résumé may change several times over the course of your job search and many times throughout your life. But now you have a formula, a strategy, and insight into what employers are looking for that most of your competitors don't. Now, here's a blank template for you to use to construct your first Fearless Résumé! Begin by filling in the contact block.

_____ _____

_____ _____

_____, _____ _____

_____ - _____ - _____

_____ - _____ - _____

_____@_____. (net, com, org)

OBJECTIVE

_____

_____

_____

SUMMARY

_____

_____

_____

_____

_____

_____

WORK HISTORY

_____

_____

_____

_____

_____

_____

_____

_____

_____

_____

_____

_____

_____

_____

_____

_____

_____

_____

EDUCATION

_____

_____

_____

_____

_____

_____

[Optional Blocks: please insert in the template in the proper place.]

RELEVANT SKILLS

PUBLICATIONS/PATENTS

_____

_____

_____

_____

_____

_____

AWARDS AND RECOGNITIONS

_____

_____

_____

PROFESSIONAL GROUPS AND AFFILIATIONS

_____

_____

OTHER

_____

_____

_____

_____

_____

_____

You've done a terrific job! But let's not stop here. As one of my very special *Fearless Résumés* readers, you can visit my Web site or e-mail me to get free information on other areas of your job search, such as how to bypass human resources and get directly to the hiring manager, how to ascend to the highest rungs of your ability in an interview, and how to negotiate up to 20 percent more than the initial offer, as well as a host of job search and career transition information.

I want to see you through this whole process, until the time when you get the offer you're looking for and can run somewhere private and scream, "I did it!" Well, I might not see you. But I will be waiting to hear your scream of triumph reach me all the way to California.

All the best to you in your life and in your job search.

CHAPTER 10

Sample
Résumés

"I long to accomplish a great and noble task, but it is my chief duty to accomplish small tasks as if they were great and noble."

—Helen Keller

Adrian Takahana, Esq.   Home Phone: (208) 293-XXXX
XXX East Stokey Road   Cell Phone: (210) 367-XXXX
Carlsbad, TX 855XX   atjd2000@elevation.com

Objective
Corporate counsel position in the Fortune 500 sector.

Professional Expertise
Over 10 years as corporate counsel to Fortune 500 companies, including 4TEL Technologies and IBX Systems, specializing in complex business and corporate contracts, risk reduction, licenses, and transactions. Negotiated and provided legal documentation for over 150 customer agreements in transactions of up to $150 million. Awarded 4TEL Performance Achievement honors in 2005 and 2006. Juris Doctor (J.D.), Oxmore University; B.A. in Economics with Highest Honors. Trilingual in English, Japanese, and Cantonese. *Willing to pay for own relocation costs anywhere in United States or Asia.*

Employment Experience

<u>Director, Legal Department</u>
4TEL Inc., Austin, TX   2000–2009

- Provided risk management oversight for 4TEL Capital Sales, Operations, and Credit groups.
- Negotiated major customer agreements of up to $150 million per transaction.
- Represented 4TEL in cross-functional business development, maintaining existing accounts and winning over 86 new accounts in a 7-year period.
- Restructured existing legal process by developing, training, and delegating to dedicated in-house legal group, saving the company approximately 3 attorney salaries at an average sum of $235,000 each per year.

- Provided training to subordinates on risk reduction and taught business success tools to decrease litigation by 25%, thereby saving an average of $160 million per year.
- Created streamlined templates for contracts paperwork that saved an average of 6 hours per week per attorney.

Attorney
IBX Computers, Richmond, VA   1994–2000

- Oversaw entire southwestern United States, conducting transactions of up to $100 million.
- Represented Financial, Commercial, Health Care, and Government lines of business.
- Structured government transaction to avoid litigation from a competitor that saved up to $13 million.
- Avoided numerous class action suits and served as prelitigation counsel and mediator.

Prior Legal Experience
Adrian Takahana, Esq.
Private practice in Washington, D.C., specializing in contract law.

Education
Admitted: U.S. Supreme Court

Admitted: State of Maryland

Juris Doctor degree: Oxmore University, Baltimore, Maryland

Bachelor of Arts degree in Economics: Southern Maryland University

Sarah L. Porter   (804) 237- XXXX Home
2XX Helmsly Lane   (804) 772- XXXX Mobile
Cincinnati, Ohio 4XXXX   porter_sl373@relay.net

Objective

A position as a physical therapist aide (intern).

Summary

Competence as a Certified Physical Therapist Aide gained from a 1-year accredited college-level program. Graduated with a 3.8 grade point average including academic and practical applications of being a physical therapist aide. Empathetic, motivated, good rapport with patients.

Relevant Classes

- Human Anatomy
- Human Physiology
- Physical Therapy Practices
- Ethics and Laws Governing Physical Therapists
- Kinesiology
- Medical Terminology
- Musculoskeletal Systems
- Common Injuries and Conditions
- Introduction to Exercise Physiology
- Patient Psychology
- Administrative Procedures

Work History

<u>Server</u>
Hamlet's Restaurant, Akron, Ohio   2007–2009

- Performed a part-time job to save and pay for school.
- Handled as many as 25 customers per shift.
- Carried out cash and credit card transactions.

Education

Certificate as a Physical Therapist Aide, Hollick College, Akron, Ohio

Professional Affiliations

Association for Physical Therapy Professionals (student membership)

James F. Harris
17XX Helen Street
Willets, WY 351XX
(300) 737-XXXX
jfh@wintercom.net

Objective:
A position in customer service.

Summary

Over 3 years progressively responsible experience in customer service in the restaurant and retail industries. Specialties include retail sales, store displays, and cash register operation. Undergraduate studies at Eli Fuller College, Menton, WY. Currently enrolled in a course of study leading to completion of the Dale Carnegie Sales seminar series. Fast learner, people person, polite and organized.

Relevant Skills

Retail sales	Phone sales	Department displays
Inventory control	Customer service	Cash register
Employee training	Credit card transactions	Employee supervision

Employment History

Salesperson, Tracy's Department Store, Willets, WY
2008–present

- In charge of the men's sportswear department, which includes approximately 1,000 pieces of inventory.

- Achieved highest sales of February 2009 for all clothing departments.
- Handle up to 350 customers weekly.
- Operate the cash register and accept credit cards for up to $700 per purchase.
- Arrange clothing on the racks and displays in order to attract customers.
- Calculate returns and chargebacks.

<u>Waiter</u>, Hanley's Country Kitchen, Benfanto, WY
2006–2008

- Took orders and served from a menu of over 60 items.
- Served individuals, couples, families, and larger banquets of up to 40 people.
- Operated the cash register and processed credit cards.
- Received the "punctuality" award for never being late to work in all of 2007.

Education and Certifications

Courses, Eli Fuller College, Menton, WY

Currently enrolled in Dale Carnegie Sales seminar series, Lowe, WY

Cindy Nelson SPHR
273X 3rd Street. Boston, MA 022XX
617-206-XXXX cell   617-459-XXXX home
cindynhr@doubletech.net

OBJECTIVE
Senior Human Resources Manager/Organizational Development.

PROFESSIONAL SUMMARY
Over 8 years as a human resource professional specializing in consulting, organizational behavior, and recruiting. Performed intervention strategies with Technical Assistance Center at Boston Scientific to diagnose underlying issues and facilitate problem resolution for team and management dynamics, directly improving self-reported employee satisfaction from 3 to 4.2 on a scale of 1 to 5. Increased employee retention by 25% at Goldman Capital, saving the company many thousands of dollars on new hiring procedures. B.A. in Business Administration, Channel University; currently pursuing coursework leading to a Master of Science in Organization Development at Boston University. Thesis topic: "Employee Behavior during Mergers and Acquisitions." SPHR. Member, Society for Human Resources Management, Boston Human Resource Association, American Society for Training and Development.

EMPLOYMENT HISTORY
<u>Sr. Human Resources Manager</u>
Boston Scientific Corporation, Fremont, CA   2005–present

- Led new manager assimilation process through team facilitation, resulting in shorter ramp-up period, saving the company as much as $10,000 per first month salary for manager level and above.

- Provided employee relations support to management and employees, performing investigations and recommendations that effectively saved the company over $100 million by deescalating potential lawsuits.

- Recruited to provide generalist support for client groups ranging from 175 to 300 technical, scientific, and support associates.

- Drove high-volume planning and recruiting methodologies with staffing teams by ensuring that superior candidates were being sourced and selected within preferred deadlines.

- Worked with Human Factors to ensure compliance with the Americans with Disabilities Act.

Human Resources Manager
Goldman Capital, Boston, MA   2004

- Increased employee retention by 25%, saving the company money on new hiring procedures.
- Mentored 33 new hire sales associates and assisted with the development of business plans.
- Utilized Recruitmax to source and recruit for 175 branches of this $2 billion East Coast mortgage brokerage firm, recognized as #803 in the Fortune 1000.
- Managed administrative staff of 3: 1 administrative assistant, 1 HR intern, and 1 HR specialist.

Human Resource Generalist
Valenti Manufacturing, Townsend, MA   2001–2004

- Led and supported human resources team of 5 members in the functional areas of employee relations, recruiting, training and development, compensation and benefits, HRIS, and general human resources.
- Managed over 12 community giving events per year in conjunction with marketing teams.

EDUCATION AND TRAINING
Currently completing a course of study leading to an MS in Organizational Behavior. Thesis topic: "Employee Behavior during Mergers and Acquisitions."
Boston University

BS, Business Administration
Channel University, Rochester, NY

PROFESSIONAL AFFILIATIONS
SPHR Certification
Society for Human Resource Management
American Society for Training and Development

Harvey S. Sumner
XXX August Drive
Memphis, TN 34XXX
Home Phone: (777) 333-3333
Cell Phone: (777) 444-4443
harveys@doitnow.net

Objective

A position as a sales manager in the
automotive rental industry.

Professional Summary

Over 6 years experience as a manager in the automotive
and trucking industries, specializing in team leadership,
operations, and employee training. Exceeded monthly quotas by an average of 22% over a 4-year period while serving
as manager at ABC Car and Truck Rentals. Attained a 4.9-
star customer satisfaction rating based on a survey of approximately 600 customer responses per year. A.S. in Industrial
Technology, Tennessee State College, Memphis, TN. Reliable, personable, goal-oriented.

Employment History

<u>Branch Manager</u>
ABC Automotive, Turnpike, TN   2004–present

- Manage a branch of airport car and truck rental business
  with over 305 vehicles.
- Train and supervise 4 rental personnel and 2 customer
  service representatives.
- Maintain top-quality inventory by directing a cleaning and
  maintenance staff of 9.
- Sell and upsell car rental packages to exceed monthly
  quotas by an average of 22%.

- Record and track inventory and accounts receivable with specialized software.
- Interface with up to 25 customers per day, with a customer satisfaction rating of 4.9 stars.

<u>Weight Master Assistant Manager</u>
Washington Manufacturing, Wahlog, TN   2003–2004

- Performed data entry tracking on loads of up to 2 tons of materials and cargo.
- Applied mathematical calculations to balance incoming and outgoing truck weight.
- Operated and maintained designated equipment with a Class A License.
- Utilized Hazardous Materials certification to ensure safe and nontoxic cargo, keeping loads under 100% government compliance at periodic spot checks.

Education and Training

A.S., Industrial Technology, Tennessee State College, Memphis, TN

Class A license from XYZ Transportation Institute, Memphis, TN

Hazardous Materials Certificate from University of Tennessee Extension Program

Melanie Isaac, MS
120 South Milton Avenue   Phone: (804) 576-XXXX
Healdsburg, AZ 75XXX   m.isaac@healdsburgcounty.gov

OBJECTIVE

A teaching position in environmental health or public health administration.

SUMMARY OF QUALIFICATIONS

Over 15 years experience in environmental health and safety, specializing in site safety, community preparedness, and overseeing health and safety for large private and public projects. Received a Mayor's Community Excellence Service award for effective program design policies, procedures, and protocols on over 8 project sites. Saved over 7 facilities while ensuring the use of appropriate procedures for the safest and most cost-effective results. Lecturer in Environmental Studies, Camelback College.

PROFESSIONAL EXPERIENCE

Senior Environmental Health and Safety Specialist
Health and Human Services Department,
County of Healdsburg, AZ   1990–Present

- Developed and implemented nationally recognized health and safety programs.
- Created and implemented an employee Emergency Response Training program, achieving 100% compliance with county and state regulations.
- Led team in development and implementation of comprehensive employee drug and alcohol testing program with 100% compliance with target.
- Advised teams of construction management personnel, individual site coordinators, and client EH&S personnel, including those from hospital projects, to develop specific plans appropriate to each site, protecting workers from exposure to hazardous/infectious materials.
- Team leader for individual site safety coordinators to monitor and enforce safety compliance.

- Administrator for regional air quality and water control compliance, resulting in zero citations.

PREVIOUS POSITIONS

Lecturer in Environmental Studies, Camelback College, Tempe, AZ
Keynote Speaker, Urban Ecology Conference, Chicago, IL

EDUCATION AND CERTIFICATIONS

- M.S., Environmental Studies, with Honors, Saint Peter's University, Phoenix, AZ
- B.A., Public Health, Pennsylvania Polytechnic State University, Philadelphia, PA
- Fed-OSHA Construction Safety Instructor
- Fed-OSHA Hazardous Waste Operations and Emergency Response

PUBLICATIONS (COMPLETE LIST OF PUBLICATIONS AVAILABLE UPON REQUEST)

"Environmental Issues in Securing Ideal Level Water Tables," *Journal of Integrated Ecology*, June 2003.

"Optimizing Budgets for Hazardous Waste Removal," *Environmental Quarterly*, Fall 2000.

"Student-Centered Methods for Teaching Cost-Effective and Compliant Subdivision Construction," *American Journal of City Planning*, January 1998.

"Impact Studies for City and County Recreation Facilities," *Journal of Parklands and Recreation*, September 1997.

Thomas Hernandez
222 South Drive
Jonesmore, Iowa

Home phone: (608) 342-XXXX
Mobile phone: (608) 477-XXXX
E-mail: hernandez_t@njtek.com

Professional Expertise

Over 10 years director-level leadership experience in the Information Technology field, specializing in global network design and engineering, leading broad-based functional teams, and managing multimillion-dollar budgets. Reengineered global information technology infrastructure in less than 47 days after dangerous fragmentation, thus exceeding the previous internal customer satisfaction by 22%, to a rating of 89%. Centralized and implemented database functionality to 19 regional sites and Asian subsidiaries. Electrical MSEE, MBA with an emphasis in technology leadership with honors. Member of the American Information Technology Society.

Relevant Technical Skills

Operating Systems/Systems Management/Security
CP/M, PC/MS-DOS, Apple System 7.x, Windows (3.x, WFW, 95, 98, NT 3.x, Vista)
Symantec Antivirus, Compaq Insight Manager, Business Continuity, Risk Tolerance
Content filters, firewalls

Hardware
Compaq servers, Dell servers, Apple II-Macintosh External Storage
SCSI, USB, IBM SNA controllers, Cisco routers, printers
Fault-tolerance, redundancy, RAID storage
Remote access, wireless, telecom
TCP/IP Suite, 3COM, Wang Net, EtherTalk, Netware 2-3.x, MS-NT Server, 10BT, 10B2, Phone Net, Ethernet, NetBIOS

Software/Languages
MS SQL, dBase, FoxPro, MS Access, Lotus 123, MS Office Pro, Lotus Notes
MS Exchange, Notes Mail, Eudora, MS Project, MS Outlook
Netscape, MS Internet Server
MS SQL, BASIC, MS VB, HTML

Platforms
Linux
UNIX

138

Professional Experience

Director Information Systems
Blue Sky Integrated Systems, Des Moines, IA   2001–2009

- Planning and implementing LAN/WAN network design and engineering.
- IT capital budget of $3.5 million over 3 years.
- Reengineered global information technology infrastructure in less than 47 days after dangerous fragmentation.
- Established facilities in China and Latin America and necessary IT infrastructure, including applications servers, connectivity, e-mail, etc.
- Centralized and implemented database functionality to 19 regional sites and Asian subsidiaries.
- Internal customers satisfied, evidenced by management reports of 89% success ratings and independent audits.

Manager, Information Technology
Efficace, San Dimas, CA   1994–2000

- Managed networking operations in five divisions.
- Led a team of 550 employees/clients in Phoenix, San Francisco, Atlanta, and Lisbon.
- Planned and implemented budget of $2.1 million per year.
- Initiated end-user feedback system that saved an average of $81,000 per year.
- Eliminated downtime in the manufacturing and operations divisions by 18%, thereby saving up to $46,000 per month in costs.

Degrees & Certifications

Microsoft Certified Professional, Harris Data Systems
M.B.A. (technology emphasis), University of Phoenix Online
M.S.E.E., University of California at Long Beach
B.A., Economics, Eastern Michigan University

Professional Affiliations

Member of the American Information Technology
President, Technology Education Fund for Disadvantaged Youth

Joshua Kennedy   307-722-XXXX mobile
43XX Autumn Court, Apt. C   321-826-XXXX direct
Tilden, NH 23XXX   kennedy_josh4002@oog.com

Objective: A position as a network administrator.

Summary: Over 6 years experience in electrical engineering, specializing in LAN/WAN networking, testing and hardware/software validation, installation, and removal. Created over 9 test plans and spreadsheets for different products to capture complete test cases required for specifications and customer requirements. Reduced system downtime by 18% and increased sensitivity of the inspection systems, saving tens of thousands of dollars. A.A. in Electronics; currently enrolled in classes to obtain a Network Administrator Certificate, N.S.F.E.E.

Technical Skills

LAN/WAN networking	Flash BIOS upgrades	PCB layout and design
Failure analysis	Stress tests	Defect tracking
Install/remove HW/SW	Troubleshooting	SW/HW validation

Employment History

QA Test Engineer
Banana Belt Technologies, Binghamton, NH   2007–present

- Debugging process and failure analysis down to component level.
- Set up test equipment and product under the test in the manufacturing for control run performance test.
- Created over 9 test plans and spreadsheets for different products to capture complete test cases required for specifications and customer requirements.
- Regression, integration, and system-level test execution.

- Performed complex hardware calibrations on new products, finding failures before releasing product to the customers.
- Helped IT engineers with building new PCs or upgrading for R&D engineers, including BIOS upgrades, installing licensed operating/debugging software, various hardware required for diagnostics or functional testing process, and configuring dial-up, LAN/WAN networks.

Manufacturing Assistant Engineer
Center Stage Electronics, Las Vegas, NV   2003–2007

- Conducted failure analysis and repair of printed circuit boards (alignment, memory, autofocus, laser's preamp, motor driver PCBs, and more) down to component level on multimillion-dollar equipment.
- Performed optical and laser alignments, electronic calibrations, and electromechanical adjustments to meet sensitivity qualifications.
- Reduced system downtime by 18% and increased sensitivity of the inspection systems.
- Initiated several test procedures in regard to systems assembly and subassembly troubleshooting, mechanical and electromechanical calibrations, and laser alignment.

Education
Currently enrolled in classes to obtain a Network Administrator Certificate, N.S.F.E.E, Hartmond, NH

A.S., Northeast Technical Institute, Bellevue, NH

Part Two

Fearless
INTERVIEWING

How to Win the Job
by Communicating with Confidence

CONTENTS

One can never consent to creep when one feels an impulse to soar.

—Helen Keller

Why Are Interviews So Scary?

It takes courage to live a life, any life.

—Erica Jong

Have you ever felt jittery before an interview? Nervous or even terrified? Have you ever wished you had answered a question differently or negotiated your salary more skillfully? Do you panic when you imagine the possibility of "failure"? Do you just want to make sure you get it right the first time?

Let's face it. Interviews are not like normal conversations. Being interviewed can be scary, even for ordinarily outgoing people. When you're sitting in the hot seat, the interviewer is an authority figure, and he or she has all or most of the power in the interview.

Guess what? Studies show that more than 60 percent of interviewers have never been trained in the task of interviewing. Most of these managers report that they feel "nervous, anxious, confused, stressed" and even "incompetent" when taking on the responsibility of conducting a job interview.

Now that you're reading *Fearless Interviewing*, take another look at who's being trained and who's not!

It's likely that you're actually going to be more prepared for the meeting than the interviewer.

Think again. Now who holds the power? By the end of this section, you'll find that you too have control over what goes on at the interview, especially when you learn to harness your fear into excitement, energy, and enthusiasm. To make this transformation you'll need to learn the techniques of fearless interviewing.

Here's how one of my clients, Christine, used fearless interviewing to turn her timidity into power.

Christine's Story

Christine came to see me for some career coaching after a series of failed interviews. She told me that she had interviewed at several high-profile financial firms for a position as a financial analyst. She had a B.A. in accounting and a master's in business administration, plus eight years' experience as a senior accountant and financial analyst for a midsized company in Montana.

From my evaluation of the résumé she sent me, neither her qualifications nor her education were the problem.

When Christine came to my office for an appointment, she told me that she had been out of work for several months and added emphatically that interviewing had been "torture" for her. She said that she felt timid at the interviews she had gone to and that she felt intensely uncomfortable about being asked questions that required her to call attention to herself and her skills.

Though perfectly well qualified for just about any financial analyst position, Christine suffered from what is sometimes known in psychology as the *imposter syndrome*. The imposter syndrome presents itself as the feeling that, even though we have accomplished something, we somehow feel that we don't deserve the recognition or prestige that goes with it.

According to Christine, "I've never had a problem talking about a friend's accomplishments, but when it comes to my own, I find it embarrassing." She reports, "I'm afraid that others will think I'm arrogant. I feel that if I boast about myself at an interview, the company might hire me and then find out I can't do the job at all."

At first, as Christine learned the techniques of fearless interviewing, she told me that she felt uncomfortable relating her strengths in such a straightforward manner. "It feels like bragging," she said. But as we worked together to reframe her notion of "bragging" into one of simply "reporting the facts," she began to relax and handle questions about herself more easily.

When Christine built her skills arsenal and constructed her Q statements (as you'll do in Chapters 2 and 3, she realized that her strengths were not just fabrications; they were real. Furthermore, they could be *proven* by citing examples of what she had actually done in the real world!

> **Her accomplishments, she soon learned, were not exaggerations at all; they were simply statements of facts.**

Christine's next interview was with a Fortune 500 financial organization for a job as a financial analyst. I heard from her about 2 weeks after the interview took place. She sent me a greeting card with the face of a sad, cute little puppy on the front of it. The inside of the card said, "Before, I felt like a scared puppy; now I feel like a lion! Thank you for helping me land the job!"

Just like Christine, many of us shy away from "tooting our own horns."

> **But that's just what an interview is for. It's your opportunity to tell an employer what you've accomplished in the past and how you'll help them in the future.**

When Christine was able to interview successfully for the financial analyst position, nothing new or magical was added to her personality. She simply picked up the tools that we're going to discuss in the coming chapters.

Most important, she learned to let the employer understand, in clear and specific terms, that she *could* and *would* make a significant contribution to that firm.

> **This is the key to fearless interviewing: knowing your strengths, being able to provide concrete examples of those strengths, thereby building the lasting confidence to present yourself and your skills in the best possible light.**

In the next several chapters, you'll learn the following:

- What interviewers are *really* looking for
- How to charm your way into the interviewer's heart in the first 20 seconds of the interview
- How to express your strengths and skills with power and laserlike precision
- How to handle even the most difficult questions
- How to use body language in your favor

- How to leverage multiple job offers
- The most important questions to ask the employer
- How to be a master at negotiating your salary

My Story

In the next chapter, we'll take a look at some of the fears you too are going to leave behind, but before we explore the rest of the techniques I've told you about, I'd like to tell you a little bit about how I became a career coach and how I came to write this text.

I became a career coach in 1989 for many reasons, but there's only one reason that really counts. I simply *love* talking to people about their work! Even before I was a counselor, I had a sort of innate sense that every person has a certain career destiny. I was absolutely fascinated by people's career choices—how they started doing what they were doing, if they liked their work, and especially if they had a secret dream about what they'd really like to be doing. For some reason it seemed just as natural to me to talk about people's careers as it was to talk about their pets, their gardens, or a movie they had seen.

But even though talking about careers seemed to come naturally to me, becoming a career counselor wasn't nearly as easy as that. I faced many of the same feelings of rejection and frustration as other people sometimes feel in interviews. Shortly before I took up career coaching as a profession, I decided to ask a few professional career counselors whether they thought I was suited to the occupation, what I could expect from being a career counselor, and what the job prospects were like. All ten of the people I talked to said I would "never make it" without a master's degree in counseling or education. I didn't have one, and I didn't plan to get one soon.

One said: "None of the agencies are hiring—the economy's too soft. There's a waiting list of over a thousand people from all over the world trying to get the one job at the local community college." (Sound familiar?)

Still another professional warned: "I'd hate to see you waste your time trying to build a career coaching business in this town. It's too small, and I've never known any counselor to succeed at it."

After ten of those less-than-inspiring "pep talks," I was ready to move out of town—and get a job doing just about anything else *except* career counseling! But I didn't. Somehow their warnings posed a challenge for me. I had broken into other difficult fields when everyone said it was impossible. I knew I could do it again.

I immediately started offering free talks to all sorts of organizations on goal setting, self-esteem, and résumé writing. I attended some professional seminars and conferences on career development. I read every single book I could get my hands on about careers and jobs, and I took some graduate courses in career development and counseling.

Within 6 months of deciding to become a career counselor, I had appointments booked for 2 months with a waiting list!

I worked with clients in industries as diverse as publishing, biotechnology, semiconductors, sales, the arts, entertainment, telecommunications, medicine, law, computers, defense, Web design, engineering, hospitality, foods, and even wine making. I taught workshops and worked individually with people in all walks of life—students and executives and entry-level employees and Ph.D.s.

One day, in one of my classes, a woman exclaimed, "You know, you should write a book!" I liked the idea, mostly because it represented another challenge and because I realized that indeed, I could keep teaching job-seeking skills to 10 or 20 people at a time, or I could reach thousands of people all at once!

I wrote the first chapter you're reading right now and submitted it to the top literary agent in San Francisco. I was sure he would love my idea and see it as an instant success.

Two weeks later, I got a generic rejection letter, without even a real signature. When I called and asked him about it, the editor said, "Good title, but who would read it? I'm sorry, we can't represent your book."

I was crushed; but I refused to let the rejection stop me. I was convinced that I had a valuable message for job seekers, one with important tools that would ensure their success. After a few more disappointments from other literary agents, I decided to take matters into my own hands and publish the book myself.

Sure I went into debt. Sure I was scared. But soon—after I'd flown all over the country giving Fearless Interviewing seminars, appeared on radio and TV, and been written about in magazines and newspapers—my efforts paid off.

One morning while I was going through my usual routine, I picked up the phone, and it was the beautiful voice of a New York editor! She told me that she had seen an article written by me, and that she was interested in my book. I was so stunned after she said "hello" and introduced herself that I said, "Excuse me. Would you hold on for just a moment? I've got to find my body and then get back into it."

The motto? Perseverance. Maybe interviews 1, 2, or even 3 didn't go as well as you liked. But with the ammunition in this section, we'll turn numbers 4, 5, and 6 into offers. I *know* you can do it!

CHAPTER 1

An Assault against Anxiety

> The door of opportunity won't open unless you do some pushing.
>
> —Anonymous

Tim was the head of a lighting crew for a local television news station in Salt Lake City, Utah. After four years of working on the crew and finally becoming the chief lighting designer, he figured he had paid his dues and was ready to move to Los Angeles to get a job in the film industry.

With no binding family ties or other obligations, he packed up his pickup truck and headed for Hollywood. It was four months before he landed his first interview, a meeting with the director of photography for a network movie-of-the-week. He was willing to start at the bottom, but unfortunately, the interview failed to yield the chance to do even *that*.

"It was like an interrogation," he protested when he called me. "I never expected to have to tell my life story just to get a job on a movie! Their questions were impossible. I'm not a brain surgeon."

"I don't know what happened," he reflected. "When they asked those questions about my weaknesses and my failures, my mouth went dry, and it was like my jaw couldn't move. I just sat there and totally froze! They must have thought I was a moron! I walked out of there shaking inside, feeling like I was a total idiot. There's *no way* I'm ever going to go through anything like that again!"

You're certainly not alone if you have some negative feelings about interviewing. Most people consider interviews to be somewhere between mildly unpleasant and absolutely terrifying. This section will give you specific strategies for conquering that anxiety and quieting those negative voices.

The Most Common Interview Fears

The 11 most common fears that people have voiced to me about interviewing are contained in the following checklist. Check the box next to any of these fears you have right now. Be sure to use a pencil! You're going to go back over this list at the end of reading this section, and I can safely predict that many of the fears you have now will most certainly have been "erased" by then.

☐ *I fear they will ask me a question I don't know the answer to.* Chapters 2 through 5, plus the sample interviews at the end of the section, will leave you with no doubt about how to strategically answer any of the four types of interview questions.

☐ *I'm afraid I'll sound like I'm bragging.* Many of us learned in childhood or later that "blowing your own horn" is a sign of being on an ego trip. But providing information about the nature of work you have done is not doing that. In Chapter 3, you'll see the difference between bragging and simply stating the facts.

☐ *Do I have to say I was fired from my last job? Can they find out?* There are laws that protect you from potential employers' prying into your past in ways that are inappropriate. We'll discuss those laws as well as how best to deal with questions that pertain to past employment situations.

☐ *Everyone says I am under/overqualified. What should I do?* Usually the employer who says he or she is worried about either of these issues actually has a hidden agenda. We'll find out exactly how to address and defuse that agenda in Chapter 5 when we talk about "questions behind questions."

☐ *Do I have to submit to drug testing, credit checks, or personality tests?* Drug testing, credit checks, and personality tests are a reality of today's workplace and hard to avoid. You may simply decide you don't want to work at a place with such restrictive entrance procedures.

☐ *What should I do if an interviewer asks me an intrusive or illegal question?* Some topics, such as disabilities, marital status, or sexual orientation, are off-limits during an interview. We'll talk about how to avoid these incriminating and illegal questions.

☐ *I don't know what to do with my hands during an interview.* This is a very common worry. Once you know the one most potent secret of nonverbal behavior in an interview, you'll find your hands will just fall into place, and you won't even have to think about them!

☐ *I fear I will just "freeze up" in the interview.* You'll learn the technique of "stalling and accessing," which is a convincing and comfortable way out of this one. It will seem very natural, once you learn it.

☐ *I had to answer technical questions. They were easy, and I knew I had answered them right. The interviewer said I answered them wrong. What do I do in a situation like that?* Sound familiar? If you're an engineer or scientist, you've very likely faced this type of scenario. It can be unnerving! We'll teach you how to answer the question and keep your cool in Chapter 5, in the section on "stress questions."

☐ *Do I have to reveal how much money I made at my last job? How and when should I bring up the issue of salary?* We'll discuss every nuance of salary negotiations in Chapter 7. Not only will you be able to handle salary discussions, you'll be able to master them.

☐ *How do I explain that I was laid off?* There's a simple way to phrase information about a layoff that leaves you blameless and dignified. It's contained in Chapter 5.

In addition to helping you float with ease in the shark-infested waters of these common fears, the fearless interviewing approach will do for you what most other books on the subject fail to do, and that is to focus on mastering four categories of questions and answers. Being prepared this way will enable you to answer questions with ease and authority.

Strategy versus Memorization

Most books on interviewing treat each question as a separate entity. For example, they may suggest 100 answers to the most common interview questions, with the expectation that you will remember whichever ones seem relevant when the time comes. That's fine if you have an encyclopedic memory, but a strategy is even better. Fearless interviewing is an entirely new approach to the process of interviewing that uses *strategy* instead of memory.

You won't be memorizing endless pages of interview questions, and I won't be telling you the exact words to say. You won't have to memorize anything that doesn't come naturally to you. Instead, we'll be learning strategies—basic principles that leave you free to express yourself in the most comfortable way possible.

You'll learn how to divide questions into four major categories and develop an overall plan for answering each type of question. For example, the questions "What are your strengths?" and "What are your weaknesses?" actually belong to two entirely different categories. The first is what I call a straightforward question, and the second is what I call a stress question. Each requires a different, almost opposite, strategy to answer successfully. You'll learn the most advantageous approach for each of these questions, and many more, in the following pages!

> **With fearless interviewing techniques, you'll have to keep track of only four categories instead of hundreds of questions.**

Interviewing Can Be Fun!

As you read this section, I hope that you'll go through the process of "reframing" what an interview means to you. Reframing is the process of transforming how you perceive a situation so that you can look at it in a different, usually better, way. By gaining confidence in your interviewing skills, you'll cease to see the interview as some sort of uncomfortable interrogation, and you'll begin to see it as an incredible opportunity for learning, pleasure, and even fun.

Once you do an inventory of your skills (which we will do in the next chapter), you will see that the interview is merely a forum for you to enjoy talking about what you do best and love doing most. Imagine that! A job interview that's fun!

Learning how to interview fearlessly is like learning how to dance. There are some basic steps to master. At first you learn and practice each step slowly, but before long you find yourself gliding across the floor. You've picked up the right book to help you learn those steps, and with just a little bit of practice, you'll be flying. Let's go for it!

CHAPTER 2

Building Your Skills Arsenal

> *The road to happiness lies in two simple principles: Find what it is that interests you and that you can do well, and put your whole soul into it—every bit of energy and ambition and natural ability that you have.*
>
> —John D. Rockefeller

Marie first telephoned me on a Wednesday sounding upset and confused. "I've blown the seventh interview in two months. I think I need an interview coach."

"I just can't understand it," she continued. "I had my résumé done professionally. You should see it. It can't have to do with my appearance. Every time before I go to an interview, I get my hair done, I have a manicure, and I always wear my best suits. I really don't know what to think. It makes me wonder if I'm in the wrong profession! If another person with less experience gets the job instead of me again, I'm literally going to scream!"

Marie faxed me her résumé the day before our appointment together. On paper, she looked terrific. It was clear from her résumé that she had a 10-year background in sales, had managed over 75 people, and had handled some formidable accounts of up to several million dollars each. Given the right presentation at an interview, Marie could probably have her pick of a number of sales positions in the tech industry.

She came for her coaching appointment on a Friday. In the first few seconds, it was clear to me that she had excellent social skills. Her greeting was professional, and she had a winning smile and a firm businesslike handshake. She looked me straight in the eye and stood tall, appearing to have a lot of confidence. She was dressed and accessorized impeccably. There certainly was nothing *not* to like about her. It was clear to me from the outset that first impressions were not her problem.

Marie and I decided that we would do a mock interview where I would play the interviewer and she would play herself. The first question I asked her is probably the most common first question asked in any interview: "Tell me about yourself." I followed with some other common questions like, "Tell me about your skills," and "What is your greatest strength?"

> **What evidence did I have that she was, in fact, a top performer? How did she plan to apply her skills to make profits for my company?**

Marie's answers to my questions, though technically correct, were fraught with generalities and gave only a vague impression of what she actually could offer as a marketing director. Had I been an employer, I might have had questions and doubts as to whether she could really perform as well as she said she could. How, specifically, could she prove her skills?

- For example, what did she mean when she said she was "extremely experienced"?
  - ✓ Did she mean two years' experience? five years'? Perhaps 20?
- And she says she has an "exceptional record of service."
  - ✓ What exactly is it that made her service exceptional?
  - ✓ Did she mean she had exceeded her quotas?
  - ✓ Did she mean she had handled accounts with an unusually high monetary value?
- What about her comment that she has "an outstanding sense of the needs of the marketplace"?
  - ✓ Was she adept at market research?
  - ✓ Could she give me a specific example of being able to understand the needs of a customer?

I was not surprised when she said that her greatest strength was good communication skills. Most of us, in fact, believe that we have good communication skills. The challenge is that, in an interview, you have to be able to prove it.

- ✓ Could she tell me about some presentations she had made that won accounts?
- ✓ Had she engaged in negotiations that resulted in the favor of her company? When? With whom? How much money was involved?
- ✓ Perhaps she meant she was good at resolving conflicts through communication.

It was hard to know exactly what Marie meant since she didn't really have the specific data to back up her assertions. This kind of crucial data is exactly the kind of ammunition we'll be gathering in the next two chapters. You don't have to make the same mistakes that Marie made. You will know your skills and exactly how they can make a positive impact on whatever organization you're applying to. Unlike Marie you *won't* do the following:

- Think your résumé will speak *for* you.
- Speak in generalities and expect the interviewer to "connect the dots" for you.

No wonder, Marie kept getting turned down for jobs in spite of her friendly and businesslike demeanor. Employers want proof of your abilities! The reality is that, before an employer pays Marie over $100,000 per year to act as his or her sales director, the employer will want to have some specific examples of where and how Marie had used those skills to produce positive results for another company. Marie cannot expect her résumé to "do the talking" for her. Instead, she has to learn to clearly and succinctly verbalize those results.

In the next two chapters you will learn how you can easily avoid the pitfall of sounding too vague simply by knowing your skills and knowing how to communicate them with confidence.
Let's move on to the good stuff!

Assessing Your Skills

Taking an inventory of your skills is the beginning of being successful in any job interview. Ninety percent of employers say that the primary reason they do not hire a candidate is because the interviewee *could not clearly state his or her skills*. Read that last sentence again. That doesn't mean they didn't *have* the skills necessary to do the job. It means that they could not verbally *state* those skills in a convincing way.

When you've finished the exercises in the next two chapters, you'll have built the foundation for an enormous constellation of personal skills and accomplishments that I call your "skills arsenal." In this chapter, we'll take an inventory of your skills. What are your general skills? Your job-specific skills? Your personal traits that add value? Your areas of exceptional competency? Your special gifts and talents that make you unique?

Building those "stories" from your list of skills is something we'll tackle together in Chapter 3, where you will learn the most concise and powerful way to verbally express your skills—the Q statement. No question will be able to catch you off guard because you will always be prepared to offer stories about accomplishments that will impress and maybe even dazzle the interviewer.

In this chapter we'll be discussing five types of skills:

- General skills
- Job-specific skills
- Personal traits
- Competencies
- Gifts

Identifying your skills in each of these categories is the first step in crafting stories and examples that will help you explain your skills and experience to interviewers clearly in a convincing (and interesting) way.

General Skills

First, let's take a look at general skills and see why they can be so important to you in the interview, whether you're planning to stay in the same occupation or you're thinking about making a move into an entirely new profession or a new industry.

Using General Skills in an Interview for a Career Change

"Managing" is one example of a general skill. It is called a "general skill" because it can be found in almost every industry—sports, computers, retail, manufacturing, health care, and even entertainment. And occupations like sales manager, department manager, production manager, project manager, program manager, office manager, and accounts manager require the use of management skills.

One exciting outcome of taking stock of your general skills is that it will enable you to link the set of skills you have developed in one career to the set of skills required in a different career. Someone who has managed budgets, inventory, and teams of people in the computer hardware field might find that he or she can apply those skills in another industry such as manufacturing.

In other words, if you wanted to make a jump from being a project manager in engineering to being a production manager in the film industry, *you would not be at a loss for some of the most important general skills required for that kind of change.* In the process, however, you would probably be required to answer an interviewer's questions about your abilities to make that kind of change. Your answer might look something like this:

> Although I have not had direct experience in the film industry yet, I do have management skills. I have managed budgets of up to $1 million, teams of up to 48 engineers and technicians, and schedules involving up to three different projects, each on different deadlines. Through creative scheduling and careful allocation of resources, I was able to bring one project in 18 days ahead of the deadline, thereby saving my company over $147,000. That's exactly the kind of savings I'd like to bring to your film company.

Holly, one of my clients, was a teacher, but she was able to make a career change into the much more highly paid field of training and development for a human resources department of a large computer firm. Though the occupations were different, she was able to identify several important general skills that they shared. Her general skills list looked like this:

- Curriculum planning
- Research
- Presentations
- Teaching
- Evaluation

When the human resources director asked her how she thought she could apply her teaching skills to training, Holly said something like this:

> When I took over the fourth-grade class at Bowden Street Elementary in Minneapolis, the grade point average for the preceding five years had been a C minus. Using my skills in researching age-appropriate program planning, interactive learning approaches, and developing innovative presentations, I was able to bring up the class average to a B plus. It's an achievement I'm very proud of—just the kind of improvement I expect to make in your employee morale and performance.

Using General Skills to Get a New Job

General skills can, of course, also be used when you are applying for the same type of job in the same type of industry. If you were applying for a job of a social work case manager at an agency where the caseload was particularly heavy, you might want to emphasize some of your general skills having to do with organization. Suppose your list of general skills looked like this:

- Assessing
- Counseling
- Researching
- Reporting
- Coordinating
- Organizing

If an interviewer were to ask you, "What are your strengths?" you might choose to answer in the following way, *introducing* your three most salient strengths and then *elaborating* on one of the strengths, such as in the answer cited below:

QUESTION: *What are your greatest strengths?*

ANSWER: Well, some of my greatest strengths lie in the areas of counseling, reporting, and organization. An example of an experience in which my organizational skills were very important is a position I had with Ford Human Services in Richmond, Virginia. I was responsible for a caseload of over 75 clients, which meant that I had to keep careful notes and records, and, of course, I had to review these notes before each meeting with a client. I was commended for the attention to detail in my reports, which I was able to provide because I had kept such well-organized files on my clients. I am proud that because of my organizational skills, I was able to handle such a large client base. I'm confident I will give your clients the same level of respect and detailed, in-depth attention.

You can see a pattern emerging:

1. You mention *three* skills that you used in a prior job that would also be of value in your next occupation. (We'll discover, in Chapter 8, how to assess which skills are important to your interviewer.)

2. You pick *one* skill that you believe would be *most important* for the particular job you're applying for.

3. You tell a very short story about that particular skill. You can elaborate on this story by providing specific numbers, percentages, feedback, rankings, and dollar amounts. (We're going to explore this technique more fully in Chapter 3 on Q statements.)

4. You mention that you are proud of your achievement.

5. You link your past accomplishments or results with your future performance at the company you're applying for, by saying, "And that's exactly what I'd like to do for your company." (We'll talk about why this is so important in Chapter 5.)

General Skills Inventory

Now it's time for you to take a look at the general skills you possess:

1. Scan the following list of general skills.
2. Make a checkmark next to those skills you have used reasonably well. It's possible that you have used a skill only once but are still reasonably proficient with it so that you could use it again if you had the chance.

    Be generous with yourself as you decide whether you have these skills. You need not be an expert in them, nor is it necessary that you have used them in a work environment. Think carefully back to school, recreational, social, or volunteer situations in which you may have used these skills:

___ Advertising

___ Advising

___ Analyzing data

___ Analyzing situations

___ Arranging events

___ Assessing performance

___ Assessing progress

___ Assessing quality

___ Assisting

___ Attending to detail

___ Auditing

___ Building structures

___ Building relationships

___ Building credibility

___ Building cooperation

___ Budgeting

___ Calculating

___ Classifying

___ Client relations

___ Coaching

___ Corresponding

___ Communicating in writing

___ Communicating verbally

___ Communicating nonverbally

___ Communicating feelings

___ Communicating ideas

___ Communicating instructions

___ Conceptualizing

___ Consulting

___ Correcting

___ Counseling

___ Data processing

___ Decision making

___ Decorating

___ Delegating

___ Developing designs

___ Developing systems

___ Developing talent

___ Diagnosing

___ Directing

___ Drafting

___ Drawing

___ Driving

___ Editing

___ Educating

___ Empathizing

___ Enforcing

___ Engineering

___ Evaluating

___ Filing

___ Financial planning

___ Forecasting

___ Formulating

___ Fund raising

___ Healing

___ Helping others

___ Implementing

___ Imagining

___ Influencing

___ Initiating

___ Intuiting

___ Intervening

___ Inventing

___ Investigating

___ Leading people

___ Lecturing

___ Lifting

___ Listening

___ Managing tasks

___ Marketing

___ Marketing and communications

___ Massaging

___ Nurturing

___ Observing

___ Operating computers

___ Organizing

___ Prescribing

___ Program managing

___ Programming computers

___ Project managing

___ Promoting

___ Public speaking

___ Recording

___ Repairing

___ Reconstructing

___ Reporting

___ Researching

___ Sales and marketing

___ Selling

___ Servicing equipment

___ Servicing customers

___ Supervising

___ Surveying

___ Team building

___ Team leading

___ Telephone calling

___ Tending

___ Tooling

___ Training

___ Troubleshooting

___ Understanding

___ Using equipment

___ Using the Internet

Other general skills not mentioned:

_____

_____

_____

_____

_____

_____

_____

_____

3. Now, go back over the list again from beginning to end. This time around, *circle* those skills that are checked off *and* that you want to *continue* to use in your next job.

4. Now you have a list in which some of the skills have *both* a checkmark *and* a circle, which means the following:

   a. You can use them.

   b. You like to use them.

   c. You would like to *continue* to use them in your next job.

5. There is one more step, and this is the most challenging one yet. Pick out *six* of the skills that you have on your list that are circled *and* checkmarked.

When it comes to narrowing down the number of your skills to six, it's likely that you may be thinking, "I'd like to use almost all of these skills. I enjoy using them so much that I hate to narrow down the list to just six." Think about this for a moment: The last time you bought or leased a car, did you actually consider *every single* feature the car had—from the axle to the hoses to the spark plugs to the tail lights?

Would you have been enticed to purchase the car if the advertisement or the salesperson had just said "This car has all features" and did nothing to explain specifically what the most important features of the car were?

Wouldn't it have been more engaging if the advertisement or salesperson had mentioned six or seven *special* features that you were actually looking for, like air-conditioning, an audio system with six speakers, or a five-year unconditional factory warranty?

The "special features" on this car are like the selected skills you bring with you to the interview.

By mentioning the "features" you *know* you have and you know the employer wants, you show the employer that you're equipped to solve the kinds of problems inherent in the job. (We'll learn some easy ways to determine *which* skills are important to the employer in Chapter 4 on the topic of research.)

Job-Specific Skills

You may be saying, "Fine, I'm a manager with good organizational skills, but there's a lot more to my job than that!" You're right. You have very specific knowledge and expertise that you use in your particular vocation. Job-specific skills are those abilities that you need to succeed in your particular job in your particular company in your particular industry. These are the abilities that another person who has the same job title as yours would have to have to meet the job's basic requirements.

Scan the lines below for some examples of job-specific skills for different occupations. You may not see *your* occupation listed, but you'll get an idea of the difference between these skills and the general skills we talked about before. Your job-specific skills are usually listed on your résumé, but remember the key to interviewing: It's not enough just to *possess* a skill or even have it written on your résumé. You have to be able to *verbally express* it.

Please take a look at the following list of some job-specific skills areas in which proficiency is necessary in these selected occupations. I think you'll see how they differ from general skills:

Occupation	Selected Job-Specific Skills
Accountant	Accounts payable Accounts receivable Payroll
Marketing specialist	Press release writing Trade-show coordinating Forecasting
Financial advisor	Series 7 license Knowledge of stocks, bonds, mutual funds Knowledge of retirement planning and living trusts
Football player	Understanding football strategy Staying in shape off season Playing the position (quarterback, linebacker, tight end)
Environmental planner	Knowledge of geology and biology Knowledge of causes and treatments for pollutants Knowledge of the ecology of a given geographic area
Semiconductor assembler	Component parts of a wafer Clean-room and safety procedures Superior fine-motor control
Psychotherapist	Diagnosis of a client's health Knowledge of nonverbal behavior Cognitive-behavioral therapy techniques
Publisher	Exceptional literacy The publishing process from "pitching" to marketing How to evaluate books for publication
Computer programmer	Computer languages Computer platforms C, SQL, Perl, Java, JavaScript

Occupation	Selected Job-Specific Skills
Surgeon	Knowledge of human anatomy and physiology How to make a diagnosis and prognosis Ability to perform surgery
Office manager	Order office supplies within a budget Microsoft Office, Lotus, Peachtree software Operation of multiline phone system

Now I'd like you to try your hand at identifying some of the job-specific skills *you* possess.

Job-Specific Skills Inventory

List six to ten of your job-specific skills here. What abilities must you possess to get a job in your chosen industry? It's helpful if the skills you include are those in the job description for the new position you're interviewing for. When the employer asks you the inevitable questions, "What are your strengths?" and "What are your skills?" you will have the best of your skills for that job right at your fingertips.

1. _____
   _____

2. _____
   _____

3. _____
   _____

4. _____
   _____

5. _____
   _____

6. _____

   _____

7. _____

   _____

8. _____

   _____

9. _____

   _____

10. _____

   _____

Personal Traits

Great! Now we're ready to move on to another set of skills called personal traits. They are every bit as important as your general skills, and they usually make up a set of personal characteristics that you possess. These skills have more to do with who you *are* than what you *do*, and they bear heavily upon your attitude, your work habits, your ethics, and the way you relate to other people.

When the employer asks a question like "What would your former boss have to say about you?" or "What did your former coworkers think of you?" it's very useful to be able to describe yourself using three or four of the adjectives in the next exercise.

Personal Traits Inventory

Go through the following list twice. The first time, go through the list and place a checkmark beside the traits that apply to you. *There's nothing to be gained from being modest.* If you asked any good friend or coworker, he or she would probably agree that you do, indeed, possess those qualities!

___ Accepting

___ Accurate

___ Achievement oriented

___ Action oriented

___ Aggressive

___ Ambitious

___ Analytical

___ Artistic

___ Assertive

___ Aware

___ Balanced

___ Brilliant

___ Businesslike

___ Calm

___ Caring

___ Challenging

___ Charismatic

___ Committed

___ Communicative

___ Compassionate

___ Competitive

___ Concerned

___ Confident

___ Considerate

___ Courageous

___ Courteous

___ Creative

___ Dedicated

___ Dependable

___ Detail-oriented

___ Determined

___ Diligent

___ Diplomatic

___ Direct

___ Driven

___ Dynamic

___ Economical

___ Effective

___ Efficient

___ Emotionally strong

___ Energetic

___ Entertaining

___ Enthusiastic

___ Entrepreneurial

___ Ethical

___ Exemplary

___ Expressive

___ Fair

___ Friendly

___ Generous

___ Genuine

___ Gifted

___ Hard working

___ Helpful

___ Honest

___ Humorous

___ Independent

___ Innovative

___ Insightful

___ Inspirational

___ Intellectual

___ Intelligent

___ Intuitive   ___ Responsible

___ Inventive   ___ Responsive

___ Knowledgeable   ___ Results-oriented

___ Logical   ___ Scientific

___ Loyal   ___ Self-controlled

___ Mature   ___ Self-motivated

___ Methodical   ___ Sincere

___ Meticulous   ___ Sociable

___ Modest   ___ Spontaneous

___ Motivating   ___ Supportive

___ Nurturing   ___ Systematic

___ Observant   ___ Tactful

___ Optimistic   ___ Task oriented

___ Orderly   ___ Team oriented

___ Organized   ___ Tenacious

___ Outgoing   ___ Thorough

___ Patient   ___ Tidy

___ Perfectionistic   ___ Tolerant

___ Persuasive   ___ Trustworthy

___ Physically strong   ___ Uninhibited

___ Private   ___ Unselfish

___ Proactive   ___ Unstoppable

___ Productive   ___ Unusual

___ Punctual   ___ Verbal

___ Rational   ___ Versatile

___ Relaxed   ___ Visionary

___ Reserved   ___ Warm

___ Resilient   ___ Well groomed

___ Resourceful   ___ Well liked

___ Respected   ___ Well spoken

___ Respectful

The second time you go through the list, please select the three or four personal traits that describe you best and that you think you would like to use in your next job. You may very well possess a majority of these skills. To narrow them down for the following list, try to list those traits that seem to come to you almost naturally and effortlessly. You might also consider listing the traits you're most often complimented for. Please record them here:

1. _____

2. _____

3. _____

4. _____

Competencies

You've already uncovered some foundational skills that will surely impress your interviewer and tip the scales in your direction—your general skills, your job-specific skills, and your personal traits. Now, let's add two more types of skills that will add even more credibility to your presentation.

The first is a group of skills called *competencies*. Competencies are actually clusters of skills, and they are rapidly becoming the criteria upon which *all* employees and potential employees are judged. They can make the difference between being promoted or passed over. They can and definitely do carve out the space between people who are hired and those who are not. More and more, *interviewers are trained to look at competencies as well as skills.*

The Occupational Outlook Handbook, a useful source for career information, is updated and published yearly by the U.S. Department of Labor. It lists the job descriptions, qualifications, job market expectancies, and salaries for more than 6,000 jobs, and it is published both nationally and regionally. Accessing it on the Internet at www.bls.gov/oco/ or in hard copy at your local library is a top-notch way to find vast information on what kinds of skills, education, personal traits, and competencies employers are looking for to fulfill certain positions. Increasingly, the *handbook* is listing competencies as well as skills to draw a well-rounded picture of what employers actually demand.

For example, the *handbook* notes that for the position of "financial and securities advisor," such competencies and personal traits as "a desire to succeed," "ability to handle rejection," and "self-confidence" may actually be of *more* value to the employer than traditional skills like numerical ability or formal education.

Even in positions involving a very high level of technical skill, competencies still come strongly into play. In a Web site job description of skills necessary for a computer hardware engineer, "willingness to constantly update knowledge" is a competency that ranks as high in importance as other skills that are more technology oriented.

What Are Some of the Most Valued Competencies?

Some of the core competencies that are most important for many positions in today's rapidly shifting marketplace are the following:

- *Flexibility.* The ability to change, sometimes quickly, from one set of job duties to another, or from one team to another or to working extra or different hours.
- *Adaptability.* The ability to tolerate and maximize the potential of large organizational shifts such as mergers or layoffs. Also, the ability to adjust to new leadership and management—to change departments, divisions, locations, or job titles.
- *Problem-solving skills.* The ability to self-correct. Having the tendency to tackle problems independently and with a minimum of supervision. Having the ability to tolerate frustration and/or failure until the solution to the problem is found. Maintaining persistence despite ambiguous or incomplete information and perseverance despite initial failure or frustration.
- *Interpersonal communication.* The ability to communicate in a way that is appropriate to company culture as well as individual preferences, with empathy, clarity, and good listening behaviors. Having the ability to give feedback and having sensitivity to multicultural preferences in

communication style. Being technologically literate and able to utilize the latest forms of written and electronic communication.

- *Ability and willingness to learn.* A willingness to attend professional development workshops and seminars. The ability to self-correct and alter one's own behavior. Having a propensity to pursue outside sources of formal and informal education, and taking personal responsibility to remain abreast of advances in one's field or occupation.

I once had the CEO of a high-tech company tell me that, he personally considered adaptability to be the most important quality any of his employees could possess and that he would not hire (and would even fire) those who could not demonstrate it!

Employers are very unlikely to ask you directly whether or not you possess these skills, yet they will be looking for them in your demeanor, in the stories you tell, and in the way you tell them.

You'll be taking an inventory of your competencies in the next chapter, where I'll ask you to provide an example or "story" about how you've used each of them. In Chapter 4, you'll learn how you can adjust your competencies to match those most valued by the company by aligning them with the company mission and company culture.

Your Gift

The last skill I would like to talk about is simply what I call a "gift." It's not something you learned or something you read about. It's much more about *who you are* than *what you do*. It may have been with you since birth. Perhaps it's genetically inscribed, divinely bestowed, or perhaps part of the fabric of very early childhood experiences.

What's important about knowing your gift is that, consciously or not, it's the most compelling thing about you. It's like the sun around which all the other stars and planets of your skills revolve. Your interviewer may not be able to give it a name, but he or she will feel it when you are relaxed, easy, and natural, which is what this section is preparing you to be. Do you have a hunch what *your* gift may be?

- *What is the thing that people most often compliment you for?* Is it your wit or intelligence? Is it the ability to find humor in any situation?
- *What is a quality that you would never, under any circumstances, give up?* Is it your passion or intensity? Is it your rationality? Your devotion?
- *What quality would you like to be remembered for after your death?* Is it your perseverance against all odds? Is it your ability to inspire others? Your brilliance? Your compassion? Your technical expertise? Your leadership?
- *Is your gift . . .* Your kindness? Your refined artistic taste? Your vision? Your generosity?

Take a while and think about *your* gift. Along with all these externally oriented skills you have identified in this chapter, see if you can also bring some of this gift in to the interview. Your gift makes up some of what we call your *chemistry* with another person. If it's worth having (which it is), it's worth sharing.

Skills Summary Page

List the six skills you picked from your general skills list:

1. _____
2. _____
3. _____
4. _____
5. _____
6. _____

List your six to ten job-specific skills:

1. _____
2. _____

3. _____

4. _____

5. _____

6. _____

7. _____

8. _____

9. _____

10. _____

List your three to four strongest personal traits:

1. _____

2. _____

3. _____

4. _____

List your three top competencies:

1. _____

2. _____

3. _____

Write a few sentences about your gift.

_____

_____

_____

_____

_____

_____

I'd like you to carefully read through what you've just written. I am willing to bet, right now, that there is not another person on this planet who has the exact same list as you have, with the exact same stories to tell about how and where they used their skills.

In fact, your skills arsenal is as unique as you are. *Your talents are to be treasured.* I hope you give yourself a good, hearty pat on the back! The following chapters will help you make sure you can convince an employer that you deserve to be paid well for your particular package of talents.

CHAPTER 3

Q Statements:
Your Secret Weapon

Each of us has some unique capability, waiting for realization.

—George H. Bender

In the last chapter, you identified your skills, personal traits, competencies, and gifts—a task that's surprisingly difficult for most job seekers. In fact, this crucial bit of "homework" puts you well ahead of most other job applicants. It's an essential step toward your ultimate goal—being able to clearly describe your skills and qualifications to an interviewer. The next step will be to use these skills to create pithy, memorable, quantifiable "sound bytes" about yourself, assertions we'll call *Q statements*.

What Is a Q Statement?

A *Q statement* is a sentence (or group of sentences) that expresses a *numerical measurement* of some action or accomplishment you have performed. It is quantitative. A Q statement is not vague; it's exact. For example, rather than saying you "increased productivity," using a Q statement, you would say that you "increased productivity by 25 percent."

Why quantify a skill? Let's take a look at the following statements and see which of them bears the most weight and leaves the longest-lasting impression:

STATEMENT A: I am a good communicator.

STATEMENT B: I have lectured to more than 12,000 people worldwide on the topic of personal financial planning, and I have worked individually with clients from 19 to 90 years old.

Which of these two statements seems the most evocative? From which one can you make a mental picture? Which will you remember?

Statement B is more descriptive and more concrete. It does not simply make a claim or advance a personal opinion. Statement B uses actual facts and numbers to specifically *demonstrate* the skills. This kind of clarification gives the listener evidence of the skill and a good idea of the scope of it.

Let's take another example:

STATEMENT A: I'm an excellent manager.

STATEMENT B: I have managed 135 people on projects budgeted for over $2.1 million.

> ### Remember, this is not bragging.
> ### These are facts.

If you really *do* have an accomplishment of such magnitude as the one above, which statement would serve you better? Which statement would help the interviewer to make the best decision about your qualifications? While "I'm an excellent manager" is a fine thing to say, it would be a lot stronger if it were supported by statement B.

Interviewers these days *want* to hear specific data. If you don't provide the interviewer with concrete, quantified examples of what you did, the interviewer will very likely ask you to. It's much more impressive to be prepared to offer them yourself, without prompting. And in the opposite direction, it is most troubling if the employer asks for examples of your skills and you can't think of any. To prevent being caught off guard this way, you'll want to prepare several Q statements (targeted to each specific job) before every interview. If you can learn how to quantify your skills *now*, it will become an ingrained habit, at your command whenever you need to use it.

Let's take a look at the structure and content of some other concrete, quantified statements:

- Since I've become the director of operations, I've been responsible for helping the company to decrease waste by 20 percent, resulting in an overall savings of $1.2 million a year.
- I ran a bicycle sales and repair store with 17 employees and gross annual sales of $193,000.
- I operated a multiline phone system and personally handled over 200 calls per day.
- Since I took over as the CEO of this pharmaceuticals company, we have gone from number 347 to number 197 in the list of Fortune 500 companies.
- As a program manager, I instituted and developed a production process that increased profits by 42 percent in the second quarter.

- I acted as a regional manager for 12 offices overseeing 147 salespeople throughout the Midwest.
- As a human resources manager, I initiated and developed a retraining program that improved employee satisfaction from 2.7 to 4.1 on a scale of 1 to 5.
- As a production manager, I decreased production time by six days a month, resulting in a savings of $360,000 quarterly.
- I maintain a caseload of 65 patients.
- I built a prototype that could tolerate 15 percent more stress than its predecessor.
- My team identified four as-yet-unknown species of flora and fauna in the mountainous regions of California.
- I reduced overhead by 25 percent while increasing profits by 43 percent annually.
- I designed a microchip that is 23 percent more reliable than its predecessor.
- I introduced an on-site safety program that decreased workers' compensation claims by 18 percent in 1 year.
- I process more than 250 customer requests daily.
- I won an award for decreasing materials costs from $6.41 per inch to $5.20 per inch.
- I have overseen the landscape design on over 200 projects, costing up to $350,000 per project.

After reading all these different Q statements, you probably see a pattern emerging. First, they all contain action words—verbs such as *designed, initiated, saved, processed,* and *handled.* Second, they all end with some sort of number, expressed in monetary amounts, time, and percentages, and numerical amounts of people, actions, or things.

The "formula" for a Q statement would look something like this:

Verb + (who, what, when, where, how) + Result = Q statement

Notice that the results are *specific*, *concrete*, and *measurable*. And notice that they all, at the bottom line, lead to some sort of direct benefit or monetary profit to the company.

There are five ways to quantify your accomplishments:

1. By numbers of people, places, things, units, or actions, such as "handled 200 telephone calls per day."

2. By amounts of money saved or earned, such as "$300,000 savings" or "$100,000 in profits."

3. In percentages (or fractions), such as "70 percent decrease in waste," or "33 percent increase in production."

4. By time saved, which usually means money saved.

5. By a subjective or objective scale or rank, such as "4.8 on a scale of 1 to 5 for increased customer satisfaction" or "moving from number 360 to number 121 on the Fortune 500 list."

Quality or Quantity?

Of course, it would be absurd to try to quantify every single one of your tasks or accomplishments. Still, at the very least, you can be *qualitatively* specific. For example, instead of simply saying, "I'm multilingual," you could say, "I am fluent in French, Spanish, and Chinese." Or, instead of saying that your artwork has been shown in "many galleries," you might say that your work has been shown in "galleries in Los Angeles, San Francisco, Santa Fe, Denver, and New York."

Other statements that do not need to be quantified to convey the weight of accomplishment would be the following:

- I won an award for being the employee of the year.
- I'm president of the Society for Historical Research.
- I graduated with highest honors.
- My customers have described me as dependable, honest, and fair.
- My last boss would describe me as dynamic, innovative, and creative.

- I created a new curriculum for self-esteem in secondary schools.
- I invented a new type of kitchen sponge.

Let's Get Specific

We'll talk more about qualitative statements later in this chapter, but for now we'll stick with learning more about Q statements. Now that you've read quite a few Q statements, let's move on to creating some of your own. It's time to look back at the list of your general skills in Chapter 2. Let's say "organize" is at the top of your list. An *unspecific statement* might look like this:

I am very organized.

A *more specific statement* would look like this:

I organized meetings for top international executives in New York, Washington, D.C., and Hong Kong.

The *quantified* version of this statement would look like this:

I organized up to 40 meetings a week for over 15 international executives in New York, Washington, D.C., and Hong Kong.

Q Statements for General Skills

Now that you have a Q statement, use the skills that you unearthed in Chapter 2 to construct two or three Q statements of your own for each general skill that you chose. Add additional ones as you think of more of your quantified accomplishments.

Please note your ideas on the next few pages.

Skill 1 _____ (name of skill)

Q statement:

_____

_____

_____

Q statement:

_____

_____

_____

Q statement:

_____

_____

_____

Skill 2 _____ (name of skill)

Q statement:

_____

_____

_____

Q statement:

_____

_____

_____

Q statement:

_____

_____

_____

Skill 3 _____ (name of skill)

Q statement:

_____

_____

_____

Q statement:

_____

_____

_____

Q statement:

_____

_____

_____

Skill 4 _____ (name of skill)

Q statement:

_____

_____

_____

Q statement:

_____

_____

_____

Q statement:

_____

_____

_____

Skill 5 _____ (name of skill)

Q statement:

_____

_____

_____

Q statement:

_____

_____

_____

Q statement:

_____

_____

_____

Skill 6 _____ (name of skill)

Q statement:

_____

_____

_____

Q statement:

_____

_____

_____

Q statement:

_____

_____

_____

Great! You now have some powerful statements to use as real-life examples of how you can contribute to the bottom-line profits of a company. You can prove to the interviewer that you can produce results—because *if you have done it once, it's a good bet that you can do it again.*

Q Statements for Job-Specific Skills

Now that you've made your general skills "leap off the page," I'd like you to do the same for your job-specific skills. If you can't quantify them, try just thinking of an example, story, or situation in which you used the skill.

The more vivid the story, the more credible it will seem to the interviewer!

Please use the worksheet that follows to keep a record of your examples:

Skill 1 _____ (name of skill)

Q statement:

_____

_____

_____

Q statement:

_____

_____

_____

Q statement:

_____

_____

_____

Skill 2 _____ (name of skill)

Q statement:

_____

_____

_____

Q statement:

_____

_____

_____

Q statement:

_____

_____

_____

Skill 3 _____ (name of skill)

Q statement:

_____

_____

_____

Q statement:

_____

_____

_____

Q statement:

_____

_____

_____

Skill 4 _____ (name of skill)

Q statement:

_____

_____

_____

Q statement:

_____

_____

_____

Q statement:

_____

_____

_____

Skill 5 _____ (name of skill)

Q statement:

_____

_____

_____

Q statement:

_____

_____

_____

Q statement:

_____

_____

_____

Skill 6 _____ (name of skill)

Q statement:

_____

_____

_____

Q statement:

_____

_____

_____

Q statement:

_____

_____

_____

Q Statements for Personal Traits

After taking a breather from all of those incredible accomplishments, let's take a look at some of the more intangible qualities you bring to the interview—your personal traits. There are specific ways to *make these skills come alive* in the eyes of the employer too.

Let's say that one of your personal traits is that you're dependable. That's an important attribute, but it's difficult to quantify. However, you may have an anecdote or short story that *demonstrates* that you are dependable. To express the quality of dependability, you might say something like this:

> I'm very dependable. Every time the boss left the plant to go out on business, he left the operations of the plant and responsibility for the crew up to me.

You might also say:

> I'm very dependable. In two years of working for this company, I haven't once been late for an appointment with a customer.

As is true when talking about your general skills, it's not wise to make a claim about your personal traits without having some evidence to support it. Try to find at least one story, fact, example, or anecdote that proves you have that trait.

Please return to your skills summary page in Chapter 2, and find the list of your three to four personal traits. Write at least one example of when you demonstrated that trait or used that skill. Use the following pages to keep a record.

Personal trait 1 _____ (name of trait)

Q statement:

_____

_____

_____

Personal trait 2 _____ (name of trait)

Q statement:

_____

_____

_____

Personal trait 3 _____ (name of trait)

Q statement:

_____

_____

_____

Q Statements for Competencies

The same technique can be used to demonstrate your competencies. Again, return to the skills summary page in Chapter 2. Find examples of how you demonstrated three of those essential competencies and describe them here. *They need not have been used in a work setting.* All that's important is that you have an example or anecdote about how you used them in the past.

Competency 1 _____ (name of competency)

Q statement:

_____

_____

_____

Competency 2 _____ (name of competency)

Q statement:

_____

_____

_____

Competency 3 _____ (name of competency)

Q statement:

_____

_____

_____

Q Statements for Your Gift

Refer again to your skills summary page and see if you can be even more specific about how you've used your gift. Again, it's not necessary that you used this skill in a work setting, only that you can demonstrate it through some concrete example.

Your gift: _____

Q statement:

_____

_____

_____

Excellent work! Believe it or not, you are almost ready for your interview. The next chapter will give you a few more helpful hints on preparation before you stride into the interviewer's office.

CHAPTER 4

Research:
What Separates
the Hired from
the Not Hired

> *Great works are performed not by strength, but by perseverance.*
>
> —Samuel Johnson

An Interview Is Like a First Date

Have you ever been on a first date with a guy who talked *only* about himself? With a woman who never asked you any questions about *your* life or *your* interests? This person just blabbed on about himself or herself until the end of the evening, when you were relieved that it was finally O-V-E-R. Unless you were interested in getting to know an egomaniac, it's likely that the first date was probably the last.

An interview is a lot like a first date, in that displaying interest in the other person (in this case, the company) actually makes you *more attractive* to the person. It's flattering if you ask the person questions that allow them to "brag" a little bit. It's a pleasant surprise to the other person if you show that you actually know a little bit about some of the things that are important to him or her.

Why Research a Company?

This chapter will present a deep well of resources from which to plumb information on just about any company, large or small. Besides enabling you to "flatter" the interviewer, there are at least six central reasons to research a company before you step into the interview:

1. To find out whether or not it's a place you want to work
2. To discover what skills the job or the company most values
3. To ferret out as much as you can about the company culture and mission in order to align some of your competencies to fit the company's style and goals
4. To impress the employer when he or she asks: "Tell me, what do you know about our company, and why would you like to work here?"
5. So you can make intelligent queries when the employer asks you: "So, do you have any questions about our company?"
6. To give you an advantage because your competitors for this job are *not* researching the company to the degree that you're going to

All the Information Is Right at Your Fingertips

Think you'll never find out anything about Company XYZ because it's too small, it's highly secretive, or it doesn't have a Web site? Think again. There are people who have full-time jobs gathering information (including information about extremely private topics, like salaries of certain employees) on just about any company you can imagine.

You can locate facts and opinions about companies in a number of ways:

- From company Web sites
- Through other research on the Internet
- From proprietary, or "for-fee," databases
- From public, or "free," databases
- From one-stop job centers around the country
- In public libraries, from their books, periodicals, and computer databases
- From the interviewer, *during the interview itself!*

Can you think of any others? When you put your mind to it, there seem to be countless ways to gather information if you have just a couple of hours and the inclination to hunt for it.

How to Get Your Hands on a Computer

If you own a computer, you're in luck, but if you don't, you can easily locate one you can use for free or for a small fee at one of the following spots:

- At a computer café that charges low fees by the minute or hour
- At a public library—for free!
- At a copy center, like Kinko's
- At a local one-stop career center, if you qualify for services

A note about career centers: One-stop career centers were created for public use by the U.S. federal government in the 1990s. They can be found in every large city and many medium-sized towns across the nation. You can also participate in their free workshops on résumés, interviewing, and other job-related topics as well as obtain limited one-to-one support with a career counselor.

Because they are founded and maintained by government funding, you have to call first to see if you qualify for services. Don't count yourself out! I've seen everyone from secretaries to CEOs to writers and actors utilizing one-stop career centers. If you need to use a computer for research or wish to further investigate their offerings, go to the Internet address provided below.

If you were laid off from your last position, you definitely qualify to use these career centers. You may also be qualified for other reasons, such as income, family situation, veteran's status, age, disability, substance abuse history, and many more.

Keep in mind that one-stops are not only a place to use a free computer—they are also a terrific resource and source of support for just about every job seeker.

You can get in touch with one of the many thousands of one-stop career centers around the United States to see if you are qualified to use their services.

---

1. On a computer, go to the following:
   http://www.usworkforce.org/onestop.
2. On the first page, click on the link "one-stop Web sites."
3. You'll be taken to a page that displays a map of the United States.
   Click on your state.
4. This will bring up a new Web site dedicated to your state.
5. Continue to click on: "one-stop sites," "one-stop locations," "local one-stop centers," "one-stop maps," or "one-stop directions" until you find the names, phone numbers, and other contact information for centers near you.

I bet you're in front of a computer just about now and ready to launch the hunt! Let's pick a relatively easy company to research first, such as a large Fortune 500 company.

Company Web Sites

Almost every large company has a Web site (usually www.their-companyname.com). Many medium and very small (even one-person) companies also have a presence on the Web. The key is finding them.

Some companies will have Web sites with initials that stand for the name such as www.abc.com standing for "American Business Center." Instead of guessing, though, I suggest that you save time and go to a major search engine like Google (www.google.com) and enter the company name (in full) as your search term. This will bring you directly to a link you can click on to go to the company Web site.

Explore the site. Notice both the content *and* the "feel" of the site. Is it leaning toward a traditional type of design or toward a bold modern design? This alone may tell you a little bit about the personality of the company. What is the company message or mission? Does it have a slogan or catch phrase that reveals its philosophy? What products or services does it offer? How large is the company, and when was it founded? Who is the CEO or some of the other executive members?

Are there any names of women in those ranks? Is it very, or not at all, important to you that women be leaders of a company this size? Where does the company appear to be moving? Is it announcing any new product or service lines? What is the general feeling or attitude it seems to project regarding its customers? How about its employees?

Company Mission Statements

Steven Beasley, one of the leading researchers and lecturers on competencies in the world, counsels job candidates to *"align their competencies with the mission of the company"* for the best interviewing results.

Here's an actual mission statement from a leading Internet company that clearly spells out some of the competencies it expects from its employees. This mission statement was plainly written on their Web site.

> It is our goal to foster an environment of *creativity* and *cooperation*, where each employee can participate in the company mission: to create, and *continue to improve* upon, a product that serves the community and the world as a leader in the pursuit of knowledge and information.

Remember our list of personal traits in Chapter 2? This company is telling you right here in its mission statement what it is looking for.

Having read and absorbed the mission statement, you might want to emphasize the following qualities (and others you have that seem to match their values) if you were seeking employment there:

- Creative
- Self-motivated
- Innovative
- Team oriented
- Experienced in handling interpersonal communication
- Inventive
- Experienced in problem solving

Company Culture

By *company culture* we mean the *norms of behavior* (formal, informal, competitive, cooperative) that are or are not expected or offered in the everyday work environment. Company culture may refer to many things such as the following:

- Manner of dress (formal business attire versus casual dress)
- Means of communication (e-mail, phone, or just dropping by someone's office)
- Treatment of superiors, subordinates, and peers
- Use of first names or last names

- Work ethic and work hours
- Frequency and ease of promotions
- "Unwritten" behavior required for social acceptance
- Tolerance of differences
- Demands for conformity
- Fun or recreational time allowed during working hours
- Multicultural, sexual preference, and gender sensitivity
- Openness or secretiveness of management

It may include perks like free food or beverages on site, free dry-cleaning pickup, recreation rooms, health club memberships, or fitness classes.

Company culture information can often be gleaned from a company's Web site. One tech company, for example, uses its Web site to describe the company culture in the following way:

- All the snacks you can eat
- Free gourmet lunches served daily
- Free massage therapy
- Roller hockey
- Game room
- Gym

Now I bet half of you reading this book would like to pack up and work for this company right now! (It must be the roller hockey!) But what about those of you who don't necessarily believe in mixing work with play and who wouldn't mind bringing a bag lunch to an environment that's a bit less stressful? (Free food usually means long hours.) And maybe you'd prefer to work for a company in which the pace was a bit slower instead of high-energy, and highly demanding.

I wouldn't suggest that you decline an interview there just because of what the Web site says, but it might be *one* component of your final decision about whether or not to accept a job offer from that company (something we'll discuss in depth in Chapter 10).

Targeting Your Skills to the Company's Needs

Go to the Web site of a company that you're interested in working for. If you don't know of any companies that fit the bill, go to www.hoovers.com. In the site search section, chose "search by industry." Then enter the name of an industry you're targeting, like "fashion." Hoovers will come up with a long, healthy list of companies for you to investigate, including the corporate Web address for each of those companies.

When you've gotten to the corporate Web page of a company you'd like to explore, have a look at the section of the Web site that is announcing current job openings. Is your job there? What kinds of specific words are used to describe the job title and its responsibilities as well as the requirements for skills and education, and especially personal traits and competencies?

Now look back at your skills summary page in Chapter 2. Are your skills a good fit with this company, or do you think that you might need to pick out some other skills from your arsenal to emphasize to this particular employer?

After exploring the whole Web site, what are the personal traits and competencies that appear to be called for by this company and this job?

Is the company looking for loyalty or risk taking? Does it prefer the use of time-tested conventional methods or innovation? Is the company looking for highly independent or more team oriented people? Do they expect you to come in and "hit the ground running" or learn more slowly as you go?

Researching a company from information that *they* supply in print or on the Web can obviously put you way ahead of the competition—and more at ease in the interview, because you know whom you're talking to.

There is, however, something missing when you operate only from the information that the company *wants* you to hear about it. It's important to also look at what other people are saying about this company—analysts and others in the media who know the industry and this company's place in it.

What do major magazines and newspapers and financial and business analysts have to say about these organizations—their stability, their treatment of employees, their place among their competitors, or their outlook for the future? Here are a few things you might look for in others' assessment of a company:

- Is this a company that is in a major union dispute?
- Does this company have a reputation for receiving many employee complaints or even lawsuits?
- Is the CEO just about to resign?
- Is management trying to delay a layoff that appears to be inevitable?
- How does the public view this company—as a philanthropic community hero or as a greed-driven monster?

All of these things have a great deal to do with both your short-term satisfaction and long-term stability at a company. How do you find out about these things? My favorite places are either on www.hoovers.com or at the reference desk of my friendly neighborhood library. Both sources are free, and both have more information on company stability, image, and "culture" than you can imagine.

Let's pick a medium-sized hypothetical company from hoovers.com. We enter the company name, and we are immediately greeted by a great deal of useful information, including the following:

- The location of company headquarters and subsidiaries
- The names of executives and vice presidents
- The names and information of the company's main competitors
- The scope of the company's products and services
- A brief history of the company
- Some views on its further development

- Its ranking on a number of financial and business lists, including the Fortune 500 list.
- Archived press releases sent out by the company as well as recent (even same day) media reports on the corporation

Can you imagine an employer asking you, *"What do you know about our company?"* and your responding with the following statement:

> Well, I know you were founded in 1977 in Boston, Massachusetts, by Steven Gibbs, and that your current CEO is Karen Solomon. I believe that you first started with the production of only televisions and radios, but today the company is currently number 702 in the Fortune 1000 and has expanded its product line to a very wide array of electronic products that includes a launch of a wireless telephone device next month. I know that you have been voted as one of the top 20 companies to work for, according to *Forbes* magazine, and that all of those things would make me very proud to be a part of your team.

A little research beforehand and you'll be in command of all this data! You'll sound like you've been researching all night. Not *only* is it flattering to the employer that you know so much about his or her company, but it also says a lot about you. One would imagine that a person with this much relevant information under his or her belt would not only be well prepared but also intelligent, persistent, diligent, proactive, and persuasive—just to name a few qualities. Tell me one employer who wouldn't want an employee like that!

Use Your Library Card as a Job Search Tool

If you prefer to search for books and periodicals at the library, go directly to the reference desk and tell the reference librarian exactly what you're trying to do. Reference librarians, in my experience, are even more valuable than a good career coach when it comes to guiding people to exactly the kind of information they are looking for at this stage. He or she will expertly guide you to databases of newspapers, reports, reference books, and other written material that you can peruse until you find the information that seems most critical to the interview.

In most libraries, you can also use a database with valuable information on more than 12 million U.S. companies and 1.3 million Canadian organizations called *Reference USA*. If you want to arm yourself with even *more* facts, check out *Dow Jones Interactive, Net Advantage, Dun and Bradstreet's Million Dollar Database, Edgar-Online, CareerJournal.com,* or the *Riches' Guide*. You can even log on to these storehouses of information at home if you have a library card and a personal identification number.

> ***Initially, research will lower your anxiety level because you know with whom you're dealing.***

Finally, spouting off facts and educated opinions about a company are some of the surest ways to win over an interviewer!

CHAPTER 5

Winding Up
Your Strategy

I am seeking. I am striving. I am in it with all of my heart.

—Vincent Van Gogh

I bet by this point you're ready to grab your briefcase and run to your next interview. That's great! And your enthusiasm will help you in interviews too, but before you dash off, there are a few small (but important!) matters to attend to—those extra touches that will make you feel totally prepared and give you the confidence to stride into your interview like a champion.

1. You need to assemble some references and recommendations. (Don't worry—they don't have to be from the Secretary of State or Donald Trump.)

2. Next, you need to prepare a neat and classy presentation packet. A presentation packet is a simple paper folder with one "pocket" on the inside of each flap where you'll place some essential documents needed in the interview, like letters of recommendation, a list of references, and an extra copy of your résumé. (It'll cost you about 69 cents!)

3. Finally, you need to be *absolutely sure* that come wind, rain, or fire, you get to the interview *on time*.

Recommendations

If you are like most professionals working today, you'll probably hold several jobs between now and the time you retire. In fact, according to statistics compiled by the U.S. Department of Labor, most adults will hold over five jobs in a lifetime.

People leave jobs for many reasons: a better offer, a less demanding commute, a desire to change industries or cities, a discovery that they'd like to pursue another interest or dream, a feeling they've reached a "dead end" for advancement, or a better personality fit with their boss or coworkers.

Often these transitions are smooth; on occasion they are difficult or acrimonious. But if at all possible, try to get a letter of recommendation *on company letterhead* from a supervisor, manager, officer, or executive of the company before you leave. Most bosses, even when the separation from the company may have been less than pleasant, are still willing to write you a letter of recommendation. Even if you were fired, an employer would rather give you a positive-sounding letter and bid you luck on your way out the door than have you feel so disgruntled that you may take some negative action toward the company like suing it, or going to the media with a distasteful story. Although it's unlikely you'll receive a letter under these circumstances, a recommendation on company letterhead can help you enormously.

There are three sources of information a prospective employer can use to judge the character of a job applicant:

1. What the applicant says himself or herself, either in the résumé or the interview

2. What others say about the applicant in letters of recommendation and references

3. The applicant's own actions, which is an area an employer will know the least about until an applicant is actually hired

Naturally, the employer wants to know as much information as possible about you before making an investment in hiring you. A new hire, no matter how adept he or she is, usually means an initial loss of money for an employer while the person is being trained and getting "up to speed." It's usually months before the new employer starts to make his or her return on the investment in hiring someone.

If you don't feel comfortable asking your immediate supervisor for a letter, try approaching someone above that person, or someone even closer to the top. A letter from a coworker can also speak well for your character.

A letter of recommendation can be fairly generic (and you can use it to apply for multiple jobs) and would look like the sample letter on the following page.

If your employer is writing a letter of recommendation for you and is wondering what to include, tell him or her to outline the following:

1. Some of your most valuable skills

2. A few of your personal traits

3. Any of your outstanding accomplishments or contributions to the company

June 30, 20xx

To whom it may concern:

Jared Goldberg worked as a quality assurance director under my supervision at the Caliber Corporation from 1997 to the present. Under Mr. Goldberg's able leadership, the QA department designed and built a new database to track defective parts. I can directly attribute to Mr. Goldberg's efforts a 12 percent decrease in defective materials.

Mr. Goldberg is a trustworthy, intelligent, and professional manager in every way. He was responsible for bringing many improvements to our department as well as for instituting programs to train new employees.

In 20xx, his peers voted him the Caliber Manager of the Year Award. In addition to this, Mr. Goldberg volunteered his time in the Caliber mentoring program, and he was able to mentor six junior employees in the short time that he was with us.

We are sorry to lose Mr. Goldberg, but we recommend him unreservedly to any future employer. Please feel free to contact me at any time regarding Mr. Goldberg, and I will be happy to speak with you.

Sincerely,

Kelly Jones
Vice President of Operations
(222) 000-2276 ext. 45
k_jones@123company.com

Sample Letter of Recommendation

4. Things you may have done as a volunteer

5. Any awards or special recognition you were given

6. A sentiment that the company regrets to see you go

7. A statement that recommends you to future employers

8. An offer that he or she may be contacted in the future regarding your time at the company

Often, the manager or supervisor at your current company is willing to write you a recommendation . . . but he is so busy that it's difficult for him to finish the task. Ask if you can write your *own* letter of recommendation and have him edit and sign it.

If you can, include letters of recommendation from three different people, along with a fresh copy of your résumé, when you go to the interview. Do *not* send these letters to the employer before the interview unless you're explicitly asked to do so. Employers have only 7 to 90 seconds to spend reading materials you send before the interview. Don't overburden them with letters at this point. Since letters of recommendation are optional, and for "average" interviewers, rather rare, why not save the letters for a surprise bonus at the interview just to tip those scales even further in your direction when the time comes?

Be sure that the people who signed or wrote these letters know that you are applying for new positions so that they will be prepared if a prospective employer calls them. We don't want the busy people who supported you with a letter to say "Ellen *who*?" when it comes time for a prospective employer to check on your recommendations.

References

You need to prepare your references in the same way you prepared recommendations. Whereas recommendations are usually *written* communications, references are *verbal* recommendations. You do not need letters from these people. Pick them carefull, because employers really do take the time to check them! Any of your peers, and certainly your superiors at work, make fine references.

> **To get someone to act as a reference for you, I sug-gest asking very simply, "Would you feel comfort-able acting as a reference for me?"**

If the person says yes, that's great. Tell her a little bit about the types of jobs you are aiming for, then write a thank-you note. Send your résumé with it. Sometimes when you ask someone to act as a reference, she says no. This can happen for a number of reasons; most likely, she will tell you she "doesn't know your work well enough." Don't insist—move along to your next prospect. The first person probably wouldn't have given you a particularly good reference anyway.

Bear in mind that many companies, especially large corpo-rations, do not allow managers, supervisors, or any member of their staff to recommend an employee, either in written or verbal form. If it happens that you can't get verbal references or written recommendations from someone in your last company, try the company before that one. And then, the ones before those.

> **If you're having trouble arranging work-related references, other forms of references might be character references and academic references.**

You might also try the following:

- Ask someone you know who has a solid reputation in the community to act as a reference to your honesty, your integrity, and your dependability.

- Ask a former teacher or professor to write a letter about your ability to solve problems, learn quickly, and meet deadlines.

- Ask a member of a club, volunteer, or sports group to which you belong to attest to your skills and character.

Most people are glad to act as a reference and/or provide a rec-ommendation—it makes them feel respected and important. They would genuinely like to be of help, and they would proba-bly feel honored to be asked. Think about it—wouldn't you be flattered if someone used you as a reference? Just make sure each and every person you talk with also knows that you are beginning a job search and that a prospective employer at some point will most likely call him or her.

When preparing for an interview, you'll want to collect all the vital information about your three references together on one neat page. Type a document as shown in the following form.

References for Beverly M. Santos

1. Arthur Biggis
   Supervisor III
   Maxim Corporation
   277-900-XXXX
   abiggis@maxim.net

2. Melanie Chao
   Director of Manufacturing
   Maxim Corporation
   277-900-XXXX
   mchao@maxim.net

3. Reverand Sam Anton
   First Presbyterian Church of Newburg
   455-783-XXXX
   imthereverand9887@yahoo.com

Sample List of References

The Presentation Packet

Now that you've collected your references and letters of recommendation, how will you organize them? Both of these items will be part of your presentation packet—something you'll bring to each and every interview.

A presentation packet is an $8\frac{1}{2}$- by 11-inch folder with a pocket on the inside of each cover. It need not be expensive—just neat, clean, unstapled, and uncreased. The color doesn't matter. Make copies beforehand of everything inside because you'll be giving the packet and its contents away to the interviewer for him to keep and review. Your packet should contain the following:

1. *Left side.* Three letters of recommendation (not stapled). Place the most impressive one on top.
2. *Right side.* Your list of references (under the résumé—not stapled) and a fresh copy of your résumé (on top—staples are OK).

Present this packet to the interviewer after you've introduced yourself. Open it up so that the writing is facing in such a way that the interviewer can see it. Say, "I've brought an extra copy of my résumé and some other materials I thought might be of interest to you," and set it down with both hands in front of the interviewer. He may choose to read it later, or he may leaf through it right away and comment on it. Give the interviewer time to read it by not talking until he looks up at you and asks you a question or makes a comment.

Punctuality

There is one last aspect of interview preparation that we need to discuss before moving on to the second part of this section, in which we'll walk through the interview process step by step. It's about punctuality. Unless you know the exact route and the amount of traffic likely to occur at the time of day your interview has been scheduled for, it's a very good idea to make a dry run of your trip to the interview site a couple of days before your scheduled interview.

Take some time a day or two before the interview to locate the best route to the building. Don't forget to also identify the most convenient parking, and find out which entrance to the building you'll be using. Use the number of minutes it takes you to get to the interviewer's office on your dry run and *add* an extra half hour to it to allow for any unforeseen difficulties. Knowing exactly where you are going, how long it will take, and where to park will put you at ease and really let you know you're completely prepared for a knockout interview!

The Preinterview Checklist

☐ Do you have at least 20 to 25 skills in your skills matrix that you're good at and that you love to do?

☐ Do you have at least 20 to 40 Q statements that prove you can get results?

☐ Have you gathered your letters of recommendation and called your references?

☐ Can you answer the question, "What do you know about this company?" when the time comes?

☐ Are you absolutely committed to being on time and to doing the necessary preparation to be sure that you are?

Okay. If you feel strong on those points, let's move on to talking about the interview itself!

CHAPTER 6

Managing the First Twenty Seconds of the Interview

The world is like a mirror; frown at it, and it frowns at you.
   Smile, and it smiles too.

—Herbert Samuels

You have 20 seconds or less to impress upon an employer whether or not she should *consider* hiring you. From the moment you walk into her office to the moment you sit down in a chair, thousands of neurons will be firing in the interviewer's brain asking one of two things: "Is this person friend or foe?" It's an inescapable reflex, necessary to our survival as a species, to gauge immediately whether the stranger before us is going to help us or hurt us.

First Impressions

Whether it is morally right or wrong to judge a person the moment we meet her, it is a biological necessity that we do so. As long as we know that's a fact, we need to ensure that we use it to our advantage.

> *If you want the interviewer's initial response to be "this is a friend" rather than the opposite, you should follow a few seemingly simple instructions.*

1. Wear a smile, no matter how you feel. A smile conveys confidence, high self-esteem, competence, warmth, and enthusiasm. Plus, believe it or not, medical testing of brain activity has shown that when people smile, they actually perform better at what they are doing because they are using *more* of both the left and right sides of the brain!

2. Wear clothes that are appropriate to the occasion. It is not so much the color of your suit or the pattern on your tie that matters. It is the respect you show to the interviewer by indicating, indirectly, that the interview is an important occasion to you and that you value the interviewer's time so much that you have put serious consideration into your appearance.

3. Have a firm handshake, using the whole hand. A handshake that is too loose unconsciously communicates to the interviewer that you are not fully committed. On

the other hand, a bone-crushing handshake sends a message that you may be overly competitive. Neither of these messages is attractive to an interviewer. A handshake that is firm with one, two, or three "pumps" of the elbow is an appropriate business greeting, signaling to the employer, "Let's get down to business."

4. Address the interviewer as Ms. or Mr. _____ until you're invited to call him or her by a first name. Again, this greeting is part of being respectful of the interviewer's time and authority.

5. Introduce yourself by your first and last names and say that you are happy to be there. Do you know that only 40 percent of interviewers are trained to do the job of interviewing? My surveys of managers and directors from Fortune 500 companies indicate that they very often feel *more* nervous about interviewing you than you feel about the interview! Introducing yourself and expressing that you're glad to be there is the first step to putting *the interviewer* at ease, so that you can both enjoy a relaxed meeting.

6. Do *not* sit down until the interviewer suggests that you do. If he or she doesn't, ask politely if you may sit down. As soon as you sit down in a chair in the interviewer's office, you become part of his or her territory. It is therefore wise to wait until you are invited to sit or you have asked permission to do so.

7. Do *not*, at any time during the interview, put *anything* on the interviewer's desk. Keep briefcases, note pads, date books, and purses by your side or on your lap. The employer's desk is even more sacred and private territory than the surrounding office. Keep hands, elbows, and any other items from the top of the desk. If, however, you have been invited to sit at a conference table or a round table that is not a desk, you should feel free to take notes on the tabletop as the meeting goes on. These spaces are shared territory, unlike a person's desk, which is private.

8. Make your behavior in the waiting room impeccably professional and polite. Interviewers often ask their

receptionists what they thought about you. Many managers, directors, and executives rely on their assistants as a second pair of eyes, so you'll want them to give their bosses a good report.

Facial Expression

Let's talk about each of these steps and why they are a part of the almost choreographed ritual of getting down to the serious business of interviewing. First, the smile. You may take that for granted, but check your attitude some time and see how easily and warmly you can smile at a complete stranger. Practice smiling at strangers on the streets or from your car. Exercise those smile muscles so they'll be there when you need them.

A smile is not just another facial expression. *It's a signal to that primitive part of the brain* that makes the split-second assessment of friend or foe. It says, "I'm on your side. I will not harm you."

So, no matter how you may *really* feel that day of the interview, and no matter how silly it may seem to grin, *smile*. It will send a message to your *own* brain of being happy and at ease, and it will assure the interviewer's brain that you are there to aid, not to threaten.

Linguists and psychologists have said that 93 to 97 percent of communication is nonverbal, and the smile is one very important part of that communication.

What to Wear

Now that you're wearing that beautiful, warm smile, let's look at the rest of what you're wearing. Guess what? You don't necessarily have to go out and buy a $400 outfit to be dressed appropriately for an interview (unless you want to, of course). Maybe all you need to do is invest $5 in getting those dress slacks pressed or having that attractive blazer dry cleaned.

This is not a "dress-for-success" book. It's much more important that you look neat, clean, polished, and pressed. I'm not going to tell you what color or what shoes to wear. That's up to you. Let's keep it simple.

> ***It is almost impossible to overdress for an interview unless you are wearing a tuxedo or a beaded evening gown.***

Dressing up is not only a way to make you attractive; it is one of the many signals of *respect* you will send to the interviewer during this first 20 seconds. It says, "I respect your time enough to think carefully about my wardrobe."

Many of my clients object to dressing up for an interview. They may complain that the vice president of the company is wearing shorts and sandals and has an untrimmed beard. Or that the CEO is wearing Gloria Vanderbilt jeans and cowboy boots. The difference between you and the interviewer is that you don't have an office with your name on the door (yet).

> ***Before you get the job, take the time to be more formal and more conservative than you would normally be. (Then, when you're hired, you can don your army boots, expose your tattoos, and get down to work with the best of them!)***

Remember, it is not the price of your clothes or how well they match the latest fashion. What makes the difference is that you give the distinct appearance of having taken some time to put yourself together. A few guidelines to achieve that image follow.

Men

Shoes Hard-soled, hard-toed. The best colors are black or brown. No tennis shoes, sandals, or boots. I once heard that interviewers spend a lot of time looking at shoes! It would be a shame to go to the trouble of shaving and putting on your best black suit, only to find that the toes and heels of your shoes look scuffed and shabby. Take the time to have your shoes shined, or, if you're in the mood, do it yourself. It will help complete the picture for a knockout first impression!

Ties   Conservative: black, brown, navy, or red. A solid color or a simple pattern is best. Avoid ties that are too wide or too narrow. No potentially distracting artsy or modern patterns. No pastels or flashy colors. No bow ties.

Suits   Matching business suits are best. If you do not have a tailored, well-fitting business suit in gray, black, navy blue, or brown, you may, as a second choice, wear pants (other than jeans) with a shirt, tie, and complementary jacket.

Shirts   The only type of shirt that is acceptable for men at a job interview, in my opinion, is a button-down shirt with a collar. White or light blue, or a shirt with very narrow and light pinstripes is best. T-shirts and turtlenecks are too casual, however tempting it may be to wear them.

Jewelry   Avoid wearing more than one ring per hand. Don't wear a pinky ring. If you happen to express your own style by wearing piercings on your lips, tongue, ears, or any other place that would be visible to the interviewer, I suggest that, just for now, you take them out. Wait until after you have the job offer and have put in a few weeks at the job. Then, you can decide whether piercings seem to be acceptable in your workplace.

Scents   Other than the soap from your shower and (preferably) unscented deodorant, do not wear any colognes or aftershaves. It's surprising what a strong reaction people have to scents! They either love them or hate them. Don't take the chance that you might be wearing the same cologne as her ex-husband!

Hair   Again, the rule of thumb is conservative. No matter what the length or style of your hair, it's worth investing a few bucks for a haircut before stepping into the competitive world of interviewing. Do not wear a hat.

If you have long hair, tie it back neatly, or consider, for now, having it cut. I'm not trying to tell you how to express your own personal sense of style. I am simply conveying what is true about hiring trends in the marketplace today. Interviewers prefer less rather than more hair on both your head and your face.

I had a client who had absolutely no job offers until he shaved off his shaggy beard. When he got a job (soon after shaving), he sure missed his beard, but he didn't complain about earning $80,000 a year!

Accessories   Always bring a pad of paper and a pen or pencil for taking notes. Avoid bringing a cell phone, pager, or handheld device that may ring or sound off an alarm, which could send the whole meeting rather rudely off course. Even having a cell phone turned off and strapped to your belt, in my opinion, can make you appear to not be fully focused on the interview. Interviewers expect, and should get, your full and undivided attention.

By the way, whether or not you normally wear a wristwatch, wear one to the interview. It signals that you're conscious of time, and most interviewers want an employee who has that attribute.

Finally, I suggest that if you don't have a briefcase or masculine-looking leather portfolio, buy one. There are plenty of briefcases that look like real leather but are made from other materials and cost less than $25 at an office supply store. The same goes for portfolios. Maybe you have nothing better than a copy of the Sunday paper or the *Wall Street Journal* to put inside it. That's okay. Carrying a briefcase or handsome portfolio will make you look 100 percent prepared to do business!

Women

Shoes   Wear pumps with a medium-sized heel. Do not wear high, excessively spiky heels or boots. Black, brown, taupe, or navy is fine. Avoid flashy shoes with bright colors like red or glittery gold. No tennis shoes, open toes, or sandals. Flats may be okay for an extremely casual workplace, but low pumps are preferred.

Dresses or Suits   In the workshops I teach, I always have at least one woman who says, "I wore pants to the interview and I got the job!" That's good news, but she is the exception to the rule. It's fine if you wear pants to work if that fits the company culture, but an interview is another story.

I strongly suggest that you wear either a dress or woman's business suit. If you like, you may wear a skirt with a complementary jacket or blazer. Again, we're going for a conservative "business" look, so hems should be only slightly above the knee and necklines should not be revealing. The color of your jacket or blazer is not terribly important, but try to wear solid colors or very simple patterns so the interviewer's eyes are on your face rather than lost in the pattern of your clothing.

Of course, the most uncomfortable thing about wearing a dress or suit is dealing with those oh-so-fun pantyhose. Until scientists come up with a brand that doesn't run, you'd better be sure to bring an extra pair in your purse or briefcase just in case you get a snag on your car door or in the subway.

Jewelry   Again, it's always better to err on the conservative side. Except for a wedding band and an engagement ring, stick to one ring per hand, one bracelet per wrist. Don't wear dangly or multiple earrings that may be distracting to the interviewer. Remove, just for now, any additional piercings you may have on your ears or face.

Hair and Makeup   Keep it simple! Don't allow long or wavy hair to hide your face. Consider having a touch-up color, wave, or trim. Wear lighter or less makeup than usual. Do not apply too much foundation or eye makeup. If you use hair spray, you might consider an unscented brand. Any sort of perfumelike smell from hair spray, body lotions, cologne, or perfume can be disturbing to some interviewers.

Accessories   Don't forget that your purse, briefcase, or portfolio needs to look good too. Remember to check them for scratches or tears, and remember to bring your business card. A pad and pencil to take notes shows that you're an attentive, interested listener.

These rules may seem stringent, but try to find ways to express your style as much as you can within these guidelines. Be sure to wear clothes you feel comfortable in and colors that compliment your skin tones. When you can look in the mirror and say, "Okay, I'm ready!" you'll know you've found a good combination of businesslike attire.

Your Handshake

By now, you're beaming with an ear-to-ear smile, and you look fabulous! The next signal to the employer is your handshake. In every seminar I give, I actually have the participants practice shaking hands, after which they give each other feedback.

Is it (like the story of Goldilocks and the three bears) too soft? Too hard? Or, just right? There is almost nothing worse than a noncommittal "dead-fish" handshake. We've all felt them, and there is just something intuitively unpleasant about them. On the other hand, the macho-rearrange-your-finger-bones handshake is not too appealing either. *Your handshake signals to the interviewer that you are about to do business.* If it feels, unconsciously, like a halfway committed or overly competitive handshake, you will not be getting off to the right start.

- A firm handshake, using the whole hand in the other person's hand, is an appropriate business handshake.
- There is no reason to shake a woman's hand any differently than you would shake a man's hand. Firm and businesslike is the rule to remember.

Many people, both men and women, have no idea how their handshake feels to other people. I strongly suggest that you practice it with a few friends or family members and ask for their honest feedback. Keep testing different strengths and positions until you and the other person feel comfortable.

Your Greeting

Okay, so I've asked you to grin at strangers and pump a few people's arms. What could possibly be next, you wonder? Riding a horse backward? Scaling the face of a mountain? Well, you're off the hook. Fortunately, those are not the skills you need to succeed at most interviews. The next four points are very easy and require no extracurricular practice:

1. Address the interviewer as Ms. or Mr., and introduce yourself by your first and last names. It will sound something like, "Hello, Mr. Isaacs. I'm Susan Sallinger. Thank

you for seeing me today." You'll be smiling warmly and offering a professional handshake at the same time. After the introduction, the interviewer will ask you to sit down. Don't sit down until he or she asks you to. If he or she does not ask, say, politely, "May I have a seat, please?"

2. If it's a small office or you are very close to his or her desk, you may feel tempted to put your notepad or some other article like a purse on the desk. *Don't.* The desk is the territory of the interviewer, and he or she will feel encroached upon if you pass that invisible line of his or her space and your space. Putting any item, including your hands or elbows on the desk will be taken as a sign of disrespect and an unconscious threat. If you wish to take notes, hold your notebook on your lap.

3. Don't take any beverages into the interviewer's office—spills or choking can be embarrassing and inconvenient. Even if you are offered coffee, it's quite all right to politely decline.

4. Turn your pager and cell phone off! If you forget and it happens to ring, do not glance to see who called. Simply apologize for the interruption and turn off the device.

Your Attitude

Have you ever noticed that when someone likes you, you tend to like him or her in return? Well, it's the same with interviewers. As I said earlier, many interviewers are going to be more nervous than you would imagine at this meeting. They want you to like them, just as you want them to like you.

It may seem hard to fabricate having affection for someone you hardly know or who doesn't seem particularly likeable, but there is a way. One way that I've suggested to my clients that really seems to work is that they picture the interviewer as a friend of theirs or someone they really admire.

You can pretend it's your sister Sylvia or your brother Harold, your Aunt June or Uncle Bob. It may seem a little bit silly, but I've actually told clients to picture the interviewer as a big stuffed teddy bear. Who doesn't like a teddy bear? In any case, your warmth will come through and will probably be returned.

Another thing to remember about your attitude is that *you* are interviewing the company, just as the company is interviewing you. When you keep that fact in mind, you'll remember to notice how you're being treated before, during, and after the interview. Do you like being treated that way?

If you were left waiting for an hour in the waiting room, if you were treated rudely by the receptionist, or if the interviewer was taking phone calls during your interview when he or she was supposed to be paying attention to you, you need to remember that you most likely will be treated in that same way on the job. Ask yourself the following questions:

- Do you like the general tone of the company?
- Do you feel respected?
- Do you feel you're being listened to?
- Are your questions and answers being taken seriously?

You might even think of it this way: You are hiring a new boss! Do you want to work for this person? Would you like to be around this person almost 40 hours a week? Would you like to be a part of this organization?

When you think about it, *the power belongs not only to the interviewer but also to you!* We will discuss more about the questions you need to ask yourself about accepting offers in Chapter 9.

You Passed the Test!

That's it! You've passed the audition! Congratulations! Now we're going to go for the rest of the play. The next chapters will give you all the tools you need to have a potent, masterful, and stress-free interview.

CHAPTER 7

Answering Interview Questions

> Nothing splendid was ever achieved except by those who dared believe that something inside them was superior to circumstances.
>
> —Bruce Barton

All interview questions are not the same. Some require very specific answers. Some warrant more vague and open-ended answers. Still others do not and should not have to be answered at all. These more difficult questions require a special kind of strategy so that you can navigate around them. In the next few chapters we're going to talk about four types of questions and the special strategies required for handling each type:

1. Straightforward questions
2. Questions behind questions
3. Stress questions
4. Questions you ask the employer

We'll also talk about how to recognize and deal effectively with illegal questions. Finally, we'll review some of the most important facts about body language.

Straightforward Questions

Most of the questions in the interview will usually be straightforward. These questions are designed to assess whether you possess the kinds of skills, and to what degree you are in command of those skills, that the job requires. Your skills arsenal and Q statements should be able to help you answer almost all of these types of questions. Here are some examples of straightforward questions and recommended replies.

QUESTION: *Tell me about yourself.*

ANSWER: I have seven years' experience as a case manager, specializing in issues of adolescent behavior, substance abuse, and juvenile delinquency. I earned a B.A. in psychology from the University of Wisconsin and a master's degree in social work from the University of Texas at Austin. In my last position at the Teen Discovery Center, I developed a curriculum to train juvenile offenders for job readiness. Within a year of the implementation of the program, over 75 percent of our clients found gainful employment and kept

---

Positioning Statement Template

I have more than _____ years of experience as a
_____ in the _____
_____ industry, specializing in _____,
_____, and_____.
I have an [A.A., B.A., M.S., certificate] in _____
from the University of _____
at _____ and an [MBA, Ph.D.] from the
University of _____ at _____.
I have also taken (graduate, postdoctoral, vocational, adult
education, internship) classes in _____
and _____. An accomplishment I'm
particularly proud of is [write a very strong Q statement that
fits the needs of the company]: _____
_____
_____
_____. I've come here to talk to you about
a position as a _____, and I'd like to
bring the same or better level of success with my work to you.

Positioning Statement Template with Fill-In Blanks

Positioning Statement Template

I have more than **ten** years of experience as an **events planner** in the **high-tech** industry, specializing in **trade shows,
international travel arrangements,** and **fund raising.** I have a
**B.A. in business administration from the University of Georgia
at Atlanta,** and I have earned a **certificate in international
marketing at Simms Valley College.** One of the accomplishments I'm most proud of is **hosting a dinner with our CEO and
the Georgia state governor. 110 administrators and government
officials attended the dinner, and it ran absolutely seamlessly.
I not only was able to complete the event under budget but I
also received a handwritten thank-you letter from our CEO.
Saving money on important events** is just what I'd like to do for
your company.

Positioning Statement Template with Hypothetical Answers

their jobs for at least one year. I'm applying here today as a licensed clinical social worker because I'd like to prove we can get similar results with your clients.

Your Positioning Statement: "Tell Me about Yourself"

The question "Tell me about yourself" is most often the first question to be posed in an interview.

Although it may be interpreted as a personal question that requires a personal answer, it is really an opportunity for you to introduce some of your most important employment-related skills as well as your education and accomplishments to the interviewer. Your response to "Tell me about yourself" should be a very brief synopsis, or "sound byte," about your background.

Your answer to this question is very important because it positions you for the rest of the interview. That's why some career coaches call this statement a *positioning statement*. I have found an excellent formula for positioning statements that fits for just about every type of job and every type of industry. The template is reproduced here so that you can fill in the blanks. A template filled in with hypothetical answers follows.

I don't usually recommend that my clients memorize any answers to interview questions . . . *except* **this** *one*.

Your positioning statement is extremely valuable. It can be used not just in an interview but in certain social situations, on the phone, or any time you have the opportunity to introduce yourself to someone who could hire you or who knows someone who could hire you. It's good always to have this statement ready when you're in a career transition. I suggest that you work with the template carefully so that you construct something that's comfortable to say and that really feels like a good fit for you.

Other Common Straightforward Questions

For other straightforward questions, you'll want to use your skills lists and Q statements that you prepared earlier in the section. For example, looking back at your skills arsenal:

1. Do you remember your general skills list by heart so that you can recall them in the interview?
2. Do you have a good command over your personal traits list so that you can supply examples of them to the interviewer?
3. Do you remember your list of three competencies, and do you have anecdotes to support them all?
4. Finally, do your Q statements really paint a clear picture of what you did, whom you did it for, where you did it, and, most important, the results you achieved? If so, great!

If your memory of your Q statement and skills lists are not quite up to par, now is the time to go back and review them or make changes so that you have plenty of information to *demonstrate* to the interviewer that you are his or her top choice.

Here are some examples:

QUESTION: *What are some of your strengths?*

ANSWER: My strengths are my negotiating, training, and marketing skills. An example of my training ability is a project for which I trained a group of 16 new employees for the help desk, and they were able to function 20 percent faster than their predecessors.

To answer the question above, this interviewee:

- *Cited three* of her top skills from her skills arsenal
- *Elaborated on one* of them with a Q statement

Let's look at a different question of this type:

QUESTION: *What would your last boss say about you?*

ANSWER: I believe she would say I'm innovative, dependable, and professional. An example of my ability to innovate is that I wrote an award-winning software program for training new employees.

This time, the interviewee:

- *Selected three* top personal traits from his skills arsenal
- *Elaborated on one qualitative example* of the results of his work.

The same strategy applies for the next question:

QUESTION: *What do you think your former coworkers would say about you?*

ANSWER: I think they would say that I'm friendly, efficient, and professional. An example of my friendliness is that I always make it a policy to take a coworker out to lunch sometime during his or her first week of employment. I know how it feels to be new and how much it is appreciated when another employee makes the effort to reach out. It's important to me to help my coworkers feel comfortable. I'd like to bring the same kind of friendliness to your customers.

Confused? After a few more examples, you'll get the hang of it:

QUESTION: *What accomplishments are you most proud of?*

ANSWER: I'm most proud of producing, writing, and directing my own documentary, of winning a citywide triathlon, and of producing a show for CBS television. When I produced a movie-of-the-week for CBS, I was able to cut three days out of the production schedule, saving the company over $650,000.

Again, the interviewee:

- *Picked three* accomplishments (one from his personal life)
- *Elaborated on one* of those accomplishments with a Q statement

QUESTION: *What kinds of skills do you have that would benefit this company?*

ANSWER: I believe that my management, budgeting, and purchasing skills would benefit the company. In my last company, I initiated a new procedure for purchasing materials that ended up in a 37 percent decrease in annual materials costs. That's what I'd like to do for your company.

- The phrase "That's what I'd like to do for your company" is very powerful and persuasive when it follows an impressive Q statement. Try it!

The next question is one that might apply to a person who is completely changing careers. The question is posed to assess whether she possesses the skills for the new career:

QUESTION: *What prepares you to move from being a public health educator to a book editor?*

ANSWER: Well, although I have not yet had professional experience in book editing, I have seven years' experience in the writing, proofreading, and editing of public health education reports. I have written and edited at least 40 reports of more than 100 pages each and submitted them to the state of Florida Public Health Department for review. I was also commended twice for writing, editing, and proofreading grant applications for over $350,000, one of which was submitted to the state, and one to the federal government. In addition to editing at my last job, I took an adult education class in copyediting at Seminole College in Fairfield. I'd like to be able to make similar contributions to your company.

QUESTION: *Why should I hire you?*

ANSWER: If you want someone who is going to raise morale in the company, I believe I am the one. Under my leadership in my last company, not only did employee satisfaction increase from 1.7 to 4.9 on a scale of 1 to 5 in only 1 year, but also absenteeism decreased by over 51 percent. That's exactly what I'd like to do for your company.

If someone asks you why he or she should hire you, you *may* be tempted to say, "Because I am the best person for the job." *Don't.* Though you may be right, the interviewer can't judge that from an unsubstantiated opinion. Instead, you can win over the interviewer by pulling out one of your best Q statements and adding the tagline, "That's exactly what I'd like to do. . . ."

The person being asked the following question is applying for a sales engineer position in a pharmaceutical company:

QUESTION: *What can you contribute to this company?*

ANSWER: Well, I can contribute an excellent working knowledge of pharmaceutical products, superior presentation skills, and excellent postsales follow-up discipline. An example of my postsales follow-up procedure at my last company was that I always called my customers three days after the sale and made it a point to call every two months after that point to make sure they were satisfied. I was very happy that we earned over $2 million in repeat business from one major customer in the third quarter, due to my persistent follow-up efforts. I'd like to make the same kind of profits for this company.

Questions behind Questions

The whole secret to answering a question behind a question is to understand the real intent of the question. To do that, follow these steps:

1. Become aware that the question is not what it appears at face value.
2. Determine what the interviewer is *really* asking you.

3. Recognize the interviewer's real *fear or concern* behind the question.

4. Direct your answer *toward* the real concern behind the question.

Let's take a look at some of these types of questions. We'll examine six sets of questions and answers, and I'll explain the strategy used to answer each question. Try to guess which of the answers, (A, B, or C) is the favorable answer. After a few examples, I'm sure you too will be able to decipher the question behind the questions.

QUESTION: *What do you think you'll be doing five years from now?*

ANSWER A: I'd like to be the vice president of human resources in five years.

ANSWER B: I would really like to make just enough money here to be able to buy a plane ticket to Hawaii and pay my first and last month's rent.

ANSWER C: My goal is to grow and learn more as a professional.

Before we look at the preferred answer, let's take a look at what the question behind the question might be. What is the interviewer really aiming at? What is the real concern or fear behind the question?

In my experience, when the interviewer asks this question, he or she is really asking two things:

1. Are you going to stay at the company for a while so that the time it takes to orient and train you yields a return on our investment, or are you here just for a short stay?

2. If I hire you, are you going to try to take *my* job?

Saying you're staying just long enough to get some money and skip town violates fear 1.

Saying that you want to be vice president of human resources in five years may mean that you will have to step on the toes, or, worse, replace your interviewer on the way up the corporate ladder. This answer violates fear 2.

C is the preferred answer to this question. It is open ended and nonthreatening. It is also generic enough that you can say it without feeling that you are lying. Though you don't say you'd be committed to the company, you do say you're committed to your profession. *You also express enough ambition* ("growing and learning") to sound like you're hard working and success oriented but not interested in rocking anybody's boat.

Let's explore a few more questions in this category. Try to guess the recommended response to the following questions:

QUESTION: *Why did you apply for this job?*

ANSWER A: I was just looking through the newspaper, and I came across this one.

ANSWER B: I have been targeting my job search toward major companies in the software industry. I came across yours on the Internet and decided to research it a bit further. According to your Web site, you've introduced several new product lines in the past few years. I was impressed by your track record and wanted to find out more.

ANSWER C: I heard about it from a friend.

The question behind the question is "Did you just stumble upon our company, or did you put some thought and effort into making a choice to work with us? Have you done your homework?" Answer B would indicate that you had the most forethought. Being able to answer a question like this one is the payoff for the research you learned to do in Chapter 4.

The same sort of strategy can be used for the following question, in which the question behind the question is also "Did you do your homework?"

QUESTION: *What do you know about this company?*

ANSWER: Well, in my research I learned that your company headquarters are in Philadelphia and that you have grown from one small office to over 56 lo the last 3 years. I also know that at first you marily a brokerage firm and that now y

Certified Financial Planners to serve the full range of personal finances and retirement planning. I also read a testimonial from one of your clients in the *Des Moines Daily Reporter*, who said that she had switched to this company from another brokerage firm because she felt that the planners at your firm had integrity and put her needs before their own. That kind of integrity in a company really makes me want to be a part of it!

Many of my mature clients tell me that they are faced with other versions of the question behind a question.

QUESTION: *Don't you believe you may be overqualified for this job?*

The *real* fears behind this question are usually:

1. "Are you going to leave because you don't find the position challenging enough?"
2. "Are you going to be unhappy with the salary we offer and either demand more or leave for a more lucrative position?"

This response satisfies all of the hidden agenda behind the question:

ANSWER: After discussing the position with you and seeing the job description, I feel I have a good understanding about both the responsibilities of the job and the compensation. I feel comfortable with both, and I'm eager to work for your company.

QUESTION: *What have been your most favorite and least favorite jobs and why?*

ANSWER A: I suppose that my favorite job was my last job as a Web designer. I think that the reason I liked it so much was that it was so creative and I never stopped learning new software programs. I've really liked all of my jobs, but if I have to pick one that I liked the least, it would probably be the job I had in high school as a parking lot attendant. I liked meeting people when they passed by, but I can't really say it was my favorite job.

ANSWER B: I have really liked all of my jobs equally. I guess you could say all of them are my favorite jobs.

ANSWER C: I think my favorite job was bookkeeping because I got to work mostly on my own. My least favorite job was the one I had as a senior bookkeeper when my manager was always checking over my work and telling me what to do next.

Like many questions with the hidden agenda, the question above would probably be asked to uncover a "negative." Choice B is not really directly answering the question and sounds a little wishy-washy. Answer C poses the most negative issues because it indicates that this employee had trouble working with his or her manager and probably doesn't like working on a team. Choice A is the preferred answer because it states two positive skills that the person has (creativity and liking to learn new things) and the negative (the job in the parking lot) is fairly innocuous.

One of the most difficult and most frequently asked questions is the following:

QUESTION: *Why did you leave your last job?*

The *real* fear behind this question is that you may have been fired or that you are just changing jobs on a whim, only for the money, or that you are a "job hopper."

Let's look at three alternatives for fielding that one:

ANSWER A: I became aware that there were some excellent new opportunities in the field of biotechnology. I really wanted to expand my professional growth by finding out more about them. This company, judging by your Web site, seems like it would have some interesting opportunities.

ANSWER B: I felt pretty bored at my last job, so I just wanted something more stimulating.

ANSWER C: My last boss and I really didn't see eye to eye. He wouldn't give me a raise no matter how many times I tried to get one.

I bet you already chose A. You're right! No matter what question you are asked about your last company, your last supervisor, or your former coworkers, the intent is usually to "dig up" something negative. Both B and C imply some sort of negative response to your last job.

Sharing ANY kind of negatives about a past employer is to be avoided at all costs, even if you feel that you were treated unfairly.

What if you were laid off due to a downsizing or reorganization of your company? The three rules of thumb for explaining a layoff are the following:

1. Don't blame yourself.
2. Don't blame or sound angry with the company.
3. End your statement about the situation on an upbeat note by saying that you are looking forward to a new position with new responsibilities.

Try these answers on for size. They do not get into negatives, and they indicate that you have a clean slate and wish to move on:

ANSWER: Due to a mass reorganization of my company, my entire department was eliminated. Now I'm looking forward to exploring new options for employment.

Or . . .

ANSWER: Due to serious financial problems, my company was forced to downsize. Unfortunately, my position was affected. Now I'm looking forward to exploring some new opportunities.

Or . . .

ANSWER: My company reduced its labor force to accommodate
            a major shift in business. My function in the compa-
            ny was moved to a site 1,000 miles away, where I
            chose not to relocate. I'm eager to pursue other posi-
            tions in the local area.

If you were fired, you have *no* legal obligation to reveal it. Many
highly talented people get fired incidentally. It's nothing to be
ashamed of. At the same time, it's not something to talk about in
front of a prospective new employer.

Your ex-employer cannot legally release the information that you were fired or say anything negative *or* positive
about your performance, for that matter. The only information
an employer can legally reveal about an ex-employee is the
following:

1. His or her start date
2. His or her title at the time of leaving the company
3. His or her last day with the company

You now have a strategy for answering some of these questions in
an optimal way. Keep the interview like a first date—memorable,
fun, and not too heavy. Don't get into personal details that may
end up backfiring on you.

What-If Questions

Questions behind questions often come in the form of what-if
questions:

QUESTION: *What would you do if you discovered that another employee*
          was stealing from the company?

The real concern behind this question is not what you would do
if someone were stealing. It's more about loyalty and whether
you have good judgment. See if you can guess which of these
answers would be the best for this problem:

ANSWER A: I would tell my coworker that it's illegal to steal from the company.

ANSWER B: I would immediately tell my supervisor.

ANSWER C: I would probably tell my coworker that I had suspicions about his or her stealing and that I hoped he or she would return what was stolen. If I noticed that the stealing continued, I would have to bring it up with my supervisor.

Answers A and B both make sense. They are not necessarily the "wrong" answers. Answer C, however, is the most appropriate one because it shows that the interviewee would first attempt to solve the problem with the other employee on his or her own and then get management involved only if those strategies didn't work.

Companies generally prefer that employees try to work out their problems themselves. It shows good interpersonal skills to be able to bring up something negative with a coworker. Of course, if the problem can't be solved, it shows good judgment and loyalty to the company to broach the subject with a manager or supervisor.

You might expect to receive several questions in the what-if category. Usually what-ifs are hypothetical questions involving morality, ethics, and interpersonal relations. The interviewer is not looking for an exact answer as much as he or she is evaluating your judgment as good or poor. Consider the following hypothetical situations, and imagine how you might handle them, should the interviewer bring them up:

QUESTION: *What if you noticed a team member really slacking off? He is coming in late, taking long lunches, leaving early, or chatting on the phone when he is supposed to be helping the team meet its deadline?*

ANSWER: Well, I might say, "Hey, Harry, we really need your help here. This is an important project, and all of us need to work together to see it through. You've got the talents to help us make the deadline. I really rely on you as part of the team, and I think your involvement would help out everyone. I have a lot of respect for your ideas, and I think we really need your input." If Harry didn't show some change after our talk, I would probably have to bring it up with our supervisor.

QUESTION: *What if your boss continually gossips about one of your coworkers with you and wants you to join in on the derogatory comments?*

Your reaction to situation number 2 would probably depend a lot upon your relationship with your boss. If you know the boss well, you might be able to say:

ANSWER: I really don't feel comfortable talking about Sally in this way.

If you didn't know the boss very well, it might be risky to bring up your discomfort. In that case, you might just have to listen to the gossip but not participate by saying anything bad about Sally.

QUESTION: *What if you have an important personal engagement that involves several other people, has been planned well in advance, and also costs a considerable amount of money, but your boss needs you, just this once, at the last minute to help her close a $3 billion deal before midnight?*

This situation is probably the most common and the most difficult to deal with. Having to stay late at work when there are family or social obligations is something just about everyone has to face at one time or another. It's a tough situation because someone is bound to be disappointed no matter what you decide.

First, tell your boss about the importance of your social engagement, but also reassure her that you will do everything you can to help close the deal. You might offer to stay a little bit later and be late for your other appointment. You might also say something like "I would make myself available by cell phone all night until 1 a.m. if need be, and then be on call at my social event." If you are particularly invested in your job and perhaps up for promotion, you might just have to accept the consequences and decide to stay until midnight to help the boss out. Again, there is no universally right answer.

If you have a significant other, spouse, or family member, you might discuss beforehand what sort of choices will need to be made in this situation when work and home obligations conflict. That way, you'll know if you have the support of your family to stay at work late, or if it's absolutely essential to choose your family or friend first.

Now that you have mastered the question behind the question, you're over halfway through completing the entire interview with finesse, competence, and know-how.

There are only two more types of interview questions to consider: stress questions and questions you ask the prospective employer.

Stress Questions

Don't let stress questions stop you in your tracks. That's *exactly* what they're designed to do! The lighter you are on your feet, the better you'll do.

The object of a stress question is not to gain information from the *content* of your answer. Stress questions are designed to gain information about how you *behave* under stress. That's why they're called "stress questions"—the questions themselves are supposed to create stress.

Let's take a look at one of the "scariest" stress questions:

QUESTION: *What was your greatest failure?*

You certainly are not obligated to recall your real greatest failure in front of a complete stranger. And actually, interviewers don't expect you to. Instead, the interviewer is testing to see how you react under stress.

How do you beat it? First, take a deep breath and entertain one of these answers:

ANSWER: Perhaps my greatest failure was not going to college right after graduating from high school. Anyway, I waited until I got a few years of work under my belt and then I got a degree in physics, with highest honors. I guess it didn't turn out so badly.

Or . . .

ANSWER: Well, you know, I was entered in a tricounty triathlon, and I trained for over six months for the race. I even hired a personal trainer and radically altered my diet and weight-training program. When the day of the race came, I was totally prepared and "psyched up" to win. I was sure I could place in the top three, if not take home the blue ribbon. I did the race in less that 1 hour, 32 minutes, 7 seconds. I gave it my best shot, but I came in fourth.

Or . . .

ANSWER: Once I decided to plant an elaborate vegetable garden in my backyard. I went to the hardware store to buy all the tools and seeds. I also bought a book on how to grow a vegetable garden, and I even took a county parks and recreation course on how to grow your own food. I followed all the directions I had learned, and I planted six kinds of vegetables, but the only thing that ever came up were the tomatoes. I guess I'm really much more of a corporate executive than a gardener!

With responses like the ones above, you're pointing out "failures" that are little more than minor disappointments. You'll also notice that you're actually calling attention to some *good* qualities like diligence, persistence, willingness to try something new, or even excellence. This approach works well since this is only a stress question to test your reaction.

If you have good rapport with the interviewer and can see that he or she has a good sense of humor, you might give it a lighter touch:

ANSWER: I suppose my greatest failure was not being able to take those three strokes off my golf game. [laughs]

ANSWER: I think . . . not being able to make a perfect soufflé. [chuckles]

One stress question that you are most likely to get in almost every interview is the following:

QUESTION: *What is your greatest weakness?*

Do not tell your greatest weakness! How do you think it would sound to say, "I'm really a slob" or "I have 27 unpaid parking tickets" or, worse still, "I am always late for work and I usually leave early"? Let's take *those* weaknesses (which of course *you* don't have) and leave them outside the interviewer's door.

The best way to answer this question is to pick out a negative that you might really possess but that could also be seen as a positive. Here are some examples. See if any of these "weaknesses" apply to you. In the left column is the supposed *negative* weakness. The right column represents that weakness when it's *redirected into a positive*:

"Weakness"—Negative	*"Weakness"—Positive*
Workaholic	Works hard. Would be willing to work extra hours.
Perfectionist	Is detail oriented. Sets high standards for work.
Tries to be friends with *everyone*	Is a team player. Has good interpersonal skills. Warm.
Competitive	Sets goals. Strives to excel. Overcomes obstacles.

I know some of these sound absurd, but let's take a look how the *opposite* of a supposedly negative trait can be turned into an excellent response.

QUESTION: *What is your greatest weakness?*

ANSWER: Well, some people have told me I'm a bit of a workaholic, and I guess, in part, they're right. I just don't mind working an extra hour or two or taking some work home on a Saturday if there's a really important deadline for my department to meet. Meeting deadlines is essential in this business, and I am more than willing to do my part.

A word of warning, though: Many interviewers have heard this supposed weakness so many times that you might risk coming off as unoriginal if you use it. Here are two other possible answers to this question:

ANSWER: Some people have asked me why it is that I try so hard to get along with everyone. I just like to feel that we're all working in a team environment where people need to like and respect each other. I think that when a team really gets along well, they're also more productive.

ANSWER: I've been told a few times that I'm just too much of a perfectionist. Yes, it's true. I do make it a practice of checking my work at least once or twice to make sure that it's absolutely accurate. When working in a medical lab, I have to stay on top of every detail. If the cost of knowing tests have been done correctly takes a fraction of a minute more, that's a small price to pay when someone's life could depend on it.

Even if the preceding answers sound a little twisted, they are better than bringing up real issues like not being able to follow directions or having hostile relations with coworkers. If you bring up weaknesses of that nature, you are surely going to invite the interviewer to probe further into the problem.

Another thing to remember here is that *this is a stress question*. It's not designed to specifically gather information about weaknesses. It is designed to throw you off balance. With that in mind, all you have to do is answer calmly with perhaps a smile or a little chuckle, as if you are shrugging it off.

Sometimes stress questions are very bizarre and seem not to relate to the interview at all:

QUESTION: *Why is there fuzz on a tennis ball?*

Either of these answers, said with a smile, would be fine:

ANSWER: Good question.

ANSWER: That's certainly one to think about!

Other, fairly silly questions that are designed to make you think they are "deep" and to throw you off are:

QUESTION: *What's your favorite color, and why?*

QUESTION: *If you could have dinner with anyone, who would it be, and why?*

QUESTION: *What's your favorite animal, and why?*

My advice is just to answer such questions at face value. You don't have to decipher their meaning. Interviewers are not really trying to psychoanalyze you; they just want you to *think* they are. Give a straightforward, simple answer to these questions, and you'll do fine.

Two more questions that may come up are the following:

QUESTION: *Do you object to psychological tests?*

QUESTION: *Do you object to drug testing?*

If the interviewer asks you these questions, you can at least be assured that he or she is considering you as a serious candidate for the job. You really can't win with these questions, other than to say:

ANSWER: No, I don't object to testing of any kind.

If you do object to being tested, you might want to look for some other target companies that do not employ these practices.

In Chapter 10, you'll be able to read an entire interview, from start to finish, so you'll get an excellent idea of how stress questions (and their answers) fit into the larger scheme of things.

You'll also get a sense of the flow and rhythm of the entire conversation.

Technical Stress Questions

There is a particularly insidious variety of stress questions that is usually asked in technical engineering or scientific interviews but that could very well also be used in other fields including, but not limited to, the social sciences. *Technical stress questions*, as I call them, are not really questions. They're more like little assignments. Their purpose is to put the applicant under a good deal of pressure. They may arise in an interview with an individual or in a panel interview. Let's take a look at one scenario to see how such a question typically arises.

> Abdhur Khatik has a Ph.D. in biochemistry and is applying for a staff scientist's position in a biotechnology firm. Abdhur did well in his first interview with the vice president of the company, and he has been invited back for a group interview with three of his fellow scientists. They're about halfway through the interview when one of the interviewers says, "Mr. Khatik, would you be so kind as to go to the white board and draw a picture of a normal cell?"
>
> To Abdhur, this request seems ridiculous and simple-minded. Isn't it obvious that someone with a doctorate in biochemistry would know something so elementary as how to draw a cell? Nevertheless, he follows directions and deftly constructs a diagram of a healthy cell on the white board.
>
> "There, you have it," he says, and smiles.
>
> There is an uncomfortable silence in the room. One of the scientists sits back in her chair, hands folded over her chest, frowning. Another seems to look confused and is shaking his head back and forth. The third comments, with a distinct tone of disapproval, "You mean, that's *all*? Aren't you going to draw the rest of it?"
>
> In reality, the drawing is perfect. The job applicant knows it's right, but wonders why the other scientists don't seem to think so.
>
> "Why don't you take a few moments to finish it?" the woman says.

With what you now know about stress questions, which of the following do you think is the best response?

ANSWER A: [defensively] There's nothing wrong with that! Any eighth grader would know how to draw a simple normal cell! Perhaps you've forgotten that I have a Ph.D. in biochemistry and have been published over two dozen times, not to mention that I have lectured throughout the world on the topic of cell biology.

ANSWER B: [nervously] Oh . . .uh . . . I'm sorry. You mean you want me to change it? Sure, okay. I'm not really good at drawing. Maybe you can't tell it's a cell. I must have forgotten something. It really is a poor drawing. What a mess! Sorry, I'm sure it's not what you're looking for. Should I try it again?

ANSWER C: [calmly] That's the way a normal human cell looks to the best of my understanding.

You know by now that a stress question is designed to make you defensive, angry, nervous, or doubtful. The best way to deal with the stress question is to remain calm and answer it in the best way you know how. Therefore, C would be the optimum choice in this example.

Illegal Questions

Ninety-five percent of interviewers will not ask you illegal questions. But some—because of ignorance, inexperience, or uncharitable motives—may ask you indirectly or directly about your marital status, number of children, arrest record, physical or mental disabilities, race, religion, sexual preference, or ethnicity.

You have a legal right not to discuss these issues.

One of the best ways to get around the discomfort of these types of inquiries (other than getting up and walking out the door) is to respond as follows:

ANSWER A: Excuse me, but I'm not sure I understand. Could you please rephrase the question?

That alone will usually stop the interviewer in his or her tracks. If he or she asks again, you can say:

ANSWER A: I'm not sure how my marital status would have any bearing on my ability to carry out my job responsibilities. Could you please clarify that for me?

Or . . .

ANSWER A: Does my race have something to do with the job description? I don't think I understand the question.

As for disabilities, according to the Americans with Disabilities Act, the *only* way that it is legally feasible to ask a question about physical or mental disability is the following:

QUESTION: *Do you have any physical condition that would prevent you from doing this job?*

Your answer should be no, unless you really are aware of something that would prevent you from doing *that particular job*. You may have a bad back or a trick knee or suffer from depression or diabetes, but if it doesn't affect your job duties as described, you need not mention it. The rest is between you and your doctor. You are not obligated to reveal *any* disability that doesn't directly impair your job performance for a particular job you are seeking.

> **The question "Do you have a disability?" is illegal.**

It may be answered by a simple no.

Questions to Ask the Employer

There comes a time, usually near the end of the interview, when the employer will ask you if you have any questions about the company or the position. However curious you feel, now is not the time to ask whether you get an assigned parking space or whether you get an office or a cubicle. Those are real concerns, but not at this point.

Now is the time to use your inquisitiveness to ask open-ended questions, gained from your research, that give you information while at the same time flattering the employer. The following is a list of some good questions to ask:

- What is the company's five-year plan?
- What is the company's mission?
- Is the company culture more on the casual or more on the formal side?
- What would be the ideal candidate for this position?
- What is the typical management style?
- What would be some of my duties in the first year of employment?
- What are some of the new products, services, or improvements in the works for next year's production schedule?
- What do you [the interviewer] like most about working at the company?
- What are some of the organization's proudest moments or most unique accomplishments?
- What do you think I can personally do to drive this company to the competitive edge?

Much later, when you are in the negotiating phase, you can negotiate for a parking space. For now, keep your questions open and general.

Stalling and Accessing

In some cases, there may be a question for which you just cannot recall the answer.

> **You'd be surprised at how clever your brain is if you just give it a little time to process and access a response.**

You might take a moment to put your hand to your chin and comment: "That's a really good question. Hmm . . . let me see. I haven't thought about that one lately." This stalling behavior is perfectly tolerated by the interviewer because you are letting him or her into your thinking process. And, after all, you *are* human, and so is he or she! Interviewers don't necessarily expect you to answer on a dime.

Some questions require a moment to reflect. As you use this time (rather than panicking), allow yourself to take a deep breath or two. It's also okay to allow your eyes to roam or glance down at the floor, at a window, or to a picture on the wall.

Extensive research in how our brains access information tells us that sometimes it is necessary to look to the side, up, down, or even "into space" for a moment in order to give the brain access to stored sensory cues. These cues help us construct what to say next. Ninety-nine percent of the time you can trust your brain to come up with an answer.

If you can't think of anything relevant to say at that moment, the following answer will keep you poised, while at the same time showing that you are willing to take initiative:

ANSWER: You know, that's such an interesting question. I think the answer deserves time for some research. Can I look into it this evening and call or send an e-mail with my answer first thing in the morning?

Handling Questions in Nontraditional Interviews

What if you have an interview over the phone? You may be using the same words to communicate your answers, but you will need to pay extra attention to how you communicate warmth and enthusiasm. Here are a few strategies to use when you want your phone interview to have the same impact as being face-to-face:

1. *Stand up while you're talking.* You will breathe more deeply, and your voice will sound fuller.
2. *Smile.* Yes, smile! Professional salespeople are trained to use this technique so that they actually sound friendly and cheerful (even if they're really not having a great

day). When you are smiling, an interviewer can "hear" your smile in your voice.

3. *Listen extra carefully.* Since you can't see the interviewer, be sure you understand what he or she is asking. It's okay to ask an interviewer to repeat the question or to say, "I understand that you are asking me _____. Is that correct?"

4. *Keep your answers less than 90 seconds long.* You won't be able to see any visual cues, so it's wise to keep answers to a reasonable length so as to not let the interviewer become distracted or bored.

5. *Vary the pitch or tone of your voice more than you normally would.* A slightly higher pitch will communicate excitement, agreement, or enthusiasm. A slightly lower pitch will relay that you are about to make a very important point. Let your tone go up and down a little bit more than normal. It will keep the interview from sounding stale, as well as keep you feeling enthusiastic and excited about what you're saying.

6. *If you like, you can put a little stuffed animal or picture of someone you love near the phone and look at it while you talk.* It will make you relax and feel like you're talking to a friend. It will also fill your voice with warmth. Remember, whether it's the supervisor or a CEO who is interviewing you, that person has feelings, just like you.

In fact, 60 percent of interviewers you will talk to have never been trained at all in interviewing. Hundreds of interviewers have confided in me that they actually feel nervous, incompetent, or stressed when conducting interviews.

A little warmth in your voice, generated by looking at something cuddly, funny, or someone you care about, can go a long way to soothing the "rattled" nerves of some interviewers, thereby making the whole tone of the interview more relaxed for you as well.

7. *Do not ever discuss salary on the phone.* It's quite likely that one of the first questions asked in a phone interview will be, "How much are you making now?" or "What are your salary expectations?" It's way too soon for you to reveal that kind of information. In fact, it could cost you tens of thousands a year in lost earnings! In Chapter 8 you will see why bringing up salary at such an early stage is not advisable. That chapter will also thoroughly discuss the techniques for politely and tactfully postponing salary talk until you have a firmer idea of where you stand with the company. Note, however, that if you're talking to a professional search firm, it is okay to discuss salary early on in the job search process. The recruiters at the search firm need to know your salary range in order to find an appropriate position for you.

Group Interviews

As if *one* interviewer isn't enough, you may be asked to speak to three or four interviewers at a time. This is called a group, or panel interview. The content of the interview and your answers will not be any different than they would be with a single interviewer, but your greeting, eye contact, and follow-up will change a little. Remember these three tips:

1. *When you enter the room, shake hands with each person in the group.* It's great if you can try beforehand to get everyone's name, but that's not always possible. You don't *have* to address each person by name, nor do you have to introduce yourself by first and last names to all of them. A handshake, with direct eye contact, a smile, and a simple "Hello" or "Good morning" will do.

2. *Make eye contact with everyone in the room.* The interviewers are going to ask you questions one at a time. It's good to make eye contact with the person who asked the question and the others who are listening. Be sure that you glance into the eyes of each interviewer at least for a second on every question, no matter which one of them asked a particular question.

3. *Write thank-you notes to all of the interviewers.* It's worth your time! If you don't know their names or titles, you can ask the main interviewer or his or her secretary.

Body Language

Now that you know more about how to answer interview questions, I'd like you to know a little secret about body language. The secret is this: If you are sitting back, comfortably resting on the back of your chair, your answers will not be *nearly* as believable as if you are *sitting with your whole body tilted slightly forward in your chair*. Sitting back in your chair sends a signal, unconsciously, to the interviewer that you are not that interested in what you're saying and maybe that you're even a laid back kind of person.

Leaning slightly forward—even if you're *not* that interested in the interview—sends a signal that you are energetic and enthusiastically involved in the discussion. Who would you prefer to talk with? Someone who exhibits little energy and interest, or someone who you believe is very interested and enthusiastic? Surely the person with energy and enthusiasm would win out. As discussed in a previous chapter, psychologists and linguists estimate that a full 93 to 97 percent of our communication is actually nonverbal, so before you say anything, pay attention to *how* you are saying it.

Some other body language tips to keep in mind during your interview are the following:

- Is your body open and free to move and gesture naturally? Or is it tight, with your shoulders hunched up and your arms folded in front of your chest? Of the two, an open posture is certainly preferable.
- Do you make good eye contact? Remember, good eye contact does not mean having a staring contest. It is fine to naturally look away from time to time.
- Are you sitting slightly forward in your chair, with an open posture and without any habitual movements (like twirling your hair around your finger or clenching your

fists)? Once you get the posture right and eliminate any unnecessary habitual movements, you should feel free to gesture and move about as much or as little as is natural for you.

- Are you fidgeting or feeling unsure of where to place your hands while talking to an interviewer? Simply rest one hand on each of your legs, or fold them in your lap.

You will feel most relaxed and comfortable if you just allow yourself to enjoy expressing yourself as you would in any situation.

Just one more hint: Mirror your interviewer's rate and style of speech. If you match your rate of speech to the speed of the interviewer's speech, your interviewer will unconsciously feel more of a rapport with you. Most of the time you will not need to do this, but if you get a real fast talker or a real slow drawler, that person will tend to feel more comfortable with you if you are closer to his or her rate of speech. Practice this with a friend or with someone you meet, and see how this matching technique will help you to feel more at ease.

Before we move on to salary negotiation, let's make sure you've mastered the interviewing ingredients to get a top offer! Take a moment to test your readiness with this checklist. If you can check every box, you're an interviewing pro!

- ☐ I know that the best strategy for answering straightforward questions is to tell stories with *specifics* and to use Q statements to highlight my skills, personal traits, competencies, and accomplishments.

- ☐ I've done some research on the company so I know which of my attributes to emphasize during the interview.

- ☐ I can answer the question, "What do you know about our company?"

- ☐ I know that the strategy for answering a question behind a question is to figure out the *real fear or concern* behind the question and then to answer it in a way that puts the fear or concern to rest.

☐ I recognize stress questions, and I realize they're *intended* to be stressful. I therefore *remain calm* and answer them to the best of my ability.

☐ I know how to answer the question, "What is your greatest weakness?"

☐ I am clear that I will never bring up anything negative about my former jobs or bosses, even if I am asked.

☐ Just in case an illegal question is asked, I know how to handle it.

☐ I'm aware that the way I sit in my chair can either make me look enthusiastic or disinterested. I adopt a posture that shows I'm fascinated *and* fascinating!

☐ I have a good idea of some of the questions I would like to ask the interviewer about the company when he or she says, "Do you have any questions?"

CHAPTER 8

Negotiating Your Salary

If you have to support yourself, you had bloody well better find yourself some way that is going to be interesting.
—Katharine Hepburn

Congratulations! You've completed almost every piece of the puzzle. You have command of your job-specific skills, your general skills, your relevant personal traits, your competencies, and your gift, and you're ready to use specific examples to demonstrate them at the drop of a hat!

> **Already, you are in the top 15 percent of all candidates looking for a new job!**

In addition to that, you have realistic examples of your skills and competencies, and more than 20 Q statements to back you up. Not only do you know how to *strategically* answer the most common and some of the most difficult interview questions; you also know how to stay cool under even the most pressured of interview situations—the stress question.

Now that you're a pro, this chapter will make you a master! You're going to learn how all of your hard work in the last seven chapters will pay off. You're going to grasp the techniques for bargaining for a salary of up to 20 percent higher than you would have expected. You're going to master the techniques of open-door negotiating.

The Negotiating Challenge

Have you ever noticed that your friends are more likely to talk about the intimate details of their health or relationships than they are about how much money they make? Do you know how much money your cousin, your neighbor, or even your best friend makes? If so, you're probably in the minority. For some reason, people just don't seem to feel comfortable talking about how much money they earn. If it's "too much," they're afraid they might arouse jealousy. If it's "too little," they may be afraid others will look down on them. Most teenage children don't even know how much money their parents make, much less how their parents may have negotiated to get that amount of money.

You'll find that, in an interview situation, both you and the interviewer will have a tendency to get the salary discussion out of the way and clinch the deal as soon as possible. Unfortunately, nothing could be more detrimental to your ability to bargain with the employer for the salary you deserve.

In this chapter we're going to bring the issue of salary right out into the open. We're going to talk about several things that are important to understand before you negotiate:

- First we will talk about common fears of negotiating and some responses to those concerns.

- Next, we'll compare the stories of two negotiators, Thomas and Stephan, and exactly what choices enabled one of them to get $30,000 more in salary for the same job.

- Third, I'll present what I call the *four bargaining factors*. These are four things you need to do and/or decide *before* stepping up to the bargaining table.

- Next, we'll analyze the technique of *open-door negotiating*, the surest way to bargain for a higher salary and more comprehensive benefits.

- Finally, we'll observe blow-by-blow salary discussions of successful negotiators so that you can see the four bargaining factors and open-door negotiating techniques in action.

Common Fears about Negotiating

You might be hesitant to negotiate because of any one or all of the reasons listed below. Take an honest look at yourself now, before you go into an interview, to see if you are holding any of these ideas about earning money or negotiating a salary. Most people try to avoid salary negotiating. In fact, it's not at all unusual for people to dread this part of the interview.

Here's an opportunity to examine your objections and overcome them. The effort is worthwhile. After all, the few minutes or hours you spend talking about and settling upon your compensation package not only will bring you immediate rewards but also will set you up for *all of your future promotions and raises*.

The five most common objections to negotiating that I've heard are the following:

1. *I'm afraid if I ask for more, I'll jeopardize the job offer.* If the company really wants you for the job, you'll get the job regardless of whether you do or do not try to negotiate, so you might as well try.

2. *Negotiating is only for aggressive "wheeler-dealer" types.* Actually, negotiating involves very subtle communication. You don't have to yell or scream or flex your muscles. Thousands of shy and soft-spoken people negotiate for higher pay every day. In fact, it may actually help to lower the volume of your voice during a salary negotiation.

3. *I believe that when a company says it has reached its limit, the company really means it has no more to offer.* Do you believe it when a car dealer tells you he or she "just can't possibly go any lower" on a $28,000 car, even if he or she says it two or three times? What about when an interviewer says he or she "just can't go any higher" on your salary?

   Unless you're applying for a job within the government or academia, your *employer most likely has 15 to 20 percent more for you in the budget* than he or she will originally offer. The trick is that you have to ask for it and prove (with your Q statements) that you merit the additional funds.

4. *It embarrasses me that I might be seen as "greedy" if I ask for more money or try to bargain for better benefits.* Some of us (most, I think) desire financial security and a measure of wealth so that we can live the life we choose. Wanting to improve your lifestyle and the lives of your family, friends, and even those less fortunate is not greed. A desire for your parents to have security in their old age and your kids to get a good education is certainly not greed. It really is okay to make money, and a lot of it. It's even okay to drive a fancy red sports car!

5. *I don't believe that my skills merit more pay than average.* Go back to Chapters 2 and 3. Review your skills and accomplishments. Take a look at your list of Q statements or

even say them out loud or into a tape recorder. Look at all you know. Look at what you can do. *Look at who you are.* You didn't just pull this stuff out of thin air. You really did it! You deserve an exceptional reward for the value that you bring.

One Job, Two Different Salaries

Let's have a look at Thomas and Stephan, two men who approached the issue of salary discussions very differently and ended up with quite different results.

Thomas is a 34-year-old technical recruiter with five years' experience. He's been out of work for several months and is getting anxious about finding a job. He's already gone into debt after being laid off three months ago, and he'd really like to get an offer from today's interview. In the back of his mind, he knows he will accept any reasonable offer. Anything would be better than continuing to be unemployed.

Thomas figures he already knows about interviewing techniques because in his last job, he interviewed other people. When Thomas interviewed for this recruiting position in a staffing company, he walked away with an offer of $30,000 base salary plus commissions and a full benefits package.

Stephan has only three years' experience in technical recruiting and is 37 years old. He's done considerable research on interviewing techniques, salary negotiation, and the company he is interviewing with. Though his finances have gotten very tight during a period of three months of unemployment, he's willing to wait it out for the right job at the right salary. Stephan has an interview today at the same company that Thomas is interviewing with. Although he has less experience than Thomas, Stephan negotiates for a salary of $60,000 plus commissions with full benefits, a hiring bonus, several perks, stock options, and permission to telecommute from home two days out of the week.

What happened here?

How did Stephan, with two years' less experience command $30,000 more in salary, plus extensive benefits, perks, and stock options? The chart below examines some of the things Thomas and Stephan did differently.

Thomas	**Stephan**
1. He took the first thing offered to him.	1. He *practiced* the technique of *open-door negotiating* (which you'll learn).
2. He did not research the salary, so it came as a surprise to him.	2. He *researched* salary norms so knew what to expect.
3. He did not know his bottom-line salary.	3. He *knew* his bottom line.
4. He was afraid that negotiating would jeopardize the job offer.	4. He *planned* to bargain for 15 to 20 percent over the first offer.
5. He believed that he was worth roughly the current "market value."	5. He *believed,* and knew he could prove, that he was above "market value."
6. He figured that "full benefits" meant that the company was giving him all the benefits they had.	6. He *planned* to negotiate for more benefits and some perks.
7. He felt a strong urge to close the deal ASAP.	7. He *made a firm decision* he would wait for the right offer.

The disparity between Thomas's salary and Stephan's is not an accident. Stephan consistently applied the techniques of open-door negotiating and knowledge of the four bargaining factors. Let's take a look at what they are.

The Four Bargaining Factors

Salary negotiations can be a very delicate matter. However, the more you know going in, the more influence you can exert when the time comes. Take the time to research your salary carefully and determine where you stand on these four bargaining points:

1. *Know* the relative worth for your position in the marketplace.

2. *Clarify* what qualifies you to make more than average and more than the employer's initial offer.

3. *Determine* your target salary and benefits.

4. *Forecast* how long you are willing to wait until the negotiation resolves in your favor.

I want to see you get every penny and every advantage that you deserve. To accomplish that, let's take a closer look at each bargaining factor.

1. Know the relative worth for your position in the marketplace. It is helpful—especially if you happen to be entering a new field, going from a very small to very large company, or making a significant geographic shift—to get a ballpark salary figure for a position. Do some research to determine what, statistically, is a low, mid, and high salary range for a particular position. At no point should you confuse this ballpark figure for the actual sum you'll settle for. You should use this only as a broad guideline.

There are a couple of quick and handy ways to estimate what a reasonable range for your position might be. One is the do-it-yourself method, and another is to let a professional salary service do the work. If you would like to research your salary range and your probable benefits yourself, I suggest these free Web sites and links on the Internet:

http://www.salary.com

http://www.salaryexpert.com

http://www.jobsmart.org

http://www.bls.gov/oco/

If you'd prefer to have a professional service research your salary for a fee, I would recommend these companies:

Pinpoint Salary Services, http://members.aol.com/payraises/pinpoint.html

Personal Salary Report, http://www.salary.com

2. Clarify what qualifies you to make *more* than average and *more* than the company's initial offer. Complete the qualifications worksheet at the end of this chapter. What added value do you bring to the employer? Read the job description (if there is one), and analyze how and why you, as compared to the "average" applicant, can add more to the bottom-line profits of the company. Use your skills assessments and Q statements to make your case.

Ask yourself the following:

- Can I help the company make money?
- How about saving money?
- Could my skills be used to help speed up production, decrease waste, add a valued service, or improve customer relations?
- Do I have stories illustrating that I perform consistently over quota?
- Could I act as a manager or executive who would handle bigger budgets, manage more effective teams, and provide measurably superior leadership?
- Can I prove that my organizational skills can save the company time?
- Can I demonstrate that my public relations or customer service skills could turn the company image around?
- Can I help save training time by being an independent, bright self-starter who learns quickly and doesn't mind jumping in head first?
- Do I have innovative ideas that could bring distinction, respect, and perhaps awards to the company?
- Can I prove, with examples, that I can get it done faster, better, cleaner, safer, more beautifully, or more accurately?

Acquaint yourself with what the average job expectations are, and then use Q statements to prove you can exceed them. If there's no job description, look up a typical job description for the position in the *Occupational Outlook Handbook*—a massive encyclopedia published by the U.S. Department of Labor that features not only job descriptions but also salary reports, job requirements, and future economic outlook for more than

6,000 occupations. You can access the handbook online at http://www.bls.gov/oco/.

The basic premise of all of these bargaining factors is that you are not a position. In fact, what you bring to the table may be a lot more than what the company had in mind for the position. Since you've assessed your skills and constructed Q statements in the last chapters, you are more likely to be able to convince the employer that indeed you have more to offer the company in bottom-line profits than the average person they had in mind for the position.

At no time, especially during salary negotiations, do you want the employer to think of you as simply "filling a position." Rather, you need to be thought of as an individual with special talents who can help the employer solve problems and who can add value to the bottom-line profits of the company.

So few people actually do a thorough inventory of their abilities and are able to communicate them. I'm certain that after doing the exercises in the previous seven chapters, you'll be able to absolutely shine as that ideal candidate who brings extra value to the organization. With extra value comes a higher salary. Let's continue with the last two bargaining factors.

3. Determine your target salary and benefits. Your target salary should always be 15 to 20 percent more than what the employer initially offers. Learn to quickly multiply by 15 or 20 percent and add it to your salary figure on the spot if you need to. Distinguish between the benefits you absolutely need and those you want. (See page 289 for a list of benefits.)

4. Forecast how long you are willing to wait until the negotiation resolves in your favor. Some people feel they can wait only ten minutes; others, wisely, know that it can actually take weeks before a compensation package is settled. You may need income at this very moment, but the longer you can afford to wait for circumstances to go your way, the greater advantage you will enjoy.

> *Is it worth it to you to spend a couple of hours planning your negotiations if it means earning $20,000 or even $40,000 more a year?*

Okay, once you have determined these bargaining factors and learned the techniques of open-door negotiating, having a conversation about your salary will be like a walk in the park.

Leticia's Story

One of my clients, Leticia, was terrified about negotiating, and she told me that she had spent more than an hour holding her ground and reiterating her value to the company until, Voilà! She managed to go from an initial offer of $37,500 with medical and dental benefits to $51,000 plus bonuses, medical, dental, and vision coverage—plus a 14-day paid vacation and tuition reimbursement.

Interestingly enough, the interviewer left the room several times and insisted she had gone to her boss and that her boss had gone to the vice president, and that they absolutely refused to budge. But, because Leticia knew how to perform above and beyond the functions listed in the job description, and she had examples to prove it, the company finally caved in, though not without a lot of "drama."

It may look, in the final hour, as though the employer is about to fall flat on the floor and die before handing you the top rate for your talents, but I haven't gotten a report of a serious casualty yet. Hold out!

Open-Door Negotiating

Remember Stephan, who doubled his offer and got an expanded benefits package? Like Leticia, he used the techniques of open-door negotiating. Open-door negotiating may not be what you usually think of when you think about striking a bargain with an employer. There's no threatening behavior, no fists on the desk, no high-pitched voices, and no tones of finality. In fact, it's important that before I explain what open-door negotiating *is*, I tell you what it is *not*.

What Open-Door Salary Negotiation Is Not

I'd like to debunk some commonly held myths by telling you what negotiating is not:

- It is not a cutthroat battle to the finish, where the winner finally gets what he or she wants and the loser storms out and slams the door.
- It is not a balancing of a scale, where the two parties meet right in the middle and neither really gets what he or she wants.

Rather than using the metaphor of a "battle to the finish" or a "balancing of the scales," I'd like you to think about negotiating in terms of an "open door." In open-door negotiating, there are no declarations of finality, no threats, and no settling for something mediocre just because it happens to be in the middle. There especially isn't a passive acceptance of the first offer you get just because you fear you might lose the job if you mention a higher figure. Open-door negotiating is about creating possibilities, carefully weighing those possibilities, and coming to a civilized agreement.

The Rules of Open-Door Negotiating

There are several rules to observe in the game of open-door negotiating if you want to play it well:

- Try to postpone the salary discussion until a job offer has been made or until you are in a second interview.
- Do not be the first one to mention an exact amount of money, no matter how many ways the interviewer tries to get you to inform him or her of what you earned or what you wish to earn in the future.
- Speak in terms of ranges of salary rather than using exact figures.
- Postpone saying no to an offer until you are sure you have all the information.
- Postpone saying yes to an offer until you are sure you have all the information.
- Postpone, postpone, postpone. There is no reason to rush a salary discussion, especially when that discussion could add 15 to 20 percent to your earnings. Be patient.

Finally, remember that *your base pay is not the only thing you're negotiating for.* You're actually negotiating for a full compensation package that may include a sign-on bonus, extra benefits and perks, and many other features we'll talk about later in this chapter. Let's move on to an actual blow-by-blow account of a salary negotiation.

The Salary Discussion

Here are some possible scenarios that illustrate the principles of open-door negotiating and the use of the four bargaining factors. This is the story of Alex, a computer hardware sales engineer:

QUESTION: *What are you making right now?*

ANSWER: I'm making as good or better than a person of my skills in this geographic area.

QUESTION: *Can you give me an exact number?*

ANSWER: Well, you know, it's very difficult to compare what someone in a small company like mine makes with what someone working in a large company like this one would make. Maybe you could tell me what salary range would be reasonable for a person with my skills in this company.

QUESTION: *Oh, anywhere from $30,000 to $60,000, plus commissions.*

ANSWER: [stands up, puts his hand out for a handshake] $60,000 sounds great. When can I start?

This may sound like it's all too simple, but it works. This is a very typical salary negotiation for many of my clients. The scenario can certainly unfold in a thousand different ways, but what looks like luck here isn't. It's skill. Let's see what happened and exactly how Alex managed to pull this one off:

1. He never mentioned the exact amount of money he made, even when asked twice.
2. He did say he was in the "mid to high range."

3. He thinks of a reason (for example, it is difficult to compare salaries in a small company with those of a large company). Other reasons could be the following:

- A change of geographic area (for example, from Seattle to Atlanta)
- A change of level of position (for example, from manager to director)
- A change of industry (for example, from travel to telecommunications)
- A change in the type of pay structure (for example, from commission to hourly wages or a salary)

After he establishes that a comparison can't be made, he *turns the question back on the interviewer* by saying, "What salary range do you think would be reasonable for a person with my skills?" Notice he *still* doesn't ask for an exact number. An exact number would partially "close the door." Alex crafts his responses so that the door stays open.

Also, he does not ask for the salary range for the *position*. He forces the interviewer to look at what he, as an individual, can contribute. If he had not done this, he may have been offered only $30,000 in base pay. In the space of a moment, he was able to increase the offer by 50 percent. This is a very dramatic case, but it really does happen in this way for many of my clients.

Now that we've analyzed Alex's conversation with the interviewer, lets look at a few examples of how other job candidates have been able to receive optimum compensation. Here's a story of Wu-lei, a marketing specialist:

QUESTION: *What are your salary expectations?*

ANSWER: Actually, moving from the semiconductor industry to the clothing industry, it's very hard for me to judge. Maybe you could let me know what sort of salary range would be expected for a person with my background.

QUESTION: *We could start you anywhere between $50,000 and $62,000.*

ANSWER: [stands up to shake hands] $62,000 would be fine.
When can I start?

Let's imagine Wu-lei in another version of the story in which
$62,000 was a lot lower than what she had expected.

- If she says, "That's not acceptable," she closes the door to
any other possibilities.
- If she replies, "How about $68,000?" expecting the
employer to counter halfway at about $65,500, she still
may be cheating herself out of thousands of dollars a year.

Here are some ways Wu-lei can use open-door negotiating by
not mentioning any exact figures. She can respond to the interviewer's proposed *range* in a number of ways:

ANSWER: [leans back in her chair for a moment, thinking, then
leans forward with direct eye contact] To tell you the
truth, I was expecting something *somewhat* higher.

Or . . .

ANSWER: (Leans back and then forward) I was actually *expecting* a substantially higher figure.

Or . . .

ANSWER: Thank you, but I'd be much *more inclined* to accept an
offer closer to the seventies or eighties.

Or . . .

ANSWER: Hmm . . . I think I would find the offer more *attractive* if it were closer to $70,000.

Clients often ask me what to do if the interviewer absolutely
insists that they reveal an exact dollar amount for their current
salary. There's a method for handling that one too:

QUESTION: *We can't proceed unless you tell me an exact dollar amount
of your current salary.*

ANSWER: My base salary is $78,350 a year, and that is one of
the reasons I'm looking for another position. I would
like to be making more.

Or . . .

ANSWER: My base salary is $78,350 a year with an excellent
           benefits package worth $12,000, so that puts my
           entire compensation package somewhere in the
           nineties.

If you're at a first interview and are reasonably sure of a second interview, or if you're being screened on the phone, you should not get into serious negotiations. The question "How much do you expect to earn here?" is just a screening question to get you in or out of the next interview. The best answer is sometimes "flexible," "open," or "negotiable."

Even if the interviewer mentions that the position pays an amount that isn't amenable to you, don't reject it in the first interview. You haven't even tried to negotiate yet!

Your objective in the first interview is to get to the second interview.

Hang in there. You don't *have* to accept the figure that is mentioned. Simply say you'd be willing to "consider" it. By the second interview you'll have a lot more bargaining power. You know the company is very interested in you. You may be one of only two or three candidates. You may be their only candidate. You're in the seat of power.

Another client of mine, Gary, was offered what he considered to be an unacceptably low salary in the first interview. He continued with the interviewing process and made it to the second interview. Gary was able, after a 45-minute negotiation, to get the employer to raise his salary from $35,000 to $49,000.

Gary did it by continuing to stress his skills and using Q statements. He was sure to let the employer know of the value he could contribute to the company, and he made himself absolutely irresistible. Earning $14,000 in the space of a 45-minute negotiation is certainly time well spent!

Benefits and Your
Total Compensation Package

You don't have to end your salary negotiations with the salary discussion. You can negotiate for just about anything. Here are some obvious and not-so-obvious factors to be considered in your total compensation package:

- ☐ Relocation fees
- ☐ Sign-on bonus
- ☐ Life, disability, and accident insurances
- ☐ Medical, dental, vision, and counseling benefits
- ☐ Paid holidays
- ☐ Vacation days
- ☐ Health spa or gym membership
- ☐ Company car
- ☐ Mileage reimbursement
- ☐ Training and education reimbursement
- ☐ 401(k)
- ☐ Profit sharing
- ☐ Commission structure
- ☐ Bonuses
- ☐ Performance and salary review after 90 days
- ☐ Stock options
- ☐ Telecommuting (working from a computer at home)
- ☐ Flextime
- ☐ Child care reimbursement
- ☐ Company-sponsored discounts on goods and services
- ☐ Parking reimbursement
- ☐ Commuting reimbursement
- ☐ First- or business-class airfare
- ☐ Expense accounts and company credit cards

. . . and more.

Creative Negotiations

Pat is a client who negotiated her compensation package creatively when the company she applied to "wouldn't budge" on salary. She got them to agree on $80,000 a year (more than they initially offered), but she felt she needed to make a better deal with them to feel satisfied working there on the long term. She had a great idea on how to narrow the gap between what she wanted and what the company offered.

- She said she would be glad to accept $80,000 if she could work a 32-hour week. In effect, she increased her salary by $20,000 a year.
- Pat asked that her medical and other health benefits begin immediately rather than after 90 days. She got that too.
- She asked for tuition reimbursement for a master's degree program that would further her knowledge of her field. She got that benefit also, and it was a lifesaver at $330 per graduate unit (about $1,000 per class).

Use the techniques of open-door negotiating, along with the rock-solid confidence you have built while assessing your skills, gifts, and accomplishments. Take the risk! It will pay off. I leave you with a phrase I once heard in the movie *Desert Hearts*: "You can't win if you don't play the game."

CHAPTER 9

Following Up: Juggling Multiple Offers

> *Let me tell you the secret that has led me to my goal: my strength lies solely in my tenacity.*
>
> —Louis Pasteur

Focus Letters

You're back from the interview. Easy, even exhilarating, wasn't it? Celebrate, but don't pop the champagne cork yet if your offer is still pending. We still have a little more strategizing to do together.

Now is the time to get out a pen and paper or boot up the computer. I bet you think I'm going to suggest that you write a thank-you note. Well, yes and no. Now is a time when you can *continue to ride the wave of positive persuasion* that you created at the interview.

The note we're going to write now is a different kind of note. I call it a *focus letter*. Its purpose is to leave no doubt in the employer's mind that you are the candidate to hire.

A focus letter includes a gesture of appreciation for the interviewer's time, but also, and more importantly, it imparts a meaningful message of your newfound perceptions of the company . . . and how your expertise is indispensable to solving the problems of their business. On the following page is an example of a focus letter from a marketing executive seeking a position as the senior vice president of marketing at a software corporation.

How to Compose a Focus Letter

1. Determine the problem the employer is attempting to address in hiring someone to fill the position you are applying for. Some examples of the types of problems addressed in hiring strategies are the following:

   - Increasing the speed of production
   - Getting a better return on investment
   - Improving efficiency
   - Raising employee morale
   - Becoming more organized
   - Attracting more customers
   - Selling more products or services
   - Decreasing waste
   - Ensuring safety
   - Improving public relations
   - Saving money and time

Ms. Bettina Simmons
Executive Vice President
Ionit, Incorporated
554 Second Avenue, Suite 237A
New York, NY 103XX

Dear Ms. Simmons:

What a pleasure it was to meet you after hearing so much about you from Carol Jones! I must say I was very flattered that you extended our meeting from the half hour we had planned to almost ninety minutes. I certainly appreciate your generosity in sharing your ideas about the company and acquainting me with Bob Delts and the others on the team.

Something in our exchange rang a bell for me, and I just thought I'd share it with you. You mentioned that Ionit would be opening an office soon in Minneapolis and that a senior vice president would be needed there for a time to get the January product launch off to a roaring start.

I didn't mention it at the interview, but I happen to have experience with the marketing of DTrek 5001 and similar software. I planned and executed a similar launch in my prior position at 4Tell, and I ended up saving the company almost a quarter of a million dollars by including a direct-mailing component in the project.

I believe that I have the wisdom gained from experience to be instrumental in the same kinds of substantial savings for Ionit and, if hired, I plan to present several scenarios that I think would be beneficial for the Minneapolis effort. I also am free to relocate there until the product is off to a healthy start in the Minneapolis market.

Again thank you for your time in the interview. If you have any questions I can answer or if you would like to see a sample proposal for my ideas for the Minneapolis project, I would be happy to oblige.

Regards,

Han Nguyen
(212) 883-XXXX
h_nguyenvp@juno.com

Sample Focus Letter

- Winning an award or distinction
- Earning a place as a leader in the industry
- Changing the company image
- Outsmarting the competition
- Inventing new products, ideas, and services
- Bettering the skills of employees and managers
- Providing healthier workplaces
- Complying with government regulations
- Accurately accounting for revenue, taxes, expenditures, personnel, or inventory
- Keeping current customers happy
- Encouraging word-of-mouth referrals
- Revamping existing products or services

2. Decide on one or more strategies, based on your proven skills or your Q statements, that illustrate to the interviewer that you could be instrumental in helping the company solve its problems and reach one or more of its goals.

The Format of Your Focus Letter

- *First paragraph.* Begin with a pleasant, but not too personal, greeting stating that you enjoyed the interview and/or appreciated the interviewer's time.
- *Second and possibly third paragraphs.* Introduce the problem and establish for the employer that you have solved similar problems in the past. Mention that, if hired, you would like to get to work on helping the employer reach his or her goals.
- *Final paragraph.* Close with polite thank you. You might also mention that you will be calling to follow up in two or three days.

Tips to Remember about Focus Letters

1. Always double and *triple* check the spelling of the person's name and job title.

2. Send the focus letter within 24 hours of the interview.
   • E-mail is great.
   • Mailing or faxing is also good.
   • Dropping it off at the employer's offices may be intrusive.

Follow-Up Calls

At the close of the interview, it's a good idea to arrange a callback time. Three days is usually enough time to check in with the employer. If it happens that you have to wait for a long time to be apprised of their decision, call back in another few days. Many people are afraid they are being too pushy by continuing to call back. They're concerned that they will scare the employer away.

Just the opposite may be true. I actually had one supervisor tell me that one of the reasons she hired me was that I called back six times in one month to check on the status of the job. Each time I called her, I asked if I could call again. She interpreted my continued phone calls not as "pushy" but as "enthusiastic." An employer is always drawn to a candidate who seriously wants to work for his or her company.

It's okay to call once or twice a week. Set the pace and *make sure the employer doesn't mind.* You'll be the one still plugging away while everyone else has given up! Guess who they'll hire when the time comes?

Multiple Offers

As I mentioned before, by this time you may have several offers. It is all right to let one employer know about another offer providing it is a bona fide offer. We call this *leveraging offers*. You may be able to influence an employer to make a quicker decision, or even to raise the monetary value of the offer, but all of this should be done in a very diplomatic way.

Make sure the employer you are dealing with knows you really want to work for his or her company and you are not just "playing games." When you have multiple offers, there are usually some pros and cons to each of them. . . . *How do you decide?*

You decide based on what makes you feel good! Our personal values, to the extent that they are fulfilled, are what make us feel happy and fulfilled. Have you ever given much thought to how you prioritize the values in your life? How about in your work? Money is certainly important for most of us, but is probably not the sole criterion on which most people's satisfaction at work is based. There are other things of value like recognition, intellectual stimulation, social contact, creativity, and even spiritual fulfillment. Take a moment now to assess some of your values, so that we can use them to help you decide exactly which job offer is the right one for you.

Values Assessment

Please rank the following values from 1 to 22, with **1** as the most important and **22** as the least important value.

____ Financial security

____ Aesthetics

____ Competition

____ Great wealth

____ Social contact

____ Recognition

____ Helping others

____ Using my technical expertise

____ Spiritual fulfillment

____ Intellectual stimulation

____ Excitement

____ Variety

____ Independence

____ Minimum stress

____ Flextime

____ Short commute

____ Minimum stimulation

____ Challenge

____ Mastery

____ Leadership

____ Routine

____ Opportunity for advancement

Now please pick your top nine values and write them below.

1. _____

2. _____

3. _____

4. _____

5. _____

6. _____

7. _____

8. _____

9. _____

Good! Here's an example of what I would like you to do with the values you've chosen. Let's imagine we have a job seeker named Tanya. Imagine she is trying to choose between a very large company and a very small company in the computer industry. Her top values (in order of their importance) are the following:

1. Great wealth

2. Competition

3. Recognition

4. Intellectual stimulation

5. Variety

6. Excitement

7. Challenge

8. Independence

9. Using my technical expertise

Evaluating Offers

Using a chart like the one that follows, on which the left side represents the small company and the right side represents the big company, we're going to compare which situation would best meet Tanya's needs for the fulfillment of her top values. If a small company would *better* satisfy a particular value, we will list it on the left side. If a value would be better fulfilled in a large company, we'll note it on the right side.

Here's how Tanya's list looks when it's finished.

Small Company	*Large Company*
Recognition	Great wealth
Variety	Using my technical expertise
Independence	Intellectual stimulation
	Competition
	Excitement
	Challenge

Tanya might make the choice to go with the larger company because it fulfills most of her values. A person with a different set of values would have a completely different profile.

Let's say we're looking at the same companies but with a different person. Carlos is recovering from a heart attack, and his doctors have told him he *must* slow down. Carlos's top values are as follows:

1. Minimum stress
2. Minimum stimulation
3. Short commute
4. Mastery
5. Independence
6. Spiritual fulfillment
7. Financial security
8. Social contact
9. Flextime

In our comparative chart, his values line up this way:

Small Company	*Large Company*
Minimum stress	Short commute
Minimum stimulation	Mastery
Flextime	Financial security
Social contact	
Spiritual fulfillment	
Independence	

On the basis of the values fulfillment indicated by the chart above, Carlos may want to go with a smaller company.

How do *your* values line up, and what will *you* choose?

Before deciding on that offer, please take a look at the interviews in the next chapter. No matter what you're like and what type of job you're interviewing for, there's something for you!

CHAPTER 10

Sample Interviews

You don't get to choose how you're going to die. Or when.
You can only decide how you're going to live.

—Joan Baez

Now is the time to put together all you've learned into a complete interview conversation. This chapter contains three sample interviews. One with Jerry Aronson, a marketing manager, another with Sarah Auschansky, an information technology engineer, and the third with Kei Soto, a director of launch operations.

Jerry's and Sarah's interviews include only what the employer and interviewee are saying, and they have only a few notes, so that you can get the sense of how an entire interview might unfold, uninterrupted. The salary negotiations illustrate a fairly straightforward manner of negotiating, which you'll recognize from Chapter 8.

The third interview includes detailed notes about why the interviewee is using certain tactics, to help you remember the reasons as they were given in previous chapters of the book. It also contains a more detailed and comprehensive salary negotiation, illustrating the nuances of the actions Kei takes to gain an optimum salary in a more complex situation.

As you read the interviews, let yourself get a feel for the flow and rhythm of the entire question and answer process. Don't try to analyze them too much—you already know all of what's going to take place from reading the previous nine chapters of the book.

Now is a time to actually imagine *yourself* in the scenarios about to be presented.

Jerry Aronson,
Marketing Manager

It's 10:30 a.m. Jerry Aronson arrived at the Walton Corporation half an hour early. He found a parking spot in the area that he had scouted out the day before, and then he took a few moments in the car by himself.

He checked to see that he had all of the materials in his presentation package, and then he put it in his briefcase. He left his cell phone and pager in the car. He was feeling relaxed, excited, and confident.

He entered the building at about 10:50 a.m. and introduced himself politely to the receptionist at the front desk, using his full name and saying he had an 11 a.m. appointment with Elena

Gross, the marketing director. In a few minutes, a woman came out to greet him.

"Jerry?" she asked.

"Yes, Ms. Gross," he said. "My name is Jerry Aronson. Thank you for inviting me today."

"You're welcome," she said. They walked into a small conference room. Jerry stood until she asked him to be seated.

"I've brought a fresh copy of my résumé and some other materials if you'd like to see them," he said.

"I would. Thanks," she said.

He handed her the presentation package, being sure not to place anything else on the conference table. The first 20 seconds had passed, and he had done it! He was feeling at ease, calm, and confident.

"Tell me about yourself," Ms. Gross said.

Jerry took a deep breath. "I have more than ten years of experience as a marketing manager, specializing in strategic planning, forecasting, and customer service. In my last position, I oversaw a help desk of 65 employees handling up to a thousand calls daily. I have a B.A. in marketing with honors. I'm currently pursuing an MBA with an emphasis in marketing at the University of Phoenix."

"Okay," she said. "What do you consider to be your greatest strengths?"

"I have strengths in the areas of quality improvement, product development, and training. An example of my quality improvement ability is a project that I completed in which I merged several phone line divisions into one unit, resulting in a savings of over $266,000 for the company and 20 percent improved quality reports from customers."

"What would your last boss say about you?" Ms. Gross asked.

"I believe she would say I'm innovative, reliable, and proactive. One example of an innovation I made at my last company was revising the curriculum for the employee orientation and training programs. The employees finished their training three days faster, and their work proved to be 15 percent more efficient than that of their predecessors," Jerry said.

"Hmm . . . good. Tell me, Jerry, what is your greatest weakness?"

"Well, I guess you could say I'm somewhat of a perfection-ist. Details and accuracy have always been important to me. For example, if I'm writing a report for my department head, I want to make extra sure that I have exactly the right numbers before passing it on. That saves her time, in the long run."

Ms. Gross smiled at him. "Just for fun, what's your favorite song?"

He laughed. "Oh, let's see . . . probably 'Don't Rain on My Parade,' by Barbra Streisand. It's so optimistic!"

"Jerry, why did you leave your last company?"

"Well, as you can see, I am relocating from New York to California. One reason for that is, obviously, this great weather out here. Also, as I mentioned I'm finishing up my degree with the University of Phoenix. Most of the classes are online, but we go to one seminar a month in California. I figured it would be more convenient and cost effective to finish the degree out here, then settle down and buy a home in California."

"You have some excellent qualifications, Jerry, but we're also considering a handful of other highly qualified candidates for the position. Tell me, why should I hire you rather than one of the other candidates?"

Jerry paused and took his time answering. "I think one of the most important reasons is my excellent track record with presentations. In particular, one of the recent presentations that I designed and delivered to an audience of European executives won my company a $4 billion contract. That's exactly the kind of contribution I'd like to make to your company."

"What do you see yourself doing five years from now?" Ms. Gross asked.

"Well, as I mentioned before, I am working on a master's degree. I don't want to stop there. I'd like to take many more professional development courses so that I stay abreast of devel-opments in the field. I think in five years, I would just like to con-tinue to grow and hone my skills as a marketing professional."

"Do you have any questions about this company?"

"Yes, as a matter of fact I do. I noticed in my research t'   'n the last two years, the company has moved from number number 97 on the Fortune 500 list. What do you attribute

"We have an incredible executive team at the he] the last three or four years, we've really streamlined /

line and redefined our market niche. We're all very proud of the progress we've made." Ms. Gross took a moment to glance at Jerry's résumé and one of the letters of recommendation.

"Hmm . . . good recommendation. Jerry, what are your salary expectations?"

"Well, frankly, making the move from a smaller company in New York to this large corporation in Santa Clara, it's rather difficult to know what to expect. What do you think a reasonable salary range would be for a person of my skills in this part of the country?"

"Oh, I'd say we're just slightly higher than back east. I would say you would start anywhere from $92,000 to $120,000."

Jerry stood up and extended his hand to Ms. Gross. "$120,000 would be fine! When can I start?"

Sarah Auschansky,
Information Technology Engineer

Sarah hopped onto the subway and mentally rehearsed the exact route she would walk to the office when she did her "practice run" the day before. She knew she should be at her stop in another five minutes and that it would take another ten to walk to her destination. As she got off the subway and made her way down the street, Sarah actually began to look forward to the interview!

That morning, Sarah had felt at ease and totally prepared, with her skills arsenal in her mind and her Q statements at her fingertips. Before she got to her stop, she made sure she had her presentation package, and she turned off her cell phone and pager.

Wow! This is getting exciting, she thought as she walked toward the office.

She arrived at the office with about 15 minutes to spare. She waited outside until ten minutes before her scheduled interview time, then made her way inside the building. On the twelfth floor, she politely greeted a secretary, who asked her to have a seat in the waiting room. "Mr. Gandy will be free in just a moment," the secretary said.

Sarah glanced through a magazine, enjoying the pictures, until the secretary came to escort her to the interviewer's office.

She smiled the moment she walked in the door, extended her hand for a handshake, and said, "Hello, Mr. Gandy. My name is Sarah Auschansky. Thank you for having me today."

"Would you like a cup of coffee?" he asked.

"No, I'm fine, but thank you." She waited for a moment. "May I sit down?"

"Of course, please do."

The first 20 seconds had just ticked away and Sarah was still smiling! She sat down, tilting her body slightly forward in the chair. She resisted the impulse to put her purse on his desk and instead, put it on the floor at her side. She placed a notepad on her lap.

The interviewer was shuffling through some papers on his desk. "Sorry. I think I must have lost the résumé you faxed to me. You don't happen to have another one, do you?"

"Yes, as a matter of fact, I do. Here's a fresh copy along with some letters of recommendation you might want to see." She handed him her presentation package.

He glanced over the résumé for just a second. "Hmm . . . very thorough. Tell me," he said, "something that's *not* on your résumé."

"What my résumé *doesn't* say is that I'm incredibly persistent. I can troubleshoot Ethernet, token ring, LAN, WAN, and frame relay. I don't stop until the problem is solved and the job is done. Once, at my last job, the whole system went down right on the last day of the quarter. Some of the other networking people panicked. I just stayed flexible and tried several different tactics. I ended up getting the system up and running within 90 minutes."

"Good." Mr. Gandy quietly took a few minutes to look over the résumé more carefully. "Your résumé looks good. Tell me, what would you do if another employee told you he had stolen something expensive from the company?"

"I think that first I would have to confront him face to face and try to persuade him to return it. If he said no, then I would have to let him know I felt obligated to tell the boss if he didn't return it. If that didn't work, I would probably have to have a talk with my supervisor about it."

"What development applications do you know?"

"I'm adept at Fortran, C++, COBOL, and SQL. I also have experience with Visual Basic and object-oriented programming. I actually trained ten of the other IT specialists in SQL."

"Why do you want this position?"

"From the job description I read on your Web site, I think it's an excellent match for my skills. I know that you specifically require an expertise in networking, and that's my strongest area. In addition to the skills I mentioned before, I'm also an expert at TCP/IP, protocols, routers, switchers, and AppleTalk."

"How soon are you available for work?"

"I'd like to give my present employer at least two weeks' notice. After that, I'd like to start work right away."

"What are you making at the company you work for now?"

"My salary is in the midrange for an IT engineer in this geographic area."

"Exactly how much is that?"

"In the high eighties."

"I need an exact number before we can move on."

"I'm making $86,700 a year, and that's one of the reasons I'm seeking a position with another company. I believe a person with my skills and expertise can command a substantially higher salary than that. As to the exact amount I'm looking for, it's negotiable at this point."

"Do you think you could accept something in the mid-nineties—say, $95,000 to $97,000?"

"A salary of $97,000 would be fine. Thank you." Sarah got up and shook Mr. Gandy's hand. "Can I see some literature on your benefits package please?"

"Sure. I have some of the information on file." He handed her a packet. Sarah was pleased with the compensation package, which included medical, dental, vision, paid holidays, paid vacation, a membership to a gym, tuition reimbursement, and stock options. "This looks very good to me," she said.

"Well then, congratulations! You're hired. Welcome aboard!"

Kei Soto,
Director of Launch Operations

Kei Soto arrived early at the restaurant, where he was scheduled for a 2 p.m. lunch interview with the chief executive officer of a company called Panatel. He had flown in from Austin, Texas, where he was the president of Soto Partners, a small consulting firm specializing in interactive communications. Kei had already passed one phone interview with the director of human resources, as well as a face-to-face interview in Houston with the executive vice president of marketing. Now it was his chance to shine. He believed that today, if all went well, the CEO would be making him an offer.

Kei had flown in the night before so that he would be rested for the interview. He had gotten up early, worked out, showered, and dressed in a navy suit with a red tie. He had had his hair trimmed and a shoe shine several days before, so he was looking crisp and professional. He climbed into his rental car, briefcase and presentation packet in hand, and drove to the appointed meeting place, arriving about a half hour early.

Kei was already seated at the table, but he had not yet ordered when the CEO arrived and introduced herself. Kei stood up to greet her and shake her hand.

"I'm Tina O'Connell," she said. "You must be Kei."

"Yes, Ms. O'Connell," Kei said. "I'm pleased to meet you."

"Please call me Tina. How was your flight?"

"Oh, a little bumpy over the Gulf, but otherwise, couldn't have been smoother, thanks."

"Would you like a cocktail or something from the bar?" she asked.

The waiter approached. "What can I start you off with this afternoon?"

"I'll have a glass of the Stonehouse Chardonnay," Tina said.

"Mineral water is fine with me, thank you," Kei responded.

[Kei knew that ordering alcohol—even over lunch when the interviewer is drinking—would not be appropriate for an interview situation. Kei waited until the CEO ordered first and then was careful to order nothing more expensive than her choice from the menu.]

"Well, I'm glad we have this time together," Tina offered. "I've heard good reports from both Nancy and Ari about your work. Even though our company is a multinational conglomerate, I still tend to think of it kind of like a family. I always personally interview every executive from the director level on up, so I'm glad you could make it out to Florida today."

"I like that philosophy," he replied. "As you may know, I came from a small but successful company where we were just like family. There's nothing like trust and teamwork to build a strong foundation for an organization."

[Kei purposely answered this way because he saw that words trust *and* teamwork *were prominent in the Panatel mission statement when he was researching the company Web site before the interview.]*

"Tell me what you know about Panatel and why you want to work with us," Tina said.

"Well, that's easy. With a rating of 12 in the Fortune 500 companies, I think Panatel is a household word. Frankly, I've always admired not only the innovativeness and durability of your products but the fact that you are so active in giving charitable donations to adult literacy and cancer research. I would be very proud to work for Panatel because I believe in the lasting power of its products, like the VoicePan 2000 and TelEase Release 201BV. I also appreciate that it shares profits with the community and people in need, like 'Ready, Go, Read' and The American Society for the Prevention of Breast Cancer."

[Kei also found these details by doing Internet and library research into news archives about the philanthropic efforts of the company.]

"I must say, I'm very impressed with how much you know about our company," Tina said.

"I guess I just really enjoy doing research," Kei responded. "I like to go into any endeavor with as much knowledge and information as I can so that I can analyze the situation before coming up with a plan of action. I'd really like to tell you about a project at my former company for which I spearheaded some research into a product launch in the previously untouched Latin American market. When we finally launched the voice recognition software into that market, we were able to report a return on investment within only nine months, because of careful research and forecasting."

[Note that "research" was one of the critical key words in the job description. Kei carefully guided the conversation to one of his key accomplishments, even though he wasn't directly asked to do so.]

"Good. Kei, I understand you currently live in Texas. Will relocation be a problem for you?"

"Not in the least. I've already discussed the possibility of making a move with my family, so we've been expecting a change for quite a while. You see I have another offer pending from Nusite in Denver that would also require relocation. My wife, in fact, was quick to let me know that she'd prefer being here in Fort Lauderdale than in Denver. We have an extended family here in Florida, and since my wife completed her MBA at Florida State

University, she still has quite a few contacts here. We'd be happy to be closer to the family and friends. By the way, we're completely prepared to pay all relocation costs. I anticipate the move will be smooth, quick, and efficient."

[Kei recognized that the question "Will relocation be a problem for you?" was actually a question behind a question. The interviewer may be fishing for whether Kei would require expensive relocation fees. In this case, he anticipated her concern and quickly quelled it by saying that he was going to pay for relocation costs.]

Lunch arrived, and Kei was careful to wait to take his first bite until after Tina had taken hers.

"I know you were president of your own company. Does making a move to the director level seem like a step down to you?"

"Not at all. In fact, when I think of working for a company as prominent as Panatel, it seems to me to be more of a lateral move, considering that my company was relatively small and unknown. I've read the job description of director of launch operations, and it sounds like a very interesting challenge for me, something I would like to sink my teeth into over the long term. I'm also very aware of what might be the possible salary range for the position, and it sounds reasonable for me financially. I'd be very pleased to make a long-term commitment to work here as a director, and I think the position will pose some very interesting problems to solve, which is exactly what I love to do most."

[Again Kei recognized that the question behind a question about moving down in rank was really a question about whether he might be overqualified for the position and therefore unhappy with either the job description or the salary. He recognized the concern behind the question and addressed it immediately by saying he would be happy in the position and satisfied with the salary.]

"I'm wondering what sort of salary you're expecting."

Kei replied, "Moving from Texas to Fort Lauderdale and from a small company of my own to a major Fortune 500 company, it's rather difficult for me to come up with an exact number. Perhaps you could tell me a reasonable range for a person with my skills."

"What range did you have in mind?"

"Well," Kei replied, "for a person with more than ten years' experience in marketing and an MBA, I consider myself a candidate for the mid to high range of a director's position in this geographic area.

"What exactly would that be?" Tina queried.

[Kei knew that the advertised range for the salary was between $129,000 and $146,000 a year. However, he calculated that the company would most likely have 15 to 20 percent more to offer him.]

"Well," he said, "I would say that starting at something above $165,000 would be reasonable."

"Kei, our salary range for this position is from $129,000 to $146,000, and I'm not sure we'll be able to go beyond that."

"Although $146,000 sounds like something I would consider, I would actually be more inclined to accept a substantially higher offer. Since I've led launches of over 20 products that have earned a return on investment in as quick as 9 months, I'm more than certain that I can bring Panatel this same aggressive approach to making immediate profits. If we can agree on a sum that's somewhat higher, it would ensure that I would find this offer more attractive than the one I've received at Nusite."

[Notice that Kei said he would "consider" $146,000. That indicated that he was interested in the position, but he didn't have to get stuck on that sum. He also kept the door open by not rejecting the offer at this early stage of negotiations.

You'll see that he strategically used the phrases "substantially higher" and "somewhat higher" to avoid mentioning an exact number. Phrases like "I'd be more inclined . . ." and "the offer would be more attractive . . ." also lend themselves to keeping options open and follow the guidelines of open-door negotiating.

Kei used the technique of "leveraging offers" when he alluded to (but does not go into detail about) the real offer he had from Nusite. He also reminded the CEO that he offers considerably more value than just "filling a position," by highlighting one of his more impressive past accomplishments, adding that he planned to use those same talents to add value to Panatel.]

Tina listened and agreed: "All right, I'm prepared to offer you closer to what you're asking for. Are you prepared to take a stab at finding a suitable number?"

"Thank you. I appreciate that. I think an appropriate salary for the contribution I plan to make would be something closer to the high $160,000 range."

[He got closer to a number here but still did not lock himself into an exact figure.]

"Then how about $169,000 to start?" she offered.

He quickly said, with a smile and hand extended for a hand-shake, "$171,000 and I'll sign on, providing the benefits are within my expectations."

"$171,000 it is," she agreed. "We're glad to have you on the team!" They shook hands over the table. "I'd like to have you meet with a human resources representative who handles benefits to discuss exactly what your total compensation package would be. I'll have my assistant arrange a meeting sometime tomorrow so we can bring the offer to a close. If everything is amenable to you, you should be receiving an offer letter by mail in five to seven days."

Kei was delighted. "Thanks. I think we've had a productive meeting today, and thank you for lunch by the way. After meeting with human resources, I'd like to take 48 hours to evaluate the entire compensation package, review what we said today, and discuss the move with my wife so that I can officially accept the offer."

[He actually used this time to go back to Nusite with a counteroffer to the $165,000 they had originally offered, seeing if he could leverage the Panatel offer for an even higher salary at Nusite.]

"That'll be fine," said the CEO. "It looks like we'll be in business by the beginning of next month."

"Tina, I really appreciate the job offer, and I think that our agreement will be mutually beneficial and profitable. Thanks again for your time. It's been a pleasure to meet and talk with you." They shook hands. "Enjoy the rest of your day."

"Sure thing. Have a safe trip home. Good-bye."

Kei returned home after meeting with human resources and negotiating for medical; dental; vision; 401(k); and vacation, sick, and holiday time. He also received a membership to the local gym, first-class airfare for any business-related travel, a life insurance policy, and stock options.

To seal the deal, after Kei got back to Texas, he wrote a focus letter, reiterating his promise to seek a quick return on investments and thanking all the people who had interviewed him for their time. He and his wife decided that although Nusite raised their offer to $173,000, they would rather spend their time and retire in Florida than Colorado.

The official offer letter from Panatel arrived in the mail a few days later. Apparently, they had decided to offer him $12,000 in relocation fees after all, on top of everything else he'd negotiated for. He smiled and signed on the dotted line.

CHAPTER 11

Practice Questions

> *Perhaps I am stronger than I think!*
>
> —Thomas Merton

In the following practice section, feel free to refer to the various chapters if you like. Chapters 2, 3, 7, and 8 will be most useful to you in this process. As you answer the questions, ask yourself, "What category of question is this, and what strategy do I need to answer it?"

Tell me about yourself.

_____

_____

_____

_____

_____

_____

_____

What are some of your strengths?

_____

_____

_____

_____

Tell me about some of your skills that apply to this job.

_____

_____

_____

_____

What accomplishment do you feel most proud of?

_____

_____

_____

_____

What would you do if you caught a coworker stealing?

_____

_____

_____

_____

What was your favorite class in school?

_____

_____

_____

_____

Tell me what you think your former coworkers would say about you.

_____

_____

_____

_____

What did you think about your former boss?

_____

_____

_____

_____

Why are you leaving your former company?

_____

_____

_____

_____

Why would you like to work for this company?

_____

_____

_____

_____

What do you see yourself doing five years from now?

_____

_____

_____

_____

Don't you think you might be too inexperienced/overqualified for this position?

_____
_____
_____
_____

Do you have a disability?

_____
_____
_____
_____

Why did you never finish your degree?

_____
_____
_____
_____

What do you usually do on weekends?

_____
_____
_____
_____

Just out of curiosity, what's your favorite color?

_____
_____
_____
_____

What do you consider to be your greatest failure?

_____
_____
_____
_____

What weaknesses do you think you have?

_____
_____
_____
_____

Have you ever been late for work or an important appointment?

_____
_____
_____
_____

How much do you know about our company?

_____
_____
_____
_____

Would you object to personality or drug testing?

_____
_____
_____
_____

How do you explain that you were at your last company for only one year/one month?

_____
_____
_____
_____

What were you doing between the time you worked for that company and today?

_____
_____
_____
_____

What is the most difficult interpersonal situation you have had to deal with at work, and how did you handle it?

_____
_____
_____
_____

What do you expect to earn here?

_____
_____
_____
_____

What was your salary in your last position?

_____
_____
_____
_____

Are you looking for a position in many other companies?

_____
_____
_____
_____

Why do you think you deserve more than what we usually pay for this position?

_____
_____
_____
_____

Are you familiar with our company mission statement, and if so, what do you think of it?

_____
_____
_____
_____

How would you describe your personality?

_____
_____
_____
_____

When would you be willing to start work?

_____
_____
_____
_____

Give me an example of how you react to change.

_____
_____
_____
_____

What do you think you could accomplish in your first year here?

_____
_____
_____
_____

May we call your references?

_____
_____
_____
_____

We have many applicants for this position. Why should I hire you?

_____
_____
_____
_____

Confidence

> To have that sense of one's intrinsic worth, which consti-
> tutes self-respect, is to potentially have everything.
>
> —Joan Didion

I recently had a woman write to me after participating in a Fearless Interviewing seminar and tell me simply, that Fearless Interviewing had given her the confidence she needed to go through an interview. I thought carefully about the word *confidence* because so many people who've attended the seminars have also responded that it gave them just that. What is confidence?

The Latin translation of the word *confidence* means "with courage," "with faith," "with trust," and "without fear." You have actually done, through the exercises in this section, what few people have taken the time to do. You're not fumbling your way into an interview with blind faith and proclaiming, "I'm great! I'm the best! I need the job! Hire me!"

You're walking in holding your head high and wearing a smile on your face, knowing that you have a strategy for the entire meeting, from beginning, to middle, to end. It gives you a sense of rock-solid clarity to know your skills, know how to express them, and know how to persuade the employer to value them too. You know that your assertions are based on truth and that you need not be fooled by an interviewer's hidden agenda or a question designed to throw you off base. You know yourself, and you know that your pride in your accomplishments is not based on arrogance but on the palpable realization that by the effort of your own hands, heart, and mind, *you* have, in fact, achieved those things, however large or small.

At the beginning of this section, I told you that when you had progressed through a few basic steps, you'd be flying. Here you are, on the launching pad! (To those of you already beginning your flight, wait a minute: Can you stay in your chair for just a moment more?) I want to talk to you before you go out there and unleash yourself onto the world.

You are a precious, smart, and courageous human being. Unless you believe that we live in a cruel universe (which I don't), then this universe will provide for you an occupation— a way to spend your time and energy—and a livelihood, a way to make a living.

There is a rite of passage into that occupation. We call it an *interview*.

An interview is simply an opportunity for you to talk about what you enjoy doing most and what you do best. Yes, there are snares and traps along the way, just as there are in any journey worth taking, but you see, we've uncovered them all! You *know* where to look, you've *planned* where to step, and you've already taken this journey safely in your mind. You're there! Your spirit is filled with confidence.

Nothing can stop you.

Part Three

Fearless

CAREER
CHANGE

The Fast Track to Success in a New Field

CONTENTS

INTRODUCTION

Have you been thinking about making a career change? Would you rather be doing something you love instead of something you just "fell into"? Perhaps your company downsized and you're out of work. Regardless of why you want to change careers, now may be the perfect time to start thinking about something new.

The idea of making a career transition may sound appetizing, but the reality could be a bit uncertain—even scary. Perhaps you've thought that changing careers sounded great but found yourself wary of taking action because

- It just doesn't seem practical to you.
- It would probably cost too much anyway.
- You don't want to have to wait years to amass new education and experience.
- You're afraid of failure or even success!

> ***Or, if you feel fearful about making a move for any other reason, this book was written for you!***

It doesn't have to take a year or more to begin working in a career you love. In fact, I'll show you how to do it in about 90 days and for less of an investment than you've ever imagined. *Fearless Career Change* guides you easily, rapidly, and economically through a process of identifying and actually getting a real dream job in the real world. Through this book,

- You'll see the strategies with which hundreds of my own career counseling clients found a career in a field they loved in a matter of a few months or less.

331

- You'll discover the secrets that have worked for people of all ages—entry level to executive, artsy to technical. They've even worked for people who didn't think they had the skills to enter a new occupation.

- You'll find that some of the people I'll introduce to you have made radical and rapid career transitions for less than it costs for a tank of gas.

Yes, it's possible to begin designing your own new career now. In my 13 years plus as a career coach, I've seen this happen time after time. Take Maria, who went from being a gardener to an environmental planner (while tripling her salary) and did it in *less than three weeks and for a sum of about $450.*

Then there's Scott, an insurance salesperson who broke into the film industry in just *one* day with just one perfectly phrased phone call and with his bank account virtually untouched.

You'll learn the strategies that Alice used to double her salary in less than a month (for about $300 and two days of intensive training) by going from sitting behind a desk to delivering babies for a living.

And how Nancy went from being a public health official to a book editor for just $50 in about three months. You'll find plenty of examples of people who have made transitions just like the one you may make, and you'll discover, blow by blow, exactly how they did it and exactly how you can do it too.

My Career Change Success Story

Despite the perceived difficulties in changing careers, billions of us do. The U.S. Bureau of Labor (www.bls.gov) statistics estimates that the average American adult will change *jobs* from five to seven times and change *careers* from three to five times in his or her life.

I myself have already had numerous jobs, and I've changed careers three times. When I say "jobs," I'm referring to a set of duties I perform in exchange for a paycheck. When I use the word "career," I am referring to an ongoing learning experience in a field that I deliberately advance in and enjoy, while making a living.

One day, when I was between careers and not sure of what move to make next, I picked up a book that would change my life. It was called *Wishcraft*, and it was written by a now very prominent author and television personality named Barbara Sher.* (Ms. Sher has some fascinating ideas about careers and career changes on her Web site at www.barbarasher.com.) When I read Sher's *Wishcraft*, it seemed completely different from other books I had seen about career change.

I thought about my next career change for quite some time, and one day, I decided I wanted to become a career counselor. It seemed odd, at first, that something I always enjoyed doing at parties (asking people about their careers) could be something I could be paid for.

I enrolled in a three-day course about teaching job search methods, and I became a Certified Job Search Trainer for about $250. I interviewed ten different career counselors, and *all* of them told me that I would never make it as a career counselor without a master's degree and that there was too much competition in my area.

Fortunately, I scheduled a visit to see a very wise career counselor. When I told her about how much I wanted to be a career counselor and when I related the negative information that others had given me, she had only one thing to say to me, *"If that's where your heart is, then do it."* So I did.

Despite all the negative reports, I set out to make it possible for me to make this career change. I enrolled in a master's level class in counseling (for about $350) at a local university that allowed open enrollment. If I did not already have a graduate degree, at least I could *create the perception* that I was in the midst of getting one. And it worked.

I did a four-month internship at a local government agency before I started out as a professional. Despite all of the people who said I had to have a master's degree, I have, to date, coached over 10,000 clients, worked as a career consultant for the top two career management firms in the world, and become known for my writings on career topics around the world.

The Fearless Career Change Process

In the next chapters we're going to pinpoint the exact strategies that many others have used to make swift but meaningful career

* Barbara Sher (with Annie Gottlieb), *Wishcraft, How to Get What You Really Want*, 2d ed., Ballantine Books/Random House, New York, 2003.

changes. The first three chapters of the book are crafted to help you decide "from the inside out" what career most closely matches your natural talents and gifts. We'll also talk about getting over the fear of taking a risk and how you can condition yourself for success.

Making a career change is going to involve both thought and action from you. Too often, fear can cause a kind of paralysis that prohibits positive action and even inhibits constructive thought. That kind of paralysis can lead to procrastination, bury our dreams, or even bring us to a screeching halt.

Many of the exercises in the book are designed to beat your fear by

- Identifying just what is stopping you.
- Reminding you of constructive ways you've dealt with fear before.
- Applying the positive attributes *you already have* to breaking through the obstacle of fear.
- Showing you the methods by which other real people have beat their fear and moved on to great careers.
- Getting you on the right path of decisive action toward the career goals you set for yourself.

The middle of the book will carefully illustrate how, in little time and with little money you can actually make the transition from where you are now to where you'd like to be. You'll learn eight strategies that will propel you to your new position with ease.

Finally, I'll let you in on the *fastest* techniques, based on many years of research, to actually break into your new field and get a job offer or start your own business. We'll take it step by step, together.

You'll be able to pick the particular styles and techniques that suit your personality and preferences. Used alone, or in combination, these techniques will propel you to passionate and powerful career choices, and help you design a map that shows you how to get there.

CHAPTER 1

Overcoming Your Fears

Signs of Change

While some people find a career change to be exhilarating, others may experience the uncertainty of the transition as terrifying. But for people in both categories, the first question often is, How do you know it's time to change? If you're still employed, you may have noticed the stirrings of mild discontent with your work have finally become so pronounced that they cannot be ignored. Going to a different job in the same field won't fix the problem. You might come to realize that a more profound change is needed.

The end of a career may start with feelings of uneasiness or frustration or even depression. These feelings may fester into burnout and exhaustion, or they may take the form of self-sabotaging behavior like being late to work or not meeting deadlines. Or, for some people, the need to change careers comes more rapidly through a sudden occurrence like a layoff. These people have to face an event that is out of their control and that is significantly disruptive. Perhaps their whole field or profession is temporarily dormant or struggling, and they have to find an entirely new way of making a living.

The signals that a career may be coming to an end may appear in unexpected ways, as in a dream. The need to cease what you're doing or how you're doing it may manifest as physical symptoms, such as tendonitis, neck pain, or back pain, or as psychophysical issues like overindulgence with food or alcohol, problems with sleeping, gastrointestinal problems, or sexual difficulties.

For some people, there is no precipitating event that forces them to change careers. Instead, there is perhaps just a faint whisper in the soul that "there *must* be something better." At some point, often quite spontaneously, these same people summon the courage to embark on doing something they've always wanted to do.

Your career change need not be turbulent or dramatic. It may just be part of a natural cycle, and it may happen more than once.

If you're like many people, you've thought of what it might be like to have that "something better," but you may be putting it off until the kids go to school, your savings account is fuller, you have an advanced degree, the kids are out of college, you lose ten pounds, you get married (or divorced), your parents, spouse, or kids approve, the economy picks up, or scores of other reasons.

The problem, though, with waiting until later is that sometimes later never comes. You keep putting it off and putting it off until, one day, you may wake up when you're 5 or 15 years older and agonize over what you *could* have done or what you *should* have done.

By reading this section, you're taking the first steps toward a future designed by wants, not by shoulds.

Common Fears about Career Change

In a word, change itself (even change for the better) can be scary and stressful. Two opposing needs—one for the security of the job you've known, and one for the freedom to choose a job that might be better—seem at odds with each other. It's frustrating to be pulled in two directions and easy to become overwhelmed and even afraid of the prospect of change.

Take a look at some common and very understandable fears I've heard my clients express when faced with the prospect of exploring a new and different occupation. If you, too, have one or more of the following fears, we're going to take a serious look at them in this chapter and utilize some techniques that can help you get around and through them.

- "Every time I mention my dream career to people, they say it's too competitive and I'm safer where I am."

- "I think I'm too young to change careers. What if I look like I'm 'job hopping'?"

- "I don't have the money to go back to school to get an advanced degree."

- "I really want a new career, but I'm afraid my savings account or severance pay will wear out before I find a new position."

- "If I have to show up at my present job for one more day, I'm going to explode with boredom (or stress). The trouble is, I have no idea about what I want to do next!"

- "I'd like to be a _____, but I don't think I'd meet the requirements."

- "I've dreamed so long about being a _____, but I'm afraid I'll fail."

- "I absolutely *hate* my job, but if I just stay a little bit longer, I'll get a bonus. I'll just think about a career change *next* year."

- "I'm completely stuck. I have several careers in mind, but I don't want to pick the wrong one. Maybe I'll just wait for a sudden inspiration."

- "I'm too old. *Nobody* starts a new business at age 74."

- "I've always wanted to be a _____, but a (parent, teacher, friend, guidance counselor) told me I would never make it."

- "If I become a big success at my new job, my friends will get jealous and reject me."

- "If I had a new career where I felt *really* happy, I don't think I could handle it. I'd have nothing to worry about anymore."

Every single person I have met who is struggling with making a career change is either limited by fear of some sort or lack of information. This chapter will help you use victories in your past to neutralize your fears and sculpt the triumphs of tomorrow. Then Chapter 3 will aid you in finding the right information to make an informed choice about your next venture.

You probably have specific fears that aren't on the list above. In either case, it helps to write them down so you know what you are up against.

My three most pressing concerns about making a career change:

1. _____

_____

_____

2. _____

_____

_____

3. _____

_____

_____

Another fear, not on the list:

4. _____

_____

_____

Another fear, not on the list:

5. _____

_____

_____

Fear of Failure

Most of us have the wrong idea when it comes to failure. Do you know how many times a baby falls before she takes that first step that launches her out onto her own? Do we call her first attempts "failures" just because she ends up on the floor? Of course not, and neither does she. She gets up and tries again! I've heard the story of Thomas Edison, the genius who invented the lightbulb, many times. According to the story, Edison's friend approached him and said, "Why in the world do you stay in your laboratory, trying time and time again to make that thing work when you've failed a thousand times already?" Edison purportedly answered, "No, you're wrong—it's been 10,000 times, and I've succeeded every single time in finding yet another way not to make a lightbulb!" Think how many millions of households and factories might have had to manage with candlelight for another hundred years had there not been a man as brave as Edison. He truly "reframed" the meaning of the word *failure* into something more like a "lesson"—and a successful one at that. The fear of failure can be so constricting that you lose the confidence and the ability to take risks—and you must have both qualities if you're going to make a successful career change. My bet is that, even if you don't have confidence now or you are hesitant to take a risk, there was a time in your life when you were unafraid. We're going to uncover some of those times in the next exercise.

For the first exercise, take a look at one of the fears you listed above, and ask yourself these questions in relation to that fear.

1. What is the worst thing that can happen if I change careers?

   _____

   _____

   _____

2. What's the best thing that can happen?

   _____

   _____

   _____

3. How likely is it that the worst thing will happen?

   _____

   _____

   _____

4. How would I solve the problem if the worst thing did happen?

    _____

    _____

    _____

5. What steps could I take now to prevent the worst thing from happening?

    _____

    _____

    _____

6. How will I feel about myself if the best thing happens?

    _____

    _____

    _____

7. What steps can I take to ensure that the best thing happens?

    _____

    _____

    _____

8. If I look back on my life one year from now, I will be glad that I (describe an action here).

    _____

    _____

    _____

9. If I look back on my life 15 years from now, I'll see that making the choice now to _____

    _____

    _____ was a good one.

Career changes are not just about skill, timing, and the latest strategies. They're about mental focus, passionate motivation, and sometimes trust in things or people that we didn't even know we had before. Career changes demand a great deal of heroism, as almost every career change I've witnessed involved not only some sort of temporary sacrifice or uncertainty followed by some sort of triumph, however small or great, but also some kind of risk. If you have survived this long in this complex and demanding world, you are bound to have taken at least one risk.

Taking Risks

Let's do an exercise to find out how you did it and how you can do it again.

What are three risks I've taken in my life that have had a positive outcome for me? Describe exactly what happened before and after the positive risk and *your role* in making it turn out favorably.

1. _____
   _____
2. _____
   _____
3. _____
   _____

Ask yourself, "What do these three risks have in common? What mental attitudes and emotional attributes do they have in common? What do they say about me?" Write your answer here:

_____
_____
_____

Finally, write a paragraph or more about why you would like to make a career transition right now. Write both the negatives of your last or present job and the positives you hope for in your next job.

_____
_____
_____

You probably noticed some patterns in the successful risks you took, and you may have discovered some personal attributes that you hadn't really thought of before.

> ***Career changes are not only about doing the right things to bring about a change. They are also about being the person it takes to weather the fears, the victories, and the ups and downs of profound change.***

Here is a list of some of the personal qualities that successful career changers possess. Make a check next to the particular attributes you've noticed in these exercises or the ones that you believe you possess.

- ❑ Adaptability
- ❑ Confidence
- ❑ Courage
- ❑ Creativity
- ❑ Determination
- ❑ Drive
- ❑ Faith
- ❑ Flexibility
- ❑ Honesty
- ❑ Logic
- ❑ Motivation
- ❑ Open-mindedness
- ❑ Passion
- ❑ Perseverance (persistence in the face of "failure")
- ❑ Persistence
- ❑ Problem-solving skills
- ❑ Rationality
- ❑ Resourcefulness
- ❑ Sense of humor
- ❑ Vision
- ❑ Willingness

You don't have to have all of these attributes to achieve favorable results. In fact, if you have just one, you will have enough. When we get to Chapter 8, I would like you to look back on this list and see the richness you have to draw from. Looking at this list and consciously bringing one of your personal attributes to the forefront will help you make tough choices and weather temporary setbacks.

Building a Transition Income

Understandably, many people's fears about changing careers center on having enough money to make it through a period of unemployment and perhaps training between jobs. Most people have considerably less anxiety when they are going through this process with the cushion of a little money in the bank. Typically three months' salary would be the bare minimum to have before changing careers, although many people who haven't had more than a penny saved have had smooth transitions to a new career.

To determine how much you'll need to feel comfortable, let's build what I call a *transition income*. Take a moment to think about the *necessities* in your life, and distinguish them from your *preferences*. *Necessities* are things you absolutely must have for shelter, nutrition, health, sanity, and other basic needs.

Some examples of necessities for many of us are:

- Rent
- Mortgage
- Food
- Furniture
- Automobile insurance
- Vehicle maintenance and repair
- Pet care
- Medical and dental care
- Phone
- Transportation
- Taxes
- Cell phone
- Some degree of social and entertainment activities
- Home maintenance and repair
- Child care
- Elder care
- Gas and electric service
- An "emergency fund"
- Debt consolidation
- Money for gifts and holidays
- Retirement savings or investments
- Tithing to your church or temple
- And whatever else you need to feel comfortable

Preferences are things that enhance your lifestyle—goodies like cable or satellite TV, a state-of-the-art home entertainment system, one or more luxury cars, extensive travel, preventive health care, a housekeeper, a gardener or landscaper, a vast CD or DVD collection, a handsome wardrobe, a gym membership, charitable contributions, vacations, exercise equipment, massage, concerts, ballet, high-speed Internet connections, membership to a country club, wireless handheld devices, a fully stocked home workshop, video equipment, expensive cameras, new kitchenware, linens, or home décor, a second car for yourself or your family, first-class travel, extensive investments and retirement income, a pool—you get the picture.

Now that the difference is clear, take a minute to think about the following: What do you want, when do you want them, and what will be the cost of enjoying those things?

Please use this section to list your absolute necessities for at least a three-month period. (You may want to refer to the lists above so you don't leave anything out.) Then, do your best to estimate the monthly (and quarterly) costs of each of the items you chose. For example:

Mortgage	$1,000
Monthly housekeeper	90
Car payment	250

Fixed costs (costs that remain the same from month to month like a mortgage, rent, or car payment):

1. _____
2. _____
3. _____
4. _____
5. _____
6. _____
7. _____
8. _____
9. _____

Variable expenses (the phone, electric, and gas bills):

10. _____
11. _____

12. _____
13. _____
14. _____
15. _____
16. _____
17. _____
18. _____
19. _____
20. _____

When you're finished, total the amount.

Total $ _____ per month

_____ per quarter (1 month × 3)

What amount do you think you could live on, *at minimum*, for three months? $ _____

six months? $ _____
nine months? $ _____
A year? $ _____

It may take 90 days to a year to make your career transition, especially if you need to get some extra training, wait for your new small business to turn a profit, or establish your value in a new job so that you get a raise. If you decide on a career that takes two or more years of education, you will of course have to save or earn the money that will pay for your living expenses and education in the interim.

Take a look at your expense list again and consider it as carefully as you wish. Think about things you may be able to put aside for a while, thereby saving some extra cash for yourself as you make your way through the process of changing occupations. For example, you could use public transportation instead of putting wear and tear on the car.

You'd be surprised by how you can cut corners a bit and barely even notice it, especially if you know it's only for a limited time. You probably won't have or want to give up *all* your luxuries at once.

Would giving up three or four of those costly items be worth the joy you're going to feel when you're doing a job you love, coming home energized, feeling great about yourself, and working your way (back) to the top of a new field where you really want to be?

Your happiness is urgent. Fear may be at the back door, but you don't have to let it in. You've conquered risks before. You have what it takes to succeed. What waits for you on the other side of apprehension and procrastination is the indescribable joy of being in the right place, doing the right job at the right time. And the time is now!

CHAPTER 2

Creating Your Career Fingerprint

By far the most satisfying careers spring not just from what we want or what we are interested in but from what we were truly meant to do. How do you know what you were meant to do? Finding the answer involves becoming aware of your *authentic calling*, which many people see as divinely or naturally inscribed on your genetic code and imprinted on your soul. This chapter is called "Creating Your Career Fingerprint" because each one of us possesses a unique authentic calling, a metaphorical fingerprint, if you will, of the right career for us, unlike that of anyone else's in the world. We each have a special stamp to make in the world, however bold or faint to the eye.

> ***Each of us has an unrepeatable calling or combination of natural and unique talents in this lifetime, and it's up to us to discover them and celebrate them. Expressing your natural and unique talents outwardly, in one way or another, can lead to a kind of happiness and peace that few other experiences can rival.***

Finding your authentic calling (or special talent) may sound a little bit mysterious. From my experience, though, I can safely say that given the right circumstances, your own calling will come tumbling off your tongue and you'll wonder how it was you didn't notice it in the first place. When you are operating from your calling, it will, indeed, seem like you are not working at all but rather simply and almost magically, flowing. In my 13 years of being a career coach, I have very rarely had a client who, given the right prompting (as you'll have in this section), could not state his or her special talent within 10 or 20 minutes after talking with me. People who have done the exercises presented in this section have reported to me that, even though they were unsure of their career direction, it became clear to them as a result of gaining enormous self-knowledge from completing these exercises.

If the word calling *seems unnatural to you for any reason, try substituting the words* natural ability *or* talent.

You probably know your calling *now*—it may just take a little coaxing and my assurance to you that it's there and that you should get it down on paper. That's what the process that I call *career fingerprinting* is about: finding that single thing—a talent, a power, a special genius—that (like a fingerprint) is unique to you and only you. That's what we'll be doing in the following exercises.

What Is My Authentic Calling?

In this first exercise in the career fingerprinting process, complete each one of the following phrases using the first thing that pops into your mind. You may rest at ease even if your answers seem to make no sense at all because we're going to spend time together for the rest of this section making sure that your answers translate into a real-world career that you can fully enjoy. Right now, we're just at the beginning. There's no right or wrong answer. It doesn't matter if your answers are all the same, all different, or some sort of mixture. Try not to analyze it at all. We'll have plenty of time for analysis later. For now, let yourself have some fun.

> **You are about to encounter the wild, unencum-
> bered self that you are—the self you would be if
> you had absolutely no barriers, responsibilities,
> past disappointments, issues with money, or
> future worries—and complete these sentences
> as if you had no limitations whatsoever and
> without censoring.**

When I was a child, I was naturally talented at

_____

_____

_____

Someone once told me I was particularly talented at

_____

_____

_____

Other people have told me that I was unusually adept at

_____

_____

_____

If I asked the wisest man or woman in the world "What is my special talent?" he or she would say, "Your special talent is

_____

_____

_____

and you can use it to

_____

_____

_____

If I came to know the kindest man or woman in the universe, he or she would tell me that my authentic calling is

_____

_____

_____

and I can use it to

_____

_____

_____

Two years from now it will be clear that my authentic calling has always been

_____

_____

_____

Five years from now it will dawn on me that my calling has always been

_____

_____

_____

Ten years from now I'll realize that my calling is

_____

_____

_____

Twenty years from now I'll look back and I will see that my calling was or is

_____

_____

_____

Thirty years from now I'll reflect upon my life and know that my calling was

_____

_____

_____

When I die, the people who knew me will say I was uniquely talented at

_____

_____

_____

and I used my talent(s) to

_____

_____

_____

I believe my authentic calling is

_____

_____

_____

I have no idea at all what my calling is, but I'd like to pretend that it is

_____

_____

_____

A little "voice" in my head says my authentic calling is

_____

_____

_____

If my vision of my calling were to become crystal clear, it would look like

_____

_____

_____

I cannot find the words to express my natural and unique talent, but if I pretend now that I can hear the words, they would be saying

_____

_____

_____

People in the past have "made fun" of my natural and unique talent, but I now have the courage and strength to say that it is

_____

_____

_____

and I'm going to use it to

_____

_____

_____

In my most private moments, I really know that my authentic calling is

_____

_____

_____

Fifteen Categories of Unique and Special Talents

Did you have an easy or a difficult time doing the preceding exercise? If it seemed difficult to pinpoint exactly what your special talent is, that's okay. We'll soon explore several categories of unique abilities that you may recognize in yourself. If you found that the answers to the prompts were very easy for you, you may skip to the next chapter if you wish.

To start pinpointing your authentic calling, go through the following categories of talents as if you had no limitations, and see if any of them might include something that appeals to you. You may relate to many, one, or none of these gifts. It really doesn't matter. In the long run, *all you need is one.* By the end of this section you will have identified the one(s) most important to you.

> **If for some reason the specific talent that you believe you have is not on this list, then by all means write down your own version of your natural ability in your own words.**

❑ Are you good at making people feel genuinely important?

Do you have a natural talent for listening so intently that you are able to block out all external stimuli just to focus on whomever you're talking to? Can you give sincere compliments and uplifting comments to people that help them feel important and understood? Do you make it a habit to see and bring out the best in people? Do people tend to naturally trust you?

A few careers associated with this talent could be

- Astrologer
- Customer service representative
- Drug and alcohol counselor
- Human resources director
- Life coach
- Medical doctor
- Psychotherapist
- Real estate agent
- Registered nurse

❑ Are you good at assisting people in healing or personal growth?

Do you seem to naturally feel empathy and compassion for people? Do you gravitate toward those whom you can help? Do you feel delight when people feel better or improve their performance as a result of interacting with you? Do you thrive on inspiring and motivating others?

A few careers associated with this talent could be

- Acupuncturist
- Certified neurolinguistic programmer
- Chiropractor
- Family nurse practitioner
- Health columnist
- Herbalist
- Member of the clergy
- Midwife
- Motivational speaker
- Personal athletic trainer
- Psychic or intuitive
- Psychologist, therapist, or counselor

❑ Are you good at persuading people?

Do you have a way with bringing people around to your point of view? Do you have an innate sense of what people want or what they would find attractive? Do people tend to trust you and believe what you say? Have you ever completely changed a person's mind from one viewpoint to an opposite one? Do you enjoy when people seek you out for advice?

A few careers associated with this talent could be

- Actor
- Advertising salesperson
- Consultant, counselor, or personal coach
- Graphic artist
- Magazine, book, or newspaper writer, editor, or publisher
- Marketing and communications specialist
- Personal financial planner
- Politician or political activist
- Professor or teacher
- Public speaker
- Salesperson
- Supervisor

❑ Are you good at designing things?

Do you thrive on designing simple or complex things, processes, or projects? Is it second nature for you to be organized in anything you undertake? Do you have an eye for the big picture but also a sense for the minutest details? Do you love to orchestrate different elements to create a new and functional, logical, or aesthetic whole?

A few careers associated with this talent could be

- Biochemist
- Computer-aided drafter
- Events planner
- Fashion designer
- Food stylist (film and photography)
- Interior decorator
- Landscape architect
- Mechanical engineer
- Programmer analyst
- Software programmer
- Window dresser for a store

❑ Are you good at building things?

Do you love to work with your hands and wood, stone, metal, plants, or other materials? Do the acts of sculpting, smoothing, cutting, digging, lifting, moving, or painting appeal to you? Do you enjoy jobs and recreational pursuits in which all or part of your body can get involved? Do you like to figure out how things fit together and create, enhance, reinforce, restore, or repair them?

A few careers associated with this talent could be

- Aircraft engineer
- Auto mechanic
- Computer or office machine repair
- Construction supervisor
- Electronics manufacturer
- Fine arts sculptor
- Fine cabinetry maker
- Gardener or landscaper
- Surgeon
- Watch repairer

❑ Do you enjoy operating things?

Do you think that you may learn how to operate machinery faster or more easily than most people do? Do you enjoy the rhythm of operating a small or large machine correctly and efficiently? Do you think you have more patience than most people when you operate machines? Do machines, toys, and gadgets fascinate you?

A few careers associated with this talent could be

- Assembly line worker
- Commercial airline pilot
- Digital video editor
- Heavy-machinery operator
- Lighting technician

- Office manager
- Photographer
- Respiratory therapist
- Sound technician

- Truck driver
- Ultrasound technician
- Word processor

❑ **Are you especially adept at fixing things?**

Can you quickly analyze a situation, product, or project and come up with a solution to repair, restore, or improve it? Are you able to take many factors into account and arrive at a workable solution? Are you able to observe things, people, and processes objectively? Do you feel confident about your ability to solve problems, and do you derive satisfaction from troubleshooting difficult or not-so-obvious challenges?

A few careers associated with this talent could be

- Appliance repairer
- Automotive repairer
- Business consultant
- Car detailer
- Certified heat and air-conditioning technician
- Financial advisor

- Organizational consultant
- Plumber
- Postsales hardware engineer
- Professional mediator
- Small business machine repair

❑ **Do you love to test and stretch your intellect as far as you can possibly go?**

If your appetite for knowledge about a particular scientific or artistic field is nearly insatiable, you may want to apply your intellect to learning as much as you can about a given subject. Would you like to be considered an expert in your field? Would you like to write, research, or illuminate a certain topic or topics? Have you ever noticed that you never tire of reading everything you can find about a certain subject? Do you enjoy being in an academic environment and/or discussing intellectual pursuits with like-minded people? Do you attend lectures just for fun? Do you feel most comfortable in a laboratory, editing room, library, or classroom?

A few careers associated with this talent could be

- Biophysicist
- Environmental planner
- Fiction or nonfiction writer
- Filmmaker
- Historian

- Marine biologist
- Mathematician
- Music composer
- Political analyst
- Research scientist
- Sociologist

❑ Are you gifted with unusual physical strength, agility, grace, coordination, or fine motor skills?

Do you enjoy using talents that highlight your physical strength, agility, or coordination? Are you careful to take very good care of your body? Is it important to you to excel physically and mentally at what you do? Do you sometimes notice that you're competitive? Are you more dedicated and disciplined than most people about your physical health and/or appearance?

A few careers associated with this talent could be

- Athlete
- Athletic coach
- Dancer
- Entertainer
- Massage therapist

- Personal trainer
- Pilates instructor
- Stunt man or woman
- Yoga instructor

❑ Do you have a burning desire to share your compassion, love, and empathy with the world?

Is it extremely important to you to make a contribution in the world or a difference in the lives of individuals? Would you like to be a pivotal person in someone's growth, development, or even happiness? Do you feel driven to leave the legacy of being a loving and caring person? Do you ever have the sense that you are somehow divinely mandated to give something back to humanity, even if it means that you may not make hoards of money? Do you genuinely love being around people and rarely tire of them?

A few careers associated with this talent could be

- Artist
- Author or journalist
- Child-care worker
- Director of a nonprofit
- Entertainer
- Homeless advocate
- Life or career coach
- Lobbyist
- Minister

- Motivational speaker
- Physician's assistant
- Political advocate or activist
- Psychotherapist
- Senior citizen companion
- Teacher
- Volunteer

❑ Are you so incredibly adept with detail that you amaze your family and friends?

Do you get great satisfaction from striving for absolute perfection? Do you feel a sense of pride when you have created order out of chaos and/or organization from disarray? Is it easy and natural for you to work slowly and methodically so that you end with a perfect result? Do you have more patience than most people with detail? Can other people trust you to put things in tidy, logical order? Do you thrive on efficiency?

A few careers associated with this talent could be

- Accountant
- Archaeologist
- Assembler
- Bookkeeper
- Building inspector
- Clean-room specialist
- Database analyst
- Financial analyst
- Forensic expert

- House cleaner
- Insurance agent
- Laboratory technician
- Logistics manager
- Operations director
- Property appraiser
- Research scientist
- Surgeon
- Watch repairer

❑ Are you mathematically gifted?

Do numbers, diagrams, and numerical concepts come easily—are they fun? Do you love to work on easy or increasingly difficult numerical or geometric puzzles? Do mathematics or numbers represent something beautiful to you? Do you think you are more adept with numbers than the average person is? Can you immediately spot errors in mathematical calculations and correct them?

A few careers associated with this talent could be

- Astrophysicist
- Biophysicist
- Bookkeeper
- Business manager
- Certified public accountant
- Chemist
- Chief financial officer
- Controller
- Engineer
- Executive
- Mathematics instructor
- Mortgage broker
- Software programmer
- Stockbroker
- Tax preparer

❑ Are you gifted at leading, managing, or directing large-scale projects?

Do you love to pull together all of the resources necessary to produce a desired result? Do people seem to look to you when the chips are down? Do you feel that you have a special way of looking at things and doing things that makes you a good leader? Can you get other people to follow your vision or act on your ideas? Do you ever dream of starting a company of your own? Do you think you know how to bring out the best in people?

A few careers associated with this talent could be

- Art director
- Commercial building contractor
- Corporate or small-business executive
- Department supervisor, manager, or director
- Events planner
- Producer or director (theater, film, television, music)
- Production manager
- Program or project manager
- Trade show coordinator
- Travel agent
- Wedding planner

❑ Do you have a scientific or academic bent?

Do you love to dig into research and compare or create theories? Do you love to apply the scientific method to do experiments and conduct research? Are you interested in subjects that others might consider eso-teric? Do you have hypotheses you'd like to test and then publish the results? Are you drawn to pure science? Do you find beauty in sci-ence? Do you often find yourself wishing that you could just spend time alone reading, for days at a time?

A few careers associated with this talent could be

- Anthropologist
- Archaeologist
- Biographer
- Chemist
- Ethnographer
- Ethnomusicologist
- Experimental psychologist
- Geologist
- Historian
- Paleontologist
- Physicist
- Psychopharmacologist

❑ Are you an expert at taking physical, intellectual, emotional, and/or financial risks?

Does playing for high stakes and not knowing your outcome give you a rush? Do you thrive on pressure and do your best under stress? Do you like to be the underdog who comes out ahead at the last moment? Do you enjoy an adrenaline rush and sometimes wonder why other people are so slow? Do you live for the next challenge? Are you attracted to dangerous situations, and do you feel confident that you can do just about anything you put your mind to?

A few careers associated with this talent could be

- Adventure guide
- Boat, horse, car, wind-surfing, or bicycle racer
- Entrepreneur or small-business owner
- Firefighter
- Inventor
- Military officer
- Mountaineering instructor
- Police officer or detective
- Private investigator
- Small-airplane operator
- Stand-up comedian
- Stocks and bonds investor
- Whitewater rafting guide

❑ Are you artistically gifted?

Do you crave the opportunity to create beauty and symbolism in the world? Can a symphony, painting, or sculpture move you to tears? Have others told you that you have a gift for being artistic? Can you remember wanting to be an artist, actor, or musician since you were very young? Have people ever said that they appreciated or were moved by something you made or did? Have you always known you were an artist but kept it hidden because it seemed impractical or someone criticized you? Do you think that art is one of the most important things in the world?

A few careers associated with this talent could be

- Actor
- Clothing, manufacturing, or furniture designer
- Crafts designer
- Dancer
- Film, theater, or television director
- Fine artist
- Florist
- Graphic or Web designer
- Interior decorator
- Musician
- Playwright
- Sculptor
- Singer

You may find that one or more special talents in these sections really resonate with you. For example, you may love to make people feel genuinely important *and* you may also be particularly talented at managing or leading large-scale projects. Write down one, two, or three of the above talents (or choose ones you believe you have that may not appear in the above list), beginning with the one you believe is the strongest.

At this time I think or feel that my authentic calling is

1. _____ and I know this because

_____

_____

_____

2. _____ and I know this because

_____

3. _____ and I know this because

_____

Perhaps you found even three or more callings that apply to you. That's fine. You may be a multiply gifted person. We'll discover some guideposts in the next section that will point the way to your particular path.

Applying Your Gifts in the Real World

If you have an authentic calling for being persuasive, for example, it is doubtful that someone will pay you simply for that raw talent. Your calling must somehow be put in context by becoming part of the world in which people are paid to perform meaningful jobs. Being persuasive, for example, might be translated into the world of work as a specific job title that is generally recognized and that people receive monetary compensation for. Some jobs that match well with the calling of being persuasive are teacher, minister, attorney, salesperson, and actor.

In the next exercise you'll be scanning through a list of job titles and asking yourself the question, "How well would this job title allow me to express my authentic calling?"

With this exercise, it's important to really let your imagination and intuition flow freely. It may even mean that you suspend, for a while, your normal, rational, critical mind in order to give other, deeper, and perhaps wiser, parts of your being a chance to bring forth messages you may not have considered before. Some people call this frame of mind "thinking out of the box," and others, "emotional intelligence." Let your mind and feelings be as flexible as possible. Too often our critical minds are the culprits that landed us in jobs we found to be unfulfilling. Now is your chance to let what I call your "deeper mind" choose for you!

> ***If you haven't already seen a clear picture of
> your authentic calling, the following exercise
> will give important clues to assist you in
> clarifying your vision.***

This exercise assesses how your gifts fit into the real world of jobs. You may believe that your career needs to be *bold, heroic,* or a *status symbol* to the rest of the world. This is not the case, because when you come upon the right career for you at this time in your life, you will *feel* fantastic no matter how the world evaluates your occupation. When you are expressing something from deep inside of you through the work you choose to do, you are making a maximum contribution both to yourself and to the world. You will be living the life you are meant to live in your own quiet way. You'll be proud of yourself. You will *know* you are magnificent! We have no time to waste, so let's begin.

1. Consider the list of occupations that is provided in the next few pages of this chapter. Look at every occupation from A to Z. There are lots of entries in the list, so you might want to try this exercise in two or three sittings.

2. Circle any entry (for example, dog shampooer, event planner, filmmaker, lawyer, pediatrician, software programmer, technician, vice president, Web designer) that you feel would allow you to express your gifts. The assumption here is that you already have all the right amount of money, education, time, familial support, location, and physical and mental ability to actually try that role for a short time. In other words, just for the sake of this exercise, you have no limitations.

3. Next, go through the occupations list again and check only those listings you would be willing to try for a whole year, again with the assumption that you are completely equipped to do them. Place a check by those job titles, whether they are circled or not.

4. Finally, pick ten of these job titles that are both circled and checked.

At the end of this list, you'll have space to write down your ten selections. Go for it!

Occupations List

A

- ❑ Abortion counselor
- ❑ Accountant
- ❑ Acupuncturist
- ❑ Addiction counselor
- ❑ Adjuster, insurance
- ❑ Administrator, health
- ❑ Administrator, office
- ❑ Administrator, school
- ❑ Administrator, unspecified
- ❑ Adoption counselor
- ❑ Adult assisted living coordinator
- ❑ Adult education teacher
- ❑ Aerial photographer
- ❑ Aeronautical researcher
- ❑ Agricultural worker
- ❑ Airbrush artist
- ❑ Alarm installer
- ❑ Alzheimer's counselor
- ❑ Ambulance driver
- ❑ Anesthesiologist
- ❑ Animal trainer
- ❑ Animator, film and video
- ❑ Antique store owner
- ❑ Apartment manager
- ❑ Appliance repairer
- ❑ Appraiser, real estate
- ❑ Aquatic researcher
- ❑ Architect

- ❑ Armed forces member, enlisted
- ❑ Army member, enlisted
- ❑ Art appraiser
- ❑ Art critic
- ❑ Art museum curator
- ❑ Asbestos consultant
- ❑ Assembler
- ❑ Assistant editor
- ❑ Astrologer
- ❑ Astronomer
- ❑ Astrophysicist
- ❑ Athlete
- ❑ Athletic trainer, certified
- ❑ Attorney
- ❑ Audio engineer
- ❑ Audiologist
- ❑ Author
- ❑ Automobile design
- ❑ Automobile repairer
- ❑ Automobile salesperson
- ❑ Automotive technician, smog
- ❑ Aviator

B

- ❑ Babysitter
- ❑ Backpacking guide
- ❑ Baker
- ❑ Bakery owner
- ❑ Ballroom dancing teacher

❑ Bankruptcy consultant

❑ Baseball player

❑ Beauty salon owner

❑ Bed-and-breakfast manager

❑ Behavioral scientist

❑ Benefits, human resources

❑ Bereavement counselor

❑ Bibliographer

❑ Biochemist

❑ Biofeedback therapist

❑ Biographer

❑ Biologist

❑ Biomechanical engineer

❑ Biopharmaceutical scientist

❑ Biophysicist

❑ Birth coach

❑ Birth control counselor

❑ Blind persons support

❑ Blinds, cleaning service owner

❑ Bodybuilder, professional

❑ Bodybuilder, instructor

❑ Bodyguard

❑ Bookkeeper

❑ Broker, automobile

❑ Broker, real estate

❑ Broker, stocks and bonds

❑ Builder, construction

❑ Building code consultant

❑ Building inspector

❑ Bus driver, school or public

❑ Business consultant

❑ Business owner, unspecified

❑ Butcher

❑ Buyer

C

❑ Cabinetmaker

❑ Camera operator, film and video

❑ Campground manager

❑ Candy store owner

❑ Career counselor

❑ Carpenter

❑ Carpet seller, retail or wholesale

❑ Cashier

❑ Casino manager

❑ Casting director, film and TV

❑ Caterer

❑ Certified financial planner

❑ Certified personal trainer

❑ Certified public account

❑ Chairman of the board

❑ Chauffeur

❑ Chef

❑ Chemist

❑ Chief executive officer

❑ Chief financial officer

❑ Chief information officer

❑ Chief operating officer

❑ Chief technical officer

❑ Child's advocate

- Child-care teacher or provider
- Chiropractor
- Clergy, unspecified
- Clerk, law
- Clerk, medical
- Clerk, sales
- Clerk, unspecified
- Clothing store owner
- Coach, life and career
- Coach, sports
- Coffee house owner
- College official
- College professor
- Colonic therapist
- Comedian
- Computer-aided designer
- Computer engineer, hardware
- Computer engineer, networking
- Computer engineer, software
- Computer programmer
- Computer, unspecified
- Conference coordinator
- Contractor
- Convalescent home manager
- Coordinator, film and television
- Coordinator, office
- Coordinator, production

- Cosmetologist
- Counselor, licensed marriage and family
- Counselor, unspecified
- Court interpreter
- Court reporter
- CPR teacher
- Credit counselor
- Criminal justice, unspecified
- Criminal lawyer
- Criminal psychologist
- Criminologist
- Customer relations manager
- Customer service representative

D

- Data analyst
- Data processor
- Decorator, film and television
- Decorator, interior
- Decorator, store window
- Decorator, trade show
- Deli owner
- Delivery person
- Dental assistant
- Dentist
- Designer, costume
- Designer, fashion
- Designer, interior
- Designer, unspecified
- Desktop publisher

- Die cutter, machinist
- Diet counselor
- Dietician, registered
- Digital audio effects engineer
- Digital video effects technician
- Disabled person's advocate
- Disk jockey
- Diver
- Document controller
- Dog trainer
- Doll maker
- Drafter, computer-aided
- Dressmaker
- Driver, unspecified
- Drug counselor
- Dry cleaner

E

- Earthquake preparedness inspector
- Ecologist
- Economist
- Editor, unspecified
- Educational consultant
- Educator, unspecified
- Electrician
- Electronics manufacturer
- Electronics salesperson
- Embroiderer
- Employee benefits specialist

- Employee, temporary
- Employee's advocate
- Employment agency owner
- Employment counselor
- Employment developer
- Employment specialist
- Energy conservation advocate
- Energy consultant
- Engineer, architectural
- Engineer, chemical
- Engineer, computer
- Engineer, electrical
- Engineer, hardware
- Engineer, mechanical
- Engineer, software
- Engineer, unspecified
- Engraver
- Entertainer, unspecified
- Entomologist
- Environmental consultant
- Escort
- Escrow officer
- Espresso store manager
- Espresso store owner
- Espresso store worker
- Evangelist
- Executive coach
- Executive director, non-profit
- Executive producer, media
- Executive recruiter

- ❑ Executive search consultant
- ❑ Exercise physiologist
- ❑ Explorer
- ❑ Export store owner
- ❑ Exporter, unspecified

F

- ❑ Fabric designer
- ❑ Fabric store owner
- ❑ Facilities manager
- ❑ Farmer
- ❑ Fashion coach
- ❑ Fax machine repairer
- ❑ FBI agent
- ❑ Feng shui practitioner
- ❑ Fiber artist
- ❑ Filmmaker
- ❑ Financial analyst
- ❑ Financial consultant
- ❑ Financial officer, chief
- ❑ Financial planner
- ❑ Financial planner, certified
- ❑ Fire alarm installer
- ❑ Fire alarm specialist
- ❑ Fire protection consultant
- ❑ Firefighter
- ❑ Fish and game warden
- ❑ Fish broker
- ❑ Fisherman or woman
- ❑ Flight attendant
- ❑ Flooring contractor
- ❑ Florist
- ❑ Flower grower
- ❑ Food broker
- ❑ Food buyer
- ❑ Food manufacturer
- ❑ Food processing consultant
- ❑ Food stylist, media
- ❑ Food supplier
- ❑ Forest ranger
- ❑ Freight handler
- ❑ Freight traffic consultant
- ❑ Furniture dealer
- ❑ Furniture designer
- ❑ Furniture maker

G

- ❑ Gambler
- ❑ Game designer
- ❑ Gas station owner
- ❑ Geologist
- ❑ Geophysicist
- ❑ Gift manufacturer
- ❑ Gift shop manager
- ❑ Glassblower
- ❑ Gold seller
- ❑ Golf course architect
- ❑ Golf shop owner
- ❑ Golfer, professional
- ❑ Gourmet chef, professional
- ❑ Government official, unspecified
- ❑ Graphic designer
- ❑ Greenhouse builder

- ❑ Greensman, film and television
- ❑ Greeting card maker
- ❑ Grinder, machinist
- ❑ Grocer
- ❑ Gym manager
- ❑ Gym owner

H

- ❑ Handyperson
- ❑ Hang-gliding instructor
- ❑ Hardware store owner or manager
- ❑ Health-care practitioner, unspecified
- ❑ Health plan administrator
- ❑ Heating and ventilation specialist
- ❑ Heavy-equipment operator
- ❑ Helicopter pilot
- ❑ Herbologist
- ❑ Historian
- ❑ Holistic healer
- ❑ Horse breeder
- ❑ Horse trainer
- ❑ Horseback riding instructor
- ❑ Horticulturist
- ❑ Hospital administrator
- ❑ Hotel manager or owner, unspecified
- ❑ Human factors/ergonomist
- ❑ Hypnotherapy practitioner, certified

I

- ❑ Ice cream maker
- ❑ Ichthyologist
- ❑ Illustrator
- ❑ Immigration lawyer
- ❑ Immigration officer
- ❑ Immunologist
- ❑ Importer
- ❑ Income tax preparer
- ❑ Industrial designer
- ❑ Industrial engineer
- ❑ Industrial hygiene consultant
- ❑ Industrial or organizational psychologist
- ❑ Information technologist, unspecified
- ❑ Instructor, unspecified
- ❑ Instrumentation technician
- ❑ Insurance analyst
- ❑ Insurance auditor
- ❑ Insurance claims agent
- ❑ Insurance consultant
- ❑ Insurance salesperson
- ❑ Interior designer
- ❑ Internet access provider
- ❑ Internet consultant
- ❑ Internet game designer
- ❑ Interpreter, deaf
- ❑ Interpreter, multilingual
- ❑ Inventor
- ❑ Investigator, private

❑ Investigator, unspecified
❑ Investor, unspecified

J

❑ Jeweler
❑ Job development specialist
❑ Job search coach
❑ Journalist
❑ Judge
❑ Juggler

K

❑ Kennel employee
❑ Kennel owner
❑ Kitchen designer
❑ Kitchen equipment manufacturer
❑ Kitchen supervisor
❑ Kosher deli owner

L

❑ Labor advocate
❑ Laboratory assistant
❑ Laboratory technician
❑ Laborer, unspecified
❑ Landscape architect
❑ Lawyer, unspecified
❑ Learning disabilities specialist
❑ Legal assistant
❑ Legislative assistant
❑ Legislator
❑ Librarian

❑ Library employee
❑ Life coach
❑ Lighting designer
❑ Lighting technician, film and media
❑ Limousine driver
❑ Liquor store owner
❑ Literary agent
❑ Literary critic
❑ Lithographer
❑ Livestock rancher
❑ Living trust expert
❑ Loan agent
❑ Locksmith
❑ Logger
❑ Logistics and planning engineer
❑ Logo designer
❑ Lumberyard owner

M

❑ Machinist
❑ Magazine editor
❑ Magazine publisher
❑ Mail carrier
❑ Maintenance and repair worker
❑ Maintenance technician
❑ Makeup artist, media
❑ Manager, production
❑ Manager, program
❑ Manager, project
❑ Manager, retail

- Manager, safety
- Manager, stage
- Manager, unspecified
- Manicurist
- Manufacturer, unspecified
- Mapmaker
- Marine biologist
- Marketing analyst
- Marketing and communi-
cations manager
- Marketing and communi-
cations specialist
- Marketing consultant
- Marketing director
- Martial arts instructor
- Massage therapist
- Mechanical engineer
- Mediator
- Medical assistant
- Medical transcriber
- Metallurgist
- Meteorologist
- Midwife
- Midwife assistant
- Military, unspecified
- Mime
- Ministorage facility manager
- Miniaturist, film and media
- Minister
- Ministore employee
- Ministore owner
- Mobile phone customer
service representative

- Mobile phone salesperson
- Model maker
- Model, artist's
- Model, high fashion
- Mortgage broker
- Mountaineering guide
- Mountaineering instructor
- Mounter, photos and
pictures
- Music producer
- Musician, unspecified

N

- Nanny
- Narrator
- Naturopathic physician
- Neon artist
- Neurologist
- Newscaster, radio and
television
- Newsletter publisher
- Newspaper columnist
- Newspaper editor
- Newspaper publisher
- Newsroom director
- Nighttime security guard
- Noise control consultant
- Notary public
- Nuclear scientist
- Nurse, certified aide
- Nurse, emergency
- Nurse, intensive care
- Nurse, licensed vocational

- Nurse, pediatric
- Nurse, psychiatric
- Nurse, registered
- Nurse, unspecified

O

- Occupational health officer
- Occupational therapist
- Oceanographer
- Office clerk
- Office employee, unspecified
- Office furniture designer
- Office machine technician
- Office manager
- Office supply store owner
- Oil producer
- Online customer service representative
- Opera singer
- Operator, machine, unspecified
- Ophthalmologist
- Optical engineer
- Optician
- Optometrist
- Optometrist assistant
- Oral surgeon
- Orchid grower
- Organizational development consultant
- Organizational psychologist
- Ornament maker

- Orthodontist
- Orthopedic surgeon
- Orthotics technician
- Osteopathic physician
- Outplacement consultant

P and Q

- Painter, buildings
- Painter, fine art
- Painter, interiors
- Painter, sets (theater, media)
- Painter, signs
- Palm reader
- Paralegal
- Parapsychologist
- Parasitologist
- Parole officer
- Parts clerk
- Pastor
- Pastry chef
- Patient's advocate
- Pattern maker
- Payroll clerk
- Pediatrician
- Perfume maker
- Pet store owner
- Petsitter
- Pharmacist
- Pharmacy assistant
- Photoengraver
- Photofinisher
- Photographer

- ❑ Photography store owner
- ❑ Physiatrist
- ❑ Physical therapist
- ❑ Physical therapy aide
- ❑ Physical therapy assistant
- ❑ Pipe fitter
- ❑ Plant store owner
- ❑ Plumber, unspecified
- ❑ Podiatrist
- ❑ Police officer
- ❑ Politician
- ❑ Pollution control technician
- ❑ Precision die maker
- ❑ Probation officer
- ❑ Production manager, film and television
- ❑ Production manager, industry
- ❑ Production supervisor, unspecified
- ❑ Professor, unspecified
- ❑ Project manager, industry
- ❑ Prop master, entertainment
- ❑ Property manager
- ❑ Property owner, multiple rentals
- ❑ Psychiatrist
- ❑ Psychic
- ❑ Psychoanalyst
- ❑ Psychologist, educational
- ❑ Psychologist, unspecified
- ❑ Psychopharmacologist
- ❑ Psychotherapist

- ❑ Public health counselor
- ❑ Public health officer
- ❑ Public servant

R

- ❑ Racer, professional
- ❑ Radio announcer
- ❑ Radio station manager
- ❑ Radio technician
- ❑ Radiological technician
- ❑ Radiologist
- ❑ Railroad worker, unspecified
- ❑ Rancher, unspecified
- ❑ Ranger, forest and parks
- ❑ Rape counselor
- ❑ Reader, script
- ❑ Real estate agent
- ❑ Real estate assistant
- ❑ Real estate broker
- ❑ Real estate investor
- ❑ Real estate, timeshares
- ❑ Record store clerk
- ❑ Record store manager
- ❑ Records clerk, law
- ❑ Records clerk, medical
- ❑ Records clerk, unspecified
- ❑ Recreation therapist
- ❑ Recruiter, college
- ❑ Recruiter, corporate
- ❑ Recruiter, executive
- ❑ Recruiter, military
- ❑ Recruiter, technical

- ❑ Referee, sports
- ❑ Registered nurse
- ❑ Registrar
- ❑ Rehabilitation counselor, unspecified
- ❑ Repairer, auto
- ❑ Repairer, unspecified
- ❑ Reporter, news and media
- ❑ Researcher, legal
- ❑ Researcher, marketing
- ❑ Researcher, medical
- ❑ Researcher, scientific
- ❑ Researcher, unspecified
- ❑ Resort groundskeeper
- ❑ Respiratory therapist
- ❑ Restaurant maitre d'
- ❑ Restaurant manager
- ❑ Restaurant owner
- ❑ Restorer, art and furniture
- ❑ Retail clerk, unspecified
- ❑ Retail store manager, unspecified
- ❑ Retail store owner, unspecified
- ❑ Roads and highway worker
- ❑ Rubber stamp maker

S

- ❑ Salesperson, unspecified
- ❑ Sales consultant
- ❑ Scene designer
- ❑ School administrator
- ❑ School principal

- ❑ School psychologist
- ❑ Scientist, unspecified
- ❑ Screenwriter
- ❑ Script supervisor, film and television
- ❑ Seamstress
- ❑ Security guard
- ❑ Seismologist
- ❑ Self-employed business owner
- ❑ Senior vice president
- ❑ Shipping and receiving
- ❑ Shoe repairperson
- ❑ Shopper, personal
- ❑ Shuttle driver
- ❑ Singer, opera
- ❑ Singer, pop
- ❑ Ski instructor
- ❑ Social director
- ❑ Social psychologist
- ❑ Social worker
- ❑ Sociobiologist
- ❑ Sociologist
- ❑ Software designer
- ❑ Software engineer
- ❑ Software postsales consultant
- ❑ Software presales consultant
- ❑ Songwriter
- ❑ Sound editor
- ❑ Sound mixer
- ❑ Sound, boom operator
- ❑ Sound, Foley artist
- ❑ Special effects engineer

- ❑ Staffing specialist
- ❑ Store manager
- ❑ Store owner
- ❑ Strategic marketing analyst
- ❑ Stunt performer
- ❑ Systems analyst

T

- ❑ Tailor
- ❑ Talk show host
- ❑ Tax return auditor
- ❑ Tax return preparer
- ❑ Team leader, unspecified
- ❑ Technical director, theater
- ❑ Technical director, television or film
- ❑ Technical instructor, unspecified
- ❑ Technician, unspecified
- ❑ Telecommunications expert
- ❑ Theologian
- ❑ Tour operator
- ❑ Tractor operator
- ❑ Trainer, unspecified
- ❑ Travel agent
- ❑ Travel writer
- ❑ Tree trimming business owner
- ❑ Truck driver

U

- ❑ Umpire
- ❑ Underwater researcher
- ❑ Undertaker

- ❑ Underwriter
- ❑ Usher

V

- ❑ Vendor
- ❑ Veterinarian
- ❑ Veterinary assistant
- ❑ Vice chancellor
- ❑ Vice president, unspecified
- ❑ Visual effects engineer
- ❑ Voice teacher
- ❑ Voice-over artist

W

- ❑ Waiter or waitress
- ❑ Warehouse supervisor
- ❑ Watchmaker or watch repairer
- ❑ Water aerobics instructor
- ❑ Wedding consultant
- ❑ Welder
- ❑ Wildlife expert
- ❑ Woodworker

Y

- ❑ Youth activities coordinator
- ❑ Youth drug and alcohol counselor
- ❑ Youth social worker

Z

- ❑ Zookeeper
- ❑ Zoologist

Great! Now write your ten top job titles (or titles you added to the above list) here:

1. _____
2. _____
3. _____
4. _____
5. _____
6. _____
7. _____
8. _____
9. _____
10. _____

In the next chapter, you will take the next step and get a detailed view of each of these careers. We're going to do exercises that will give you a feel for the careers you just listed and what it would be like to be doing them.

You'll have the chance to find out the duties, working conditions, qualifications, opportunities, salaries, and more of the ten jobs you've picked so that, as you narrow down the list to just one career, you are more informed.

You'll also have a chance to imagine yourself (from morning to night) actually doing that job for a day and seeing how it might fit into your entire lifestyle. Most people don't want a job, however rewarding, that consumes their entire life to the exclusion of their health, recreational, spiritual, or family life. Considering other parts of your life in the exercises we're going to do will help you put your new career in perspective and make sure that it's a good fit with your personal life and non–work related goals.

CHAPTER 3

Testing the Waters

You may have found the exercises in the previous chapter challenging. But you completed them, and you should be proud that you've taken those brave steps because there are very few people who take the time to think about what makes them unique. You now have a list of ten potential jobs that are ideal for you. That means that you're equipped with the knowledge that will help you make a career choice that will be inspiring. Now that you've made the effort to find your talents and your top ten favorite potential occupations, we're going to see which of those occupations will best suit your needs.

What do I mean by "needs"? All of us have needs for self-expression, economic security, career/life balance, stimulation, relaxation, contribution, and more. It's essential to gauge whether or not, and to what degree, those needs are going to be fulfilled in your occupation so that you're going to truly love what you do.

To determine this, we're going to complete four active exercises together that will help you build a sense of whether or not the job described by that title is *really* right for you.

> **Some of the exercises involve reading and writing while others invite you to actually do or imagine something.**

The four activities are methods of gathering information about you and the job you want. For some, the thought of gathering information may seem daunting or even boring, but I promise it will be fun *and* enlightening.

1. Career Options Research
2. Your Ideal Work-Life Day
3. Your Transferable Skills and Satisfiers Grid
4. The Long View

Exercise 1. Career Options Research

There are two reliable and up-to-date sources you can use to delve into the details about the ten job titles you've selected. I know of absolutely no better resources for researching careers than these databases to give you a fleshed-out picture of what a particular job might really be like in the real world.

The first source is the O*NET, which is an interactive database that can be found on the Internet and that can be used by anyone at no cost. It is compiled and continually updated by the U.S. Department of Labor. It is an absolutely invaluable tool for career changers because you can search for a job not only by its title but also by its industry and/or the skills needed to do it. You can also explore the fastest-growing jobs, highest-paying jobs, wage and industry trends, and much more on this site. No other source has better quantitative or qualitative information about occupations than this. This gold mine of information can be found at http://online.onetcenter.org.

The second excellent source of information about a wide variety of vocations is the *Occupational Outlook Handbook (OOH)*, which can be found in printed form at your local library, at a college, or community career center. It is published in book form by the U.S. Bureau of Labor Statistics. Basically, it contains much the same information as does the O*NET. Its advantage is that if you don't have access to the Internet for the O*NET, you can find the *OOH* at the library. It's also available on the Internet at no cost at http://www.bls.gov/oco.

Look up each of your ten career choices on the O*NET and in the *Occupational Outlook Handbook* and take notes that you can refer to later. You're going to be using this information in the rest of this chapter, so pick out what seems important to you and have it readily at hand.

By entering a job title you're interested in, you will find the following:

- A definition of the job and explanation of the responsibilities it entails, down to the smallest details of what the job requires.
- Listings of jobs that are closely related to the title you enter, so that if that occupation isn't right for you, you can view another similar one that may be.
- The usual education, skills, and experience required for breaking into the job.
- Work environments and working conditions.
- Professional organizations that have more information about the occupation.
- Career paths (how one would advance in the career).
- The labor market prospects (the relative ease of breaking in to that position).
- Average range of earnings in the United States. Figures for these salary amounts and forecasts are taken from the Bureau of Labor Statistics. Tabulations for both state and national averages are available.
- A forecast of the job's continuing popularity in the future.
- Work values. (I call these *satisfiers* and we'll be covering this essential component of job satisfaction later in this chapter.)

Because having a concrete understanding of what a specific job is like is crucial to knowing how well you'll like it, plan to take a good chunk of your time to really plumb the depths of data on the O*NET.

The O*NET and the *Occupational Outlook Handbook* may not be an *exact* mirror image of you, the job, the requirements, *or* the salary. Instead, they provide a general picture of what the job might really be like. For example, the description may say that a master's degree is *required*, when in fact it is only *preferred*.

Your reference librarian may be able to guide you to other periodicals that cover job market details and salary information calculated for your particular geographic area, usually by county.

After reading carefully about the ten career choices you selected in the last chapter, analyze what you've read, see how it all stacks up, and check with your gut feelings about each profession. As you explore the jobs in the O*NET or the *OOH*, keep asking yourself the question:

To what extent would this occupation allow me to express my authentic calling?

Please take a moment to reflect on and rank each career according to the following criterion: If a career will completely suit your calling, rank it 10. If it is at the bottom of the scale and will not at all fit with your calling, rank it 1.

Career Choice	*Lowest*	*Highest*
1. _____	1 2 3 4 5 6 7 8 9 10	
2. _____	1 2 3 4 5 6 7 8 9 10	
3. _____	1 2 3 4 5 6 7 8 9 10	
4. _____	1 2 3 4 5 6 7 8 9 10	
5. _____	1 2 3 4 5 6 7 8 9 10	
6. _____	1 2 3 4 5 6 7 8 9 10	
7. _____	1 2 3 4 5 6 7 8 9 10	

Career Choice	Lowest	Highest
8. _____	1 2 3 4 5 6 7 8 9 10	
9. _____	1 2 3 4 5 6 7 8 9 10	
10. _____	1 2 3 4 5 6 7 8 9 10	

The next step requires you to make a tough choice. Based on the research you've done so far and the list you've compiled above, select just three job titles that sound best to you. If you know of a job title like "pilates instructor" that is not listed in either database, include it as one of your three choices.

1. _____
2. _____
3. _____

Excellent! We'll be exploring these three careers—and how you feel about them—in depth for the rest of this chapter.

Exercise 2. Your Ideal Work-Life Day

By now you should have a more fleshed-out model of your three job titles. Now it's time to use your imagination to try to understand what these three jobs would be like. For each of the job titles you're exploring, write what a day would be like if you were *really* doing that profession.

On a piece of notebook paper or your computer, describe it in as much detail as possible, using all five senses, from the moment you wake up in the morning to the moment you lay your head down to sleep. Make the day as realistic as possible.

Realistically, who is there when you wake up? What do your bed sheets feel like? What do your bedroom, bathroom, and kitchen look like? What sort of clothes do you put on—sweatpants and a T-shirt, some kind of uniform, jeans and a blazer, or a designer label three-piece suit or dress? What is your jewelry, if any, like? Do you need makeup or not? Do you leave the house or stay in your home to work? Are any children around that you have to get off to school? Do you have a maid or cook? Is a spouse, significant other, or roommate also getting ready for work?

How do you get to work? What kind of car do you drive? Do you have a chauffeur? Is your vehicle racy or practical, an SUV, an economy, or a luxury car? What color is it? How far away, ideally, is your workplace from where you live? Do you work at home? If not, how long is the commute to work? What are you thinking about as you transport yourself to your job? Are you on a train, bus, or subway, or are you walking or riding a bike? Are you listening to music, news, books on tape, learning a foreign language while commuting perhaps, or listening to motivational tapes?

Who is there when you get to work? How do they treat you? Can you imagine something they might say? Are you alone? If not, what is the quality of the interaction between you and others? Do you feel respected, valued, liked, or loved? Imagine what you might be saying to the others. How does your boss, if you have one, interact with you? Are you the boss?

What is the mood? Is it serious or light? Exciting or serene? Chaotic or orderly? Harmonious or tense? Do you feel this company has a sense of integrity? Is is honest? Does it care about its employees? Does it act in a morally upstanding way? Would you feel proud to say you work there? How do you feel about yourself when you are at your place of work doing what you'd ideally like to be doing?

Do you have an office, a cubicle, a workstation, or are you working outdoors? What, exactly, are you doing? Are you primarily using your intellect, your body, your intuition, your emotions, or some combination of all of them?

What do you love about what you are doing? Are you using your gifts? Are you the head of the company, or might you be self-employed? If the company has a hierarchy, where are you on the ladder?

What, exactly, does your place of work look like? Are you in a small, medium, or large company? Does your job require travel? If so, where? Are you in an executive office, at a factory, in a laboratory, at a school, on a movie set, at a hospital, in an airplane, a retail store, or out of doors? Do you work from a car most of the day?

Is your workload heavy, moderate, or light? How many hours do you work in your day? Do you have routine hours and deadlines or flexible time to work at your own pace?

Is it a standard nine-to-five day, or do you work fewer, different, or more hours? Do you see yourself working at night and/or on call or on the weekends?

What do you most enjoy about this scene? What do you think or feel about yourself as you imagine yourself in this day?

Write a realistic day in your ideal career in as much detail as possible, noticing the feelings and thoughts inside you as well as imagining the environment around you.

Continue in this manner until your workday is over and you return home. What time do you get home, or what time do you stop working? Are you working overtime? How is the commute home? What do you do in the evenings after work and with whom?

How much money do you make in this career? Do you have a comfortable or exorbitant amount of money to spend and invest, or do you have to stay on a more limited budget?

Do you have time for leisure activities? Do you have the energy to run errands or spend some time beautifying your garden? Is there time for a lunch out with a friend, some golf at the driving range, or a game of tennis or racquetball? How about time to go to the gym during lunch or after work? Can you get together with friends at the end of a long day for dinner or drinks? Do you have time to take care of your body and your social and spiritual life? Do you bring work home with you?

With this particular career as part of your day, how do you end your day? Do you share intimacy with someone you love? Do you need to get your children to bed? Do you fall to sleep reading, watching TV, or doing a crossword puzzle? Do you write in a journal or diary?

Maybe you make a list of your goals for the next day or read a good book and end your evening with prayer, contemplation, or meditation. At the end of the evening, do you feel "full" or "empty"?

What time do you go to bed? What thoughts do you have in your mind about your ideal workday as a _____? What feelings do you have about your life and yourself as you reflect back on your day?

Now please write two more realistic days for your other job titles, using the same attention to detail.

When you're finished, you'll have a good idea as to how your three career selections might fit into your everyday life. You'll also have a taste of how your work, home, social, financial, and recreational lifestyle might unfold with each career.

Take a minute and write your notes and observations about each career.

Career 1

_____

_____

_____

Career 2

_____

_____

_____

Career 3

_____

_____

_____

Exercise 3. Your Transferable Skills and Satisfiers Grid

The next key step in creating your career fingerprint is to match your new career to your gifts, transferable skills, and satisfiers. You are unique, and so are your personal preferences. You'll learn about each through the different steps of this exercise.

Transferable Skills

The first part of this exercise focuses on transferable skills. A *transferable skill* is a skill that can transfer from one job to another. In other words, these are skills you use at your current job that will transfer to whatever profession you choose next. Managing, organizing, and communicating are some of the most common transferable skills because they can be used in such a wide variety of industries and occupations.

Office managers, financial planners, entrepreneurs, and logistics directors are examples of just a few of the careers that entail organizational, management, and communication skills. Although the jobs seem quite different at face value, they share a core group of skills.

Understanding your transferable skills will make it easier for you to change occupations. Your skills go with you. In the next chapter, you'll learn how and why transferable skills are going to be one of the main strategies you'll be using to change careers. For now, focus on learning what your transferable skills are.

This exercise has three steps:

1. On the following list make a checkmark to the left of any of the transferable skills that you already possess, to whatever degree you know how to do them (you don't have to be an expert).

2. Then go back through the list and circle the skills you'd actually like to use in the future. It's okay to circle either checked or unchecked items.

3. Finally, pick six of the circled skills (they don't have to have a checkmark) that you'd really like to use in your next job. Go for it!

Transferable Skills Checklist

- ❑ Acting
- ❑ Advertising
- ❑ Advising
- ❑ Aiding

❑ Analyzing
❑ Arranging
❑ Assessing performance
❑ Assessing progress
❑ Assessing quality
❑ Assisting
❑ Attending to detail
❑ Auditing
❑ Budgeting
❑ Building cooperation
❑ Building credibility
❑ Building relationships
❑ Building structures
❑ Calculating
❑ Classifying
❑ Client relations
❑ Coaching
❑ Communicating feelings
❑ Communicating ideas
❑ Communicating in writing
❑ Communicating instructions
❑ Communicating nonverbally
❑ Communicating verbally
❑ Computer literate
❑ Conceptualizing
❑ Consulting
❑ Coordinating
❑ Correcting
❑ Corresponding
❑ Counseling

❑ Customer service
❑ Dancing
❑ Data analysis
❑ Data entry
❑ Data processing
❑ Decision making
❑ Decorating
❑ Delegating
❑ Designing
❑ Developing designs
❑ Developing systems
❑ Developing talent
❑ Diagnosing
❑ Directing
❑ Drafting
❑ Drawing
❑ Driving
❑ Editing
❑ Educating
❑ Empathizing
❑ Enforcing
❑ Engineering
❑ Evaluating
❑ Facilitating
❑ Filing
❑ Financial planning
❑ Forecasting
❑ Formulating
❑ Fund raising
❑ Healing
❑ Helping others

- ❏ Imagining
- ❏ Implementing
- ❏ Influencing
- ❏ Initiating
- ❏ Intervening
- ❏ Intuiting
- ❏ Inventing
- ❏ Investigating
- ❏ Leading people
- ❏ Lecturing
- ❏ Lifting
- ❏ Listening
- ❏ Managing tasks
- ❏ Marketing
- ❏ Marketing and communications
- ❏ Massaging
- ❏ Motivating
- ❏ Multitasking
- ❏ Negotiating
- ❏ Nurturing
- ❏ Observing
- ❏ Organizing
- ❏ Performing
- ❏ Persuading
- ❏ Prescribing
- ❏ Program managing
- ❏ Programming computers

- ❏ Project managing
- ❏ Promoting
- ❏ Public speaking
- ❏ Reconstructing
- ❏ Recording
- ❏ Repairing
- ❏ Reporting
- ❏ Researching
- ❏ Selling and marketing
- ❏ Selling
- ❏ Servicing
- ❏ Servicing customers
- ❏ Singing
- ❏ Supervising
- ❏ Surveying
- ❏ Teaching
- ❏ Team building
- ❏ Team leading
- ❏ Telephone skills
- ❏ Tending
- ❏ Testing
- ❏ Tooling
- ❏ Training
- ❏ Troubleshooting
- ❏ Understanding
- ❏ Using equipment
- ❏ Writing

My six preferred skills that I'd like to use in the future are:

1. _____

2. _____

3. _____

4. _____

5. _____

6. _____

We'll use this list in conjunction with the next part of this exercise, which is deciding other important career choice factors, which I call your *satisfiers*—that is, the aspects of a job that make it emotionally appealing.

Below is a list of satisfiers. You may find that many or all of these things are important to you; however, I'd like you to carefully focus on the meaning of each of these satisfiers and how they will affect your life *both* in and out of the work setting.

Each of them may sound appealing; however, in this assignment your task is to reflect on which six are the *most* important to you and are the satisfiers that you'd like to have in your next career.

Which of these satisfiers rate as your top six? (Please circle only your top six satisfiers.)

1. A company that is charitable to the community
2. A job that will accommodate my disability
3. A wide range of benefits and/or perks
4. Ample promotion opportunities
5. Beautiful and pleasing surroundings
6. Challenging responsibilities
7. Easy commute
8. Emotional fulfillment
9. Excitement
10. Flexible hours
11. Extremely high income
12. Friendly and respectful colleagues
13. Independence

14. Intellectual challenge
15. Lots of leisure time with family, friends, hobbies, and travel
16. Low stress
17. Possibility for very high earnings and/or commissions and bonuses
18. Power, influence, and authority
19. Routine
20. Spiritual satisfaction
21. Steady income

My top six satisfiers:

1. _____
2. _____
3. _____
4. _____
5. _____
6. _____

The Transferable Skills and Satisfiers Grid

In the next step in this exercise, you'll combine the information you have gathered so far. It's called the "transferable skills and satisfiers grid." I have adapted it from the work of Howard Figler in the *Complete Job Search Handbook.*

This assignment is exciting because it synthesizes the qualitative information we've gathered in this and the previous chapter and provides a subjective but quantitative look at how the pieces of your career puzzle fit together.

Finally, you'll have information that can influence your choice of one career over the other two, and a starting point to put everything you've learned into action in the following chapters.

1. Make a chart that looks like the one that follows. List your three job titles at the top of the chart. Number the jobs 1, 2, and 3 not in any particular order of preference.

	Job 1	Job 2	Job 3
SKILLS			
Skill 1			
Skill 2			
Skill 3			
Skill 4			
Skill 5			
Skill 6			
SATISFIERS			
Satisfier 1			
Satisfier 2			
Satisfier 3			
Satisfier 4			
Satisfier 5			
Satisfier 6			
GIFTS			
Gift			
Gift			
Gift			
Subtotal			
INTUITION			
TOTAL			

2. Then list all six of your preferred skills from top to bottom.

3. Next list your six satisfiers.

4. For each of your preferred skills (for example, management), ask yourself, "How well will job 1 satisfy my desire to be a manager?" If it will provide you with an opportunity to be a manager, put a checkmark in the corresponding box. If not, leave it blank.

5. Repeat the same question for each of the other two jobs.

6. Continue using the same methods for all of your skills and satisfiers. For example, "Will job 2 satisfy my need for economic security? Prestige?"

7. Each column should now have several checkmarks. The last step is to look at your gifts.

Because I believe that using your gifts in your career will make you absolutely soar, I'm going to ask that you rate "gifts" on a scale of 1 to 100 for each of the three jobs—for example, "How well will job 1 allow me to express my gifts?" If you have more than one gift, also list them on the chart and rank them from 1 to 100.

---

8. Now, add all of the checkmarks that appear vertically under job 1 and write your total.

9. Do the same as in step 8 for the other two jobs.

We're not quite finished yet, but stop and take a minute to observe how the totals look. Is one job way ahead? Do others lag behind? Do two or all three have nearly identical scores?

Now, for a final, and most important, indicator, you'll be using your intuition to help you rate these jobs. Please rank each occupation on your chart in terms of your intuitive feeling, from 1 to 100. Again, 100 would mean something like "absolutely fantastic," and 1 would be "horrifying."

What does "intuitive feeling" mean? To some, it may literally be a feeling in the gut, chest, or stomach. Others internally sense some sort of feeling of right or wrong. Others may feel that one choice is simply more clear or rings more true.

This exercise allows you to observe a lot of information at once. Carefully reflect on it. The numbers themselves do not have to decide your career for you, but they are a good indicator of how well you believe a certain occupation will fulfill many of your needs. The chart is only a tool. You must base your decision on what seems best to you. After all, it will be you doing the job, not someone else—not your parents, your spouse, your friend, or me.

Exercise 4. The Long View

Imagine you are near the end of your life, and you are very, very old. As you look back you can see yourself clearly just as you are right now, in the midst of radically changing your course in life. Assume that you have amassed a great deal of wisdom as a result of having a wide array of life experiences—knowledge about yourself, other people, and the way the world works.

Assume also that as you look back at yourself from what I call "the long view," you feel an overwhelming degree of love and compassion for yourself. You may no longer be interested in some of the outer trappings of life—how shiny your new car was, how big your house was, or whether you wore the latest fashions.

With this frame of mind, answer the following questions: *What career would I pick if I were looking with wisdom from the long view? What will make me happy? What can I look back at with a deep sense of pride and sacredness? What career will give me what I really want, deep down inside?*

Enter your discovery here:

_____

_____

_____

Congratulations! You've created your career fingerprint. Whatever career title you chose will be the one that we will use for the rest of the book as you work to quickly change careers. Now you'll see how all of the objective data and self-knowledge you've gathered can be put into *action*, and *fast!*

My No. 1 preferred career is _____.

CHAPTER 4

Eight Fast-Track Strategies for Successful Career Changers

This chapter will introduce you to eight strategies to move you from where you are now to where you want to go. Used one at a time or in combination, these proven strategies will put you on the launching pad for a new career within a few months. Coupled with the goal-setting methods in Chapter 7 and the accelerated job search techniques in Chapter 8, you'll be landed in a new job in less time than you can imagine.

People around the globe have been making swift career changes for years. So . . . just how is it done? I've done extensive firsthand research on some of the most useful actions other people have used to realize rapid career transitions, which I will pass on to you. These strategies, all based on real success stories, are the ones we'll introduce in this chapter and expand upon further in Chapter 6.

Yes, there may be more than eight strategies for career change. Some people inherit a family business or get a foot in the door to a new industry because they already have a friend in that field. Probably the most common model of career change holds that a person must go back to school or receive lengthy training in order to meet the demands of a new position. This is not the method of choice with Fearless Career Change! Of course, if you're aimed at a job that requires by law or by custom that you obtain a long-term advanced degree like an associate's, bachelor's, master's, or doctorate, you may find it more helpful to skip to Chapter 7, where you can begin setting goals for your new career.

> *For those of you who want to get on the fast track, we're going to hone in on the strategies the majority of my clients have found to be the most successful.*

The eight fearless career change strategies (one or more of which I'd like you to apply) are these:

1. Transferable talents
2. Strategic education
3. On-the-job training
4. Internship
5. Short-term education (90 days or less)
6. Volunteering
7. Just dive in!
8. Entrepreneurship

Strategy 1. Transferable Talents

A *transferable talent*, as we talked about in previous chapters, is an ability or abilities that can be used in disparate fields. Just as "communication" is a talent that can be used if you're a shoe designer, cashier, or biochemist, a transferable talent is something you can take with you as you move from career to career.

As you will see in the following chapters, a wide range of transferable talents can be used to pave the way to your new career, even if it is an entirely different field or occupation. For example, Miguel used his transferable talent of being facile with numbers when he went from being a mechanical engineer to a personal financial planner. Both fields demand some degree of mathematical talent and experience. The talent of *analysis* could be used in different contexts by a software programmer, doctor, businessperson, or sound engineer.

> **A multitude of talents are transferable. You might possess several of them without even knowing it. For example, are you a good listener and also good at solving complex problems? These are both talents that can be used in many jobs.**

Which of Your Skills Might Transfer to Your Dream Career?

Go back to the list entitled "transferable skills," which you completed in the last chapter. Carefully consider how your top six skills might transfer into abilities you might be able to use in your ideal career. Then, take a look at some of the other skills on the list. Do any of them apply to the career you're headed for?

Don't take anything for granted. You might overlook skills like reading, writing, listening, or empathizing, but, after all, people actually do get *paid* to do just those things that, at first glance, seem very ordinary.

> **Your transferable skills do not just come from your work life.**

Is your sock drawer so neat (even color coded) that some people, if they had access to your sock drawer, might think you're just a little bit "nuts"? It's likely that your skill of being organized could carry over into your authentic calling.

Are you always the friend who offers a shoulder to cry on? Your dream career may utilize these skills: listening, building rapport, empathizing, nurturing, or even giving advice.

Did you ever design a room in your home, draw a map, or compose photographs? Your spatial, coordination, and design skills might be used in scores of different contexts.

Even if the career of your dreams seems to have nothing to do with your last job, transferable skills from your social life, a hobby, schooling, intellectual, or artistic or spiritual pursuits may catapult you into something new and different in your work life.

Some talent that was buried may surface and translate or transfer to a real job in the real world. Sometimes just one skill is needed to bridge the gap to your new pursuit.

Take a moment and think creatively about how one or more of the six preferred skills in the last chapter may be the ones you can rely on or expand upon in a new vocation. If none of the six you picked seem applicable, find one to three others on the list that are applicable and do the following brief exercise.

Skills I can do and that I like, which could be used in my next career are:

1. _____
2. _____
3. _____

Strategy 2. Strategic Education

Strategic education means enrolling in one or more courses in a certificate or degree program and beginning a new job *before* completing the program or simply not completing the degree at all.

For example, Nancy used a wide range of strategies to break into the publishing field. One of those was what I call "strategic education." She enrolled in a copyediting course at a local community college to pick up some new knowledge required in her new field, and before she finished it, a book publishing company hired her.

Community (two-year) colleges do not have complex registration and application procedures. It's just about as convenient for someone who already has another advanced degree to pick up a couple of classes for general interest as it is for someone just getting out of high school to register and declare a major in order to complete an associate's degree.

These colleges are extremely affordable and offer opportunities for young and mature people alike to take one or two classes to brush up on their skills or to earn a certificate in a particular subject like Web design, real estate, physical therapy assistance, marketing, computer networking, computer programming, or early childhood education. These schools also offer two-year associate's (AA or AS) degrees in academic disciplines like psychology, biology, foreign languages, theater and television arts, and art history.

Sometimes their catalogs are sent to households in the areas they serve, or they can be found at places that have other free weekly newspapers and magazines. Otherwise, you can get a hard copy of their semester-long offerings by personally visiting the registrar's office on campus or accessing an electronic catalog online.

As with most education, training, and even seminars that pertain directly to a new or existing business you operate, many costs for education can be deducted from your taxes. It is best to ask your tax professional which courses and programs would be eligible for such a write-off.

> **The technique of strategic education can also be used to get a promotion within the company you already work for.**

It may be that, instead of making a sweeping change to another career altogether, getting a promotion or a new title in the company you already work for will satisfy your needs. Rodrigo, and many other clients I've coached, got promotions just a few weeks after beginning just *one* course in a master's program.

> **With the benefit of strategic education, you won't have to wait for years to receive a raise and a new title!**

Some people who return to school with the intention of completing a degree see their employers reimburse them later for as much as 50 percent of their tuition. You might find that enrolling in just one course is all that your boss needs to see to be convinced that you're really motivated, ambitious, and determined to master new skills.

Discussing Tuition Reimbursement with Your Boss

If your employer is going to take on part of or all of the expense for your tuition, he or she will want to know whether he or she is making a good investment. Be prepared to show brochures and computer printouts of the typical curriculum from several programs in your area, and plan a discussion with your boss so that he or she feels included in the decision-making process.

It's up to you to make a case for the value, both financially and professionally, of what you'll be gaining by returning to school and in what precise way that will benefit your organization.

Your employer will be much more likely to buy into your course of action if he or she is allowed to bear some of the responsibility of making the decision. Set aside some specially appointed time with your boss to meet and talk about your plans.

To set up a meeting, you might say something like this:

> I've been thinking about pursuing some advanced studies that would *make me more valuable* to our company. I have gathered literature on several of the best programs, and I'd like to have your opinion about them. When can we set up a brief meeting to talk about it?

You can also ask the human resources department whether your company already has a tuition reimbursement program in place. (Many companies do.) If you're working for a smaller company or one without formal tuition reimbursement perks, you might convince your employer to chip in by saying something like this:

> I'd really like to be able to *contribute* more knowledge and take on more *responsibilities* at work. Would you consider covering a percentage of my fees for an advanced degree if I could guarantee that, *in the long run,* my new expertise and training would *save the company money and increase profits?*

You must be creative in thinking about the *concrete* ways that obtaining additional training will affect the employer's *bottom line.* The best way for you to persuade your employer to support your decision to upgrade your education and take a financial interest in assisting you is to *place yourself in your employer's shoes* and ask yourself what changes or improvements in the company would be meaningful from his or her point of view.

For virtually every business, the bottom line has something to do, directly or indirectly, with *making the company profitable and successful.* Think about the following ways you might be able to impact the bottom line at your company:

- Creating or improving products or services that will draw additional revenues for the company
- Helping the company *save time* or money
- Improving the reputation, visibility, and credibility of the company to the public and its customers
- Making a measurable contribution to improving worker morale and productivity
- Decreasing waste, inefficiency, accidents, and downtime
- Troubleshooting problems more effectively and efficiently
- Becoming part of a management team
- Helping the company beat the competition

All of the results listed above impact the company's profits in one way or another. When you save time, you also save money. When the company has a more visible presence in the community, it attracts more consumers. If you can improve production or services, you will not only increase customer satisfaction but you may also be able to charge more for those items—again, generating more profits for the business.

When you help your boss connect your proposed educational choice to the kinds of changes or activities that increase revenue, he or she is much more likely to support your decision to seek additional education and quite possibly will supplement your tuition costs.

Present your proposal to receive funding from the company just as you would a formal business presentation. The use of colorful literature from colleges and universities, measurable estimates of the future improvements you expect to make, and the use of visual aids such as charts, graphs, or even simple drawings will all help the employer imagine the possibilities that lay in store for the company if you receive money for additional training.

Strategy 3. On-the-Job Training

On-the-job training usually means that you are paid an entry-level salary (or, in some cases, less) for a limited amount of time while you are learning a new profession or trade.

For example, when Scott went from being a customer service representative for a health insurance company to a film and television set dresser, he used the strategy of paid on-the-job training, among others, to facilitate his transition. We'll take a look at exactly how Scott positioned himself to receive this training in the next chapter, as well as examine how other people have used on-the-job training to break into and learn a new occupation.

Some examples of industries that offer on-the-job training are trades (construction, bricklaying, plumbing, manufacturing), fashion, film and television, financial and brokerage firms, all forms of sales, administrative and office work, manufacturing, health and human services, community activism, nonprofit organizations, cooking and fine cuisine, food and beverage, real estate, tourism, travel and cruises, and organizations involved in civic or global environmental, political, health, and education concerns.

One could almost argue that every job involves some sort of on-the-job training, at least enough to get oriented to a new environment, but the industries listed above are the ones most likely to accept inexperienced mature career changers from other fields or students looking for a first-time job.

If you want to find out about businesses that do on-the-job training, it's best to get in touch with an owner or manager of a business and simply ask if he or she, hypothetically, is willing to provide training for a person with little or no experience who also possesses some assets (for example, good problem-solving skills, flexibility, 3.5 grade point average, or a certificate or degree) or any other educational, personal, or professional background that is in your favor. Be careful that the on-the-job training pays you a wage you can live on until you step up to a regular salary.

Be careful: There may be some companies that will try to take advantage of your "trainee" status by extending your training for longer than needed or paying you far less than is reasonable.

For example, a training period that lasts more than a year while paying minimum wage is really not equitable. A two-week to six-month training period with clearly delineated responsibilities, expectations, and supervision and that pays somewhere just about or substantially above minimum wage is a much more reasonable exchange.

When a company offers you on-the-job training, ask who your supervisor will be and what you can expect to learn during the paid training period. Don't let the company use your talents unsupervised and pay you less than it pays other workers to do the same tasks any employee might routinely perform.

Consider asking for an informal written agreement with the employer that states what "milestones" you must master before becoming a full-fledged employee paid at a standard wage.

The agreement can state both what is expected of you as the trainee and what is expected from the employer. It should also clearly state the name or names of your supervisor(s) and the manner in which you will be evaluated at the end of the training period.

More about how, precisely, to target the companies with which you want to form an on-the-job training program and how to get in touch with an owner or manager is outlined in Chapter 8 under the heading "direct contact."

Strategy 4. Internship

An *internship* (sometimes paid and sometimes unpaid) trades the intern's labor and talent in exchange for his or her learning or advancing in a new occupation. Are internships only for students, right out of high school or college? Absolutely not. I've known people well into their mature years who take advantage of internships. I sought out an internship in career counseling with a government agency in Santa Cruz, California, when I was just starting out as a career coach.

I called the agency, asked for the manager of the career counseling staff, and asked whether or not they had an internship program. After I told her a little bit about myself, she said I could join in on a four-month program in which I would lead workshops for unemployed people. It was an invaluable experience, and though *I didn't receive a lot of formal training*, I got loads of *experience* helping people solve their employment problems to add to my résumé. Just as important, I left with a terrific letter of recommendation on official county government letterhead.

Whether you're volunteering or doing an internship, be sure to ask your employer (usually your immediate supervisor) if he or she would be kind enough to write a recommendation letter. It will benefit you for many years to come.

Some will say they don't know what to write but would be willing to edit and sign a letter that you write for yourself. This is no time to be modest. Write yourself a stellar letter fit for framing! After all, you've done the work for free.

Han was well into midlife when she sought a certificate in dog obedience training and then completed an internship with a more experienced dog trainer. To set up her internship, she contacted several trainers in her area and told them she had just received a certificate in animal behavior and that she wanted to continue to study her craft under a more seasoned professional.

One of the trainers agreed to let her observe and participate in a "puppy obedience" class. She was able to get a letter of recommendation from the trainer, which she now shows to clients seeking assistance with their pets.

Here is a short list of industries that widely accept, and sometimes even depend upon, internships:

- Agriculture
- Animal behavior
- Archaeology
- Counseling
- Dance and art therapy
- Environmental planning and preservation
- Fashion

Name and Title of Supervisor
Name of Business
Business Address
Phone/Fax
E-mail

To whom it may concern: June 6, 20xx

    It is with pleasure that I write this letter of recommendation for Carl Springer, who was a marketing intern at our firm for two months in spring of 20xx. Mr. Springer performed many of the duties of a regular staff member such as attending staff meetings, working on assignments, and sitting in on presentations to clients. It was with great professionalism, intelligence, and dedication that Mr. Springer took it upon himself to write several pages of new content for our company Web site that are now incorporated into our site.

    Although my firm doesn't currently have an opening for a new staff member, I would certainly not hesitate to hire Mr. Springer immediately if it did. In the short time that Mr. Springer was with us, he added a great deal of enthusiasm, team spirit, and innovative marketing ideas. I would highly recommend Mr. Springer to any company seeking a sharp and creative marketing professional.

    If you have any questions about Mr. Springer's performance as an intern here at our firm, please feel free to contact me.

Sincerely,

Signature of Supervisor   **(This is mandatory)**
Typed Name and Title of Supervisor

Sample Letter of Recommendation

- Fashion design
- Film and television production
- Geriatrics
- High technology
- Manufacturing

- Marine biology
- Mental health services
- Museums
- Printing
- Publishing
- Theater arts

The most valuable resource I can recommend on internship is Mark Oldman's book *Best 109 Internships*, in which he lists scores of companies from the nonprofit, profit, and government sectors.* The list includes such Fortune 500 giants as Hewlett-Packard, Procter and Gamble, and Microsoft as well as unexpected offerings such as MTV, NASA, the CIA, American Conservatory Theater, and even *Rolling Stone* magazine.

The author also indicates that his research shows that 80 percent of companies that hire interns also *pay them well*, even as much as $800 per week.

> **There are ways to maximize the potential of your internship to lead you right into a job, which we'll discuss in Chapter 5.**

Strategy 5. Short-Term Education

Short-term education, as I define it, is completing a prescribed program of training in a formal or semiformal setting (such as a school, college, or professional organization) that lasts for 90 days or less.

One of my clients, Carol, made the dive from administrative assistant to midwife assistant in only a few weeks using the strategy of short-term education. Before she received her training, she performed what I call *labor market readiness research*. She called ten potential employers—midwives, birthing centers, obstetricians—and

---

*Mark Oldman, with Samer Hamdeh, *The Best 109 Internships*, 9th ed., Princeton Review/Random House, New York, 2003.

made sure that the school she had chosen was recognized in the industry, and in her geographic area in particular.

It would be a shame to waste hundreds of dollars, not to mention your time, on a school that did not have a good reputation among employers. The goal of your training is to prepare you to succeed in your new vocation financially as well as professionally.

> ***Labor market readiness research will give you an idea of how willing employers in your area are to hire graduates of your chosen short-term program.***

Steps for Finding Appropriate Short-Term Training Programs

1. Search your local phone company business directory under *schools, training, vocational schools, colleges,* and *universities,* and call the ones that sound appropriate.

   Most community colleges (sometimes called *junior colleges*) have very good short-term certificate programs. Similarly, you will find excellent (and a bit more expensive) certificate programs at university extension and adult education centers.

   If you're unsure about colleges and universities in your area, go to your local library and ask the research librarian to guide you to a resource that will list institutions of higher learning near your home.

   Be sure not to ignore the possibility of studying from your own home computer via distance learning, online learning, and virtual universities.

2. Telephone or set up an appointment with the training center to ask about the following:
   - The length and cost of its program.
   - The content, depth, and breadth of its program.
   - How many years it has been in business, if applicable.
   - Its accreditation, if applicable.

- The credentials of its staff.
- Its job placement rate. (What percentage of graduating students find jobs, and how long does it take them to obtain positions?)
- The average wages for a graduate in his or her first post-training job.
- Opportunities for advancement in the field.
- Information about whether the school fulfills national, state, or local laws and regulations for your new profession, if applicable.
- Telephone numbers of at least three graduates of the program whom you can call.
- Then, repeat the same process as above using your favorite Internet search engine (such as www.google.com or www.askjeeves.com).

3. Experiment, on your chosen search engine, with different ways of saying the same thing (for example, *classes, courses, school, training, program, certification*). Construct a search term (or *search string* of multiple terms) that includes some of the following words:

   1. Name of occupation (for example, *massage therapist, real estate agent*, or *network engineer*).
   2. Type of program (for example, *school, training, certification*, or *license*).
   3. The city, state, or geographic area in which you'd like to study (for example, *Indianapolis, Broward County, Illinois, New York*, or *Nevada*).
   4. If you want to study online, add: *distance learning, online education*, or *virtual universities*.

Some sample Internet search chains are:

- Massage therapist certification Broward County Florida
- Certified life coach online classes
- Certified networking engineer program New Jersey
- Culinary arts certificate Chicago
- Distance learning business administration marketing
- Web design school Seattle

- Fine cabinetry training New Mexico
- Smog technician training Boise
- Dog obedience trainer program Maine

A big part of your homework will be calling former students from the schools or programs that interest you. The dean or owner of the school should, in most cases, be able to provide you with contact information about former students who will be willing to talk to you. When you call the graduates, introduce yourself, state the purpose of your call, and ask these questions:

- Would you recommend the program at that school? If so, why? If not, why not?
- How long did it take you to find a job (or build a business) after graduating?
- How well did the school curriculum prepare you for your new position?
- Are your wages within the range of your expectations? (Do *not* ask them for the amount of money they're earning.)
- Do you enjoy your new career? Why? Why not?
- What is an average day or week like for you?
- Is there anything you would like to change about your job?
- What other advice would you give someone just entering that occupation?

There are many ways to get short-term training for what you want to do. Ellen wanted to become a *certified life coach*, someone who helps people reach personal and professional goals. She searched the Internet for a coaching program she could afford that provided the skills she wanted to master. Ellen followed the steps outlined above and gradually built a successful business for herself.

The school you choose may sound stimulating and fun, but it will only help you professionally if it's acceptable to potential employers. Be sure to do diligent labor market readiness research to determine if your desired future employers recognize and respect credentials from your course of study. We want you to get hired, now!

Strategy 6. Volunteering

Volunteer work is usually less formal than an internship, and, of course, it is unpaid. It means that you donate your labor to a business or organization either for your own philanthropic satisfaction or to learn and practice new skills.

When Nancy went from being a public health administrator to a book editor, she cleverly repositioned herself in the world of publishing by taking a volunteer position as a proofreader at a free weekly entertainment newspaper. Then she was able to combine that experience with the strategic education she also utilized. The result: Nancy had a new job as an editor at a public health book publishing house in less than four months.

Gary became a volunteer at a local public access television station by calling the station manager and asking for an interview. After going through mandatory orientation and training, he became a volunteer camera operator and later went on to work as a professional lighting designer in the television industry.

Becoming a volunteer is much the same process as becoming an intern. Find the person in charge, introduce yourself, briefly state your background and what you'd like to accomplish there, go to an interview, and join the team. You'll not only get a lot of practice (as well as the letter of recommendation) but you'll also begin taking your first steps toward being a professional.

When you're finished with your volunteer position (which can last from just a couple of days to a year or more), you're going to want to get paid for the new skills you've mastered.

> ***It is absolutely acceptable to list a volunteer or internship position just as you would recount a real paying job on your résumé. (See Chapter 8 for sample résumés.)***

The preferred way to express that you offered your labor and talents at no charge is not by writing "volunteer" or "intern" as a title on your résumé. If you negotiate a time with your supervisor to talk about a suitable job title to place on your résumé, you can usually upgrade it to something like *associate, assistant, coordinator, specialist,* and in some cases of more advanced work, *consultant.*

For example, Carl, our marketing intern, might fashion an agreement with his employer to list the time he spent there as *marketing associate* rather than *intern.* Gary, who volunteered at a TV station, might negotiate with the station manager for a title like *camera operator* rather than *volunteer.* Here are some titles for volunteer and internship positions that may be appropriate for a résumé:

- Assistant to the director
- Associate instructor
- Biochemist associate
- Customer service associate
- Executive or personal assistant
- Fashion technologist
- Financial consultant
- Human resources assistant
- Laboratory technician
- Networking assistant
- Property management assistant
- Public relations coordinator
- Software consultant
- Technology specialist

Strategy 7. Just Dive In!

Sometimes a career change does not require special study, training, or strategy. There are instances when all that's required is guts. I call this method *Just Dive In!* For example, Rita, who was "between jobs" and working as a house cleaner, took the plunge when she submitted her first work of fiction for publication. Once she took that risk, she began submitting her work to a myriad of publication sources, and finally, she wrote two books that were handled by a major publisher.

In another instance of Just Dive In! is Jennifer, an interior designer, who came upon a way she thought women could gain control of their finances. She had a hunch that the method she discovered might work.

Without any qualifications (other than managing her own finances with this method), she put a tiny classified ad in the newspaper that advertised a six-week class and support group for women who wanted to become more financially stable, for which she would be the group leader.

She charged $10 per person for six weeks and held the meetings in her home. It worked! Soon she went from teaching one class a week to three. Years later, Jennifer's work is known around the United States. She appeared on major talk shows and she wrote several books. The current cost of a one-day seminar with her? $450.

Just diving in is not for everyone. It is really for people who feel they have a knack for something and don't want to go through an educational process to begin to do that something for a living. The notion to take steps forward into the unknown may emerge as just a hunch that may not seem at all logical to an outside observer.

Following that hunch may involve taking risks and even bearing ridicule from people who may be concerned for your welfare but do not share your vision.

That said, just diving in takes high levels of self-esteem; a willingness to fail as well as prevail: the ability to tolerate uncertainty; a love for improvisation or thinking on your feet; and the ability to learn from mistakes. Jobs that absolutely require some sort of previous experience and have laws regarding certification, like registered securities trader, are not conducive to this strategy. Other types of industries, though, like the arts, hospitality, retail, senior services, community health and improvement services, entertainment, consulting, any type of sales, public speaking, home crafts and repairs, holistic healing, and travel are good bets if you're planning to Just Dive In.

You are especially valuable in the social services such as health, welfare, and education if you speak one or more languages in addition to English, or your native tongue.

Many government agencies like the county public health department, the state department of rehabilitation, and public libraries, will forgo both educational credentials *and* experience if you are fluent in Spanish, Farsi, Vietnamese, Russian, Chinese, French, Arabic, Afrikaans, Italian, or other languages spoken by part of the populace in your community.

> *If you feel like you can Just Do It and "it" does not legally or ethically require that you have a special license, degree, or designation, then most probably you can move forward to whatever "calls" to you, as long as you're willing to take the ride of your life!*

People who use the strategy of just diving in tend to hurl themselves forward headfirst and usually enjoy learning to swim. In fact, they get an incredible *thrill* out of taking just this kind of challenge. If you think you're this type of person, you probably have an *intuition or intense inner feeling* telling you to go ahead. *I invite you to do it!*

Strategy 8. Entrepreneurship

An *entrepreneur* is someone who initiates and usually (but not always) runs his or her own business.

Ever thought you could go from being an administrative assistant to a CEO in one day? All you have to do is open your own business and put your own name at the top of the organizational chart. Alice's entrepreneurial story in Chapter 6 will tell you how she did it.

Later, in Chapter 9, we'll highlight, in detail, how you can go about making the path of entrepreneurship work for you. You'll be taking a self-assessment that will help you highlight the strengths you bring to your new enterprise as well as the areas that need improvement.

By seeking out supplemental skills or the advice of other experts and professionals, you'll be better equipped to turn your new venture into a successful one. In the chapter on entrepreneurship, you'll also learn about *just how motivated you are* to weather the ups and downs of running your own business. Resources will be offered pertaining to how to take full advantage of the ample financial and professional support available from the government for which you are, most likely, eligible. You'll even get a taste for writing a marketing and business plan.

Combining Fearless Career Change Strategies for Maximum Impact

Although we've considered each of the strategies on its own thus far, the fastest results tend to arise from combining two or more of the approaches. For example, you might take a short-term series of courses *and* volunteer in your new field, to make your credentials and expertise that much more attractive to your new employer.

Blending strategic education with a well-aimed internship could even land you a *permanent* job at the organization for which you're an intern. An entrepreneur who takes some business classes to augment his or her transferable skills is likely to be that much more well rounded in executing his or her new endeavor.

One of my clients combined strategic education (enrollment in a graduate course), short-term education (a certificate earned by attending a number of seminars), an internship at a well-respected institution, and volunteering for a community group when he made his radical career change.

Which strategies you choose to utilize depends upon the money and time you wish to invest, the requirements of your new position in the real-world marketplace, and just how much of a foundation you wish to lay out before launching your new career. A good deal will also depend on your ability and willingness to take risks—to just dive in.

You must be curious about the details of many of the stories and concepts touched on in this chapter. In Chapter 6, you'll get blow-by-blow accounts of how real people transformed their special calling into a way of life.

CHAPTER 5

Strategic Education

What Is Strategic Education?

In the previous chapter, we examined, firsthand, the tremendous benefits career changers receive from utilizing strategic education. Once again, *strategic education* means enrolling in a certificate or college degree program without necessarily having the intention to finish that program.

Of course, you might want to finish the whole program, but strategic education means that by simply being enrolled in the program and taking one or two classes, the employer will perceive you as already having a certificate or a degree.

This strategy has worked time and again for thousands of people. The reason it is so effective for career changers is that it focuses on your *future*—the *intent* of where you're going—rather than your past. When the employer perceives *where you are going*, he or she sees several positive qualities in you.

> *Ambition, drive, motivation, and willingness to learn are only a few of the positive connotations the employer infers from the fact that you are trying to better yourself and improve your knowledge through enrollment in a training or education program.*

You May Be Eligible for Government-Funded Retraining

If you have been laid off in the last 16 weeks (note that the time limit may vary from state to state), the local office of your state's *employment development department* (EDD) may be able to assist you with payment for your entire certificate program. It is doubtful that the EDD will fund a degree program, but it is quite common for someone who has recently been downsized to be able to receive funding up to $10,000 for up to nine months of classes in a certificate program.

> *It is important to note that there is a window of time within which you must inform the EDD that you wish to be considered for a retraining program.*

In the state of California, for example, you cannot enroll in any of these programs using government funding past the 16-week mark of your first unemployment claim. In other words, the faster you communicate your desire to get retraining after being laid off, the better.

If you wait until after the enrollment period, you will not be eligible for government assistance in retraining. It is also important to note that you must make a case for retraining.

There must be some *reason* that you cannot return to your former occupation. Some of these reasons could be that the job market is too slow in your former occupation, that you have some disability that prevents you from going back to your old profession, or that you need additional education to be competitive in your former career.

You also have to *prove* that the new occupation you are seeking is appropriate for you and is likely to result in your getting a job or being successful in your own business. You can do this by cutting out newspaper ads or by printing a job description from the Internet and showing how they indicate your need for additional education.

How to Find "Open" Certificate and Degree Programs

You don't have to be laid off to take advantage of the certificate programs listed in this chapter. You need only contact community colleges, vocational schools, adult education programs, or continuing education programs in your region to find many of these programs. You can also research your educational choices on the Internet.

Even though the money will be coming out of your own pocket, remember that you are not necessarily paying for the entire certificate or degree program. You may be paying for only one class as a way to catapult yourself into a new category wherein you are more employable in the new career of your choice.

Another way to utilize strategic education is to enroll at a college or university in a program of study leading to an associate's degree (usually two years), a bachelor's degree (usually four years), a master's degree (usually two additional years from the bachelor's degree), or a Ph.D. program (which sometimes requires a bachelor's and other times requires a master's degree for entrance).

Normally, many schools require that you provide them with extensive documentation before entrance into one of these degree programs. The documentation may include a detailed application with an application fee, letters of recommendation, references, an essay, or written testing.

There is, however, a way to enter colleges and universities strategically by choosing institutions that offer open enrollment, open university, or adult education courses, which do not require these documents at all. You might also find a university on the Internet with online distance learning that has the equivalent of open university. Just be sure that the university is legitimate, accredited, and reputable.

A legitimate institution should provide you with a list of its accreditations before you spend your time and money. Make sure

Most of these are certificate programs run by university extension programs or private vocational schools. This list is not inclusive of, nor is it a guarantee of, all programs that may exist in your local area.

- Accounting and/or bookkeeping
- Administrative assistant
- Air transportation worker
- Alcohol and drug counseling
- Architectural design
- Automotive repair
- Back office medical assisting
- Bioinformatics
- Biotechnology
- Business administration
- Business administration, emphasis in finance
- Business analyst
- C language programming
- Career coaching
- Career planning
- Certificate in computer and information science
- Certificate in e-commerce management
- Cisco-certified engineer
- Clinical design
- College admissions
- Computer-aided drafting
- Computer application developer
- Computer graphics
- Computer network support
- Computer programming
- Computer service technician, A+ certification
- Construction inspector
- Construction manager
- Data entry
- Data warehousing
- Database management systems
- Database specialist
- Dental lab technician and assistant
- Digital signal processing
- Early childhood education
- Earthquake engineering
- E-commerce engineering

Sample of Some Government-Funded Training Programs

- Educational therapy
- Entrepreneurial management certificate
- Environmental education
- Environmental health and safety
- Event and meeting planner
- Facilities management
- Fine arts
- Garden design
- Graphic design
- Hazardous materials management
- Heating and air-conditioning technician
- Holistic health practitioner
- Human resource management certificate
- Interactive media
- Interior architecture
- Interior design assistant
- International business
- Internet security
- Java programming
- Landscape architecture
- Linux system administration
- Local area network (LAN) administrator
- Management of Internet technology
- Marketing
- Marketing and communications certificate
- Massage therapist
- Mechanical design
- Medical front office
- Microsoft-certified systems engineer
- Net development
- Network engineering
- Nonprofit management
- Object-oriented programming
- Occupational safety and health management
- Office management
- Oracle database administrator
- Pharmacy technician
- Photography
- Professional personal coach
- Program and project management certificate
- Public relations
- Purchasing management certificate

Sample of Some Government-Funded Training Programs (Continued)

- Semiconductor technology
- Senior human resource management certificate
- Senior marketing and communications certificate
- Software engineering
- Teaching English as a second language
- Technical writing
- Telecommunications engineering
- Telecommunications technician specialist
- Training and development
- UNIX system management
- Web master
- Web page pesigner
- Wireless communications
- Word processing

Sample of Some Government-Funded Training Programs (Continued)

that the accreditation is applicable to your geographic area, and that, if you are going to complete a degree in something that requires a license in your state, such as marriage and family counseling, or nursing, the college is approved by your local licensing board.

A single class may cost from $50 in the community college up to $1,100 at a university. It isn't possible to fit in this chapter or even in this book the multitudes of institutions of higher learning that offer this type of open enrollment. The best course of action is to call the colleges and universities in your area and find out whether they offer open enrollment or open university and whether or not they have a degree program in something you're interested in that would apply directly as a qualification for your new profession.

> **Try starting with your own state university program. Government-sponsored universities are always properly accredited and may be the most likely to have an open-door policy.**

When you find one of these programs, it is very likely that all you will need to sign up for it will be your social security number, credit card, name, and phone number. With that, you should be able to start studying within a month or two, if not weeks or days.

If you take more than two or three classes, most of these colleges or universities will require that you fill in the documentation and formally apply for entrance into the degree program. The two or three classes that you have taken up to that point will, most likely, apply to the credits needed for the degree.

> *In the next chapter, you'll meet several people who were actually hired for a new position while they were still taking their first class.*

Changing Your Résumé

How can you let the employer know that you're involved at an institution of higher learning? Clearly your strategic education is something you want to emphasize so that it stands out on your résumé. In Chapter 8, we'll discuss using summary statements in your résumé. Add that you are enrolled in a program in this paragraph by saying:

Currently enrolled in the course of study leading to a _____ degree in _____ at the University of _____.

If you feel uncomfortable saying "a course of study leading to a degree," you can alternatively use one of these statements:

1. Currently enrolled in undergraduate courses in _____ at _____ College.
2. Currently enrolled in graduate courses in _____ at _____ Institute.

In those first few crucial seconds as the employer reads your résumé, he or she will know that you are making the effort to increase your knowledge through education and will be duly impressed by your *intent to learn.* That's the beauty of strategic education!

CHAPTER 6

Ten Success Stories About People Just Like You

In the ten stories to follow you'll be able to easily identify the fearless career change strategies presented in the last chapter. Don't try to memorize them all. Just watch the stories unfold and see if you find any strategies you like or any *strategy that would best fit* your individual situation. Keep in mind that it is rare to use just one strategy alone. If you're planning to make a career change as rapidly as these people did, it's possible that you may use two or more strategies to reach your goal.

> **The people in this chapter may have combined as many as three or four strategies to transport themselves into the new enterprise as quickly and inexpensively as possible.**

Fear is normal. Stepping up in spite of fear is exceptional. In this chapter, you'll see how other people overcame the anxiety that sometimes accompanies change and transformed the energy of anxiety into action. When you use these strategies, you too will have the power to instigate and complete your transition successfully. No matter how easy the changes these people made may seem, there is almost always an element of risk involved in a career change. But remember, you've handled risks before.

> **All risks are double edged. On one hand, they can be frightening, but on the other hand, calculated risks can lead to terrific triumphs.**

All of the following stories are true, almost to the letter, except for the names of the people and the companies they worked for. These individuals are not different—not more courageous, conscientious, or clever—from you. The only difference is that they took *decisive action in spite of fear and unpredictability,* and they succeeded. Let's review these ten people's stories and see what can be learned from them.

Fearless Career Changers

From Landscaper to Environmental Planner in Four Weeks Using Strategic Education

Name: Marie

Former occupation: Landscaper

New occupation: Environmental planner

Primary strategy: Strategic education

Other strategies: Transferable talents, on-the-job training

Length of time from career decision to a paid position: One month

Cost (if any) of transition: $350

At 38 years old and working as the head of her own landscaping company, Marie had plenty of compelling reasons to want to change her profession. "First," she said, "my body isn't holding up to the strain of bending, lifting, and crawling day by day. My wrists are getting tendonitis from working in rocky soil. I'm tired of running my own business, and I'd like to get on someone else's payroll." She didn't need to provide other reasons, but she did. She also expressed that she wanted more intellectual stimulation, more positive impact on the natural environment, and, in her words, more "recognition" that she believed she could get from a more "prestigious" job.

> ***Admitting that you want more power, prestige, or recognition may be considered unpopular in some circles, but it's your career and your life. In the Fearless Career Change philosophy, it's fine to want these things. But you can get them only if you first admit to yourself that you want them and then go about fashioning a career that will maximize your chances of getting those satisfiers met.***

Marie had received a BS in biology from Yale University. Before we met, she had made several attempts to break into the field of environmental planning, without success. She related that employers gave her the feedback that she was academically lacking for the position. Even though she had a bachelor's degree from one of the most prestigious schools in the United States, they could not accept her application without a master's degree. Environmental planning, she felt, would utilize the talents she already had and give her a hand at making a real impact on conserving and restoring the earth's natural environment. She felt at a loss because she didn't feel she had the time to attend graduate classes for two years or more. She especially didn't want to spend "another minute" running her own business.

Since she wanted the transition to be quick, she decided to use the fearless career change plan for strategic education. She called a local university and found out that it had a program called "Open University" in which students could enroll immediately without submitting transcripts, essays, or letters of recommendation.

The only things she needed to register were her driver's license and her social security number. When she checked the catalog for an appropriate course, she found that the university offered a master's program in environmental planning—exactly what she was looking for!

She would be allowed to take up to six units (two semesters) on an open-university basis (without formally being accepted into the degree program), which could then be applied to her master's degree in environmental planning, should she choose to go ahead with the completion of the degree. After six units, she would be asked to apply in the traditional way (with transcripts, an essay, and letters of recommendation) to the master's program.

> *If you are planning to use strategic education, be sure to check with several universities—whether local or online—to see what their policies are on open enrollment.*

If you're looking for classes that could be applied to an advanced degree program, look under *open university, continuing education, open enrollment,* or *adult education* at the institution of your choice. If you'd like to find a university or college that offers open enrollment in your town, try a series of search strings on a good Internet search engine like google.com or aol.com that include the words (whichever are appropriate for you) *open enrollment university Boston.*

For example, the search string *open university online marketing* yields Web addresses for dozens of schools. Also, *open enrollment masters degree Chicago* shows multiple offerings at universities as well as online. You might try *continuing education computer networking Miami* and find that you have several choices to investigate.

Even something as unusual as *museum curator degree open enrollment* yields some interesting results.

> *As you can see, it's important to try several different ways of entering your search strings. You must experiment with many ways of saying the same thing.*

If *open university* doesn't work for the subject that interests you, *continuing education* or *adult education* might. If *museum curator* isn't producing the results you want, *art historian* may. You may find nothing that catches your eye when you enter the word *psychology*, but discover a number of offerings if you call it *counseling*.

You'll surely come up with some degree programs that will allow you to take a limited number of classes without undergoing the time and paperwork of the regular admissions process.

Marie paid $350 for her first graduate course and attended class just one night per week. By about the second week, she tried changing the summary clause of her résumé (which you'll learn about, in detail, in Chapter 8) to include the phrase *currently enrolled in a course of study leading to a master's degree in environmental planning at California State University at Hayward.*

By specifying on her résumé that she was enrolled in a relevant graduate course, Marie immediately got interviews with three environmental planning companies that had formerly rejected her. Before she ever made it to her third week of class, Marie had *two job offers!*

Why did strategic education make all the difference? Because her potential employers were more interested in her intent, that is, where she was going, than where she had been before.

Marie finished the course but never completed the master's degree. She started her first day only weeks after registering in the class. She was helping a team of scientists clean up the swamplands on the Northern California coastline. The last time I talked to Marie, she was working for the state of California, tagging baby owls for a scientific study. "I love what I'm doing," she said, "and my salary is three times what it was when I was a landscaper."

This story may sound too good to be true, but this is exactly how it happened. You'll hear several more accounts of just how powerful strategic education can be as this chapter unfolds.

Let's review the fearless career change strategies Marie used to propel her through her swift transition:

1. Transferable talents	*Yes*	Knowledge of plants, soils, and plant ecosystems.
2. On-the-job training	*Yes*	Marie had to learn more about animal ecosystems by using a combination of continued informal study and absorbing what she could through her work experience.
3. Strategic education	*Yes*	Partial grad. Course in environmental planning.
4. Short-term education	No	
5. Internship	No	
6. Volunteering	No	
7. Just Dive In!	No	
8. Entrepreneurship	No	

From Mechanical Engineer to Financial Advisor in Seven Days Using Short-Term Education

Name: Miguel

Former occupation: Mechanical engineering project manager

New occupation: Personal financial advisor

Primary strategy: Short-term education

Other strategies: On-the-job training

Length of time from career decision to a paid position: Seven days

Cost (if any) of transition: $0.00

Miguel, who worked as a project manager in the engineering department of a Fortune 500 company, was laid off over a year ago and came to me for career coaching at the persistent urging of his wife, who, he confided, was "tired of seeing him jump from engineering job to engineering job," only to be laid off again and again due to the massive flux in that industry.

Miguel too was not pleased about being a pawn to a poor economy, but he said that he felt "insecure" about changing careers midstream, saying, "I cannot see changing careers at this point in my life. I worked for six years to get my MSEE (master's in electrical engineering) and my salary is—or was—the highest it has ever been in my life."

It was not until completing the career fingerprinting process that Miguel began to think that there might be something more for him in a different field.

> *Though he was fearful about leaving the familiar territory of high technology, the power of his true calling proved to have the thrust to override most of his trepidation.*

Miguel's unique calling turned out to be "teaching, advising and mentoring others so that they can reach their full potential." With this newfound self-knowledge, he began to cautiously consider some positions other than engineering that might fulfill his love of guiding and advising others. Miguel chose to research the positions of postsales engineering, architecture, and certified financial planning and submitted them to comparison.

He found out a lot about financial advising that attracted him. Number 1 was the intensive contact with people and the opportunity to act as a counselor and mentor to those wishing to achieve their full financial potential. The second feature of the new position that caught his eye was the almost unlimited amount of money that can be made by a financial advisor, as he would be paid a base salary plus bonuses and commissions.

Although the first year or so as a financial advisor can be challenging, while you are building a client base, later years (as early as the third, according to his research) can yield up to $375,000 and more.

Miguel had to admit that sounded good. Two ski trips a year, two new cars, a new house, retirement investments, and a vacation house in Florida were all part of a lifestyle he and his wife had dreamed about. If he could potentially have all this and *work with people* almost 75 percent of the time, he would certainly thrive!

When Miguel made up his mind about changing directions, he called several of the major finance and brokerage companies in his area to see if any of them had training programs for new brokers. One, a Fortune 500 company, brought him in for interviews and testing and then offered him a spot in their 12-week training program.

Although he was paid only minimum wage to complete the training program (as was everyone), his wife's salary as a social worker was more than enough for them to get by for a few months. When he finished the course, he took a state-administered licensing exam to become qualified to sell various financial services. He was then formally offered the position.

Miguel reports that he has loved his first year at the job. "It's really about helping people reach their full potential. Once they take control of their finances, their whole lives turn around. I love being part of that." Miguel was able to use his transferable talents of teaching and advising from his last job as a project manager and his math skills from engineering.

Most important, Miguel tells me that he is living up to his *own* potential and purpose—and getting a lot better at skiing.

To sum up, let's take a closer look at Miguel's use of the fearless career change strategies:

1. Transferable talents	*Yes*	Math and people skills.
2. On-the-job training	*Yes*	First year of job involved closely supervised training. Miguel was given a mentor at work with whom he studied sales techniques for several hours a day.
3. Strategic education	No	
4. Short-term education	*Yes*	12-week intensive paid training program
5. Internship	No	
6. Volunteering	No	
7. Just Dive In!	No	
8. Entrepreneurship	No	

From Public Health Educator to Book Editor in Three Months Using Volunteering

Name: Nancy

Former occupation: Public health administrator

New occupation: Book editor

Primary strategy: Volunteering

Other strategies: Transferable skills, strategic education

Length of time from career decision to a paid position: Three months

Cost (if any) of transition: $150.00

Nancy was a high-level public administrator who had a master's degree in public health and Ph.D. in sociology. Just after completing her degree in public health, she joined the county health department of a U.S. eastern seaboard town. Over a 12-year period, Nancy worked hard to focus her efforts on becoming the director of public health for her county. It was after her third year as director that she felt the stirrings of the need for a change. "I don't know what's wrong," she said. "I'm at the top of my field, at the top of the salary range, and yet, I feel like something's missing."

She continued, "I don't feel like going to work in the morning anymore. I feel distracted and frustrated. I can't figure out why I just don't like my job anymore. Since I have such a coveted position and I make such a good living, I almost feel like I don't have a right to complain. Most people would give anything to be in my position."

Many people like Nancy become educated in a field that interests them when they're in their twenties or thirties, but their needs and tastes change with the arrival of another decade. There is certainly no law, written or unwritten, that says just because you were *once* content with a job and did it well, that you can't change your mind. Career interests can change just as the rest of you changes—emotionally, spiritually, intellectually, and so on.

> *The key is that you are not most people. It's your career, your day, your life that you have to reckon with at the end of the day—not someone else's opinion of the ideal job.*

It was evident to Nancy that she needed a change. She didn't need a reason. Her desire to change was all the reason she needed. She told me that she felt somewhat "guilty" about leaving a career she had worked so hard to build and afraid to leave such a "sure thing." Yet, she reflected, "I feel like I'm going to stagnate and die if I continue on in this way."

In spite of her malaise, Nancy still had a few moments of enjoyment in her job. She thought about it and said that she really loved writing and editing reports. "If that were *all* I were doing," she said, "I would be completely content!"

When Nancy completed the career fingerprinting process, she realized that, indeed, her authentic calling involved writing and editing. "I don't know how I didn't see that before. All through school, and throughout my life, that is where I've felt most comfortable and the most challenged."

Nancy researched the positions of journalist, technical writer, and book editor. She concluded that a career as a book editor felt like a good fit. It would be a big change, but she already had polished transferable talents in writing and editing that would ease her transition.

She knew she would need to start near the middle of the ladder in the publishing arena, but with her education and intelligence she would easily rise to the level of editor, and even higher. Volunteering and strategic education turned out to be her recipe for a successful transition.

First, she volunteered to work at a free local newspaper that would publish some of her own writing so that she could start building a portfolio (some call it a *clip sheet*) of her work. She also was able to get some proofreading experience there. Small, underfunded newspapers are often glad to have someone offer to work for free. She got two of her own articles into print—not a bad start!

Though she was still working at her old job, her mood improved dramatically. "I'm having fun again. This feels like play!" By building a bit of a reputation at a small level, Nancy was able to get letters of recommendation from the editor-in-chief and the publisher of the weekly newspaper.

> **Letters of recommendation after a period of
> volunteering or an internship are an absolute
> necessity if you're going to use either strategy in
> your fearless career change arsenal.**

The second line of attack turned out to be strategic education. She enrolled in a semester-long class in what is called *copyediting*. Copyediting is similar to proofreading, also using a specialized group of characters and symbols to make corrections to the text on a page.

Before Nancy finished the course, she had a job offer for an associate editing position in a small educational publishing house. (We'll talk about how she was able to get an interview in Chapter 8.)

About three years later, with two promotions under her belt, Nancy and her family have traded in the cold rocky coast of Rhode Island for a telecommuting job from Santa Fe, New Mexico. Nancy does her editing, and some writing, from her computer at her desk in her desert home and still works, by fax, mail, and e-mail, for her original publishing company. When she sits out on her hardwood deck with her laptop and a cup of coffee overlooking the contours of a desert landscape, she e-mails me a simple message, "Life is good."

For a quick review of Nancy's fearless career change strategies, consider the chart below:

1. Transferable talents	*Yes*	Writing and editing from school and work.
2. On-the-job training	No	
3. Strategic education	*Yes*	Partial course in copyediting.
4. Short-term education	No	
5. Internship	No	
6. Volunteering	*Yes*	Proofreader at a local news-paper.
7. Just Dive In!	No	
8. Entrepreneurship	No	

From Customer Service Representative to Film Production Assistant in One Day Using On-the-Job Training

Name: Scott

Former occupation: Insurance company customer service representative

New occupation: Film production assistant (explained below)

Primary strategy: On-the-job training

Other strategies: Just Dive In!

Length of time from career decision to a paid position: One day

Cost (if any) of transition: $0.00

Scott was one of my students in a two-day career transition seminar in Northern California. He was working as a customer service representative for a prominent health insurance organization. Scott was laid off from his job there due to massive downsizing because of budget cuts in the company.

Scott told me at the beginning of the workshop that he would like to do "just about anything" other than work in customer service for his next career. "The customers are rude. I have to meet a daily, weekly, and monthly quota, and I'm just not cut out for this kind of work."

In the seminar, Scott had the opportunity to examine just what kind of work he *was* cut out for. He had just "fallen into" working in the insurance industry to pay the bills while he finished college. After he graduated, he just stayed in a groove (or perhaps, as he might later characterize it, a rut). He had been working for the insurance company for three years. The pay was good. The commute was short, and he was a friendly sort who enjoyed his coworkers.

His authentic calling was not at all far from the surface. He had majored in art in college with the hopes of breaking into the film industry as an art director, but he had been sidetracked in the process by the illusive security of his customer service position.

If he wanted to break into the film industry at this point, he could utilize transferable skills like aptitude for color and design and for working with paint, clay, and other media to help ease his way into a lower-rung position and then work his way up to a department head.

In film, perhaps more than any other industry (except perhaps the military), it is necessary to work your way up the ladder, one rung of responsibility to the next, if you are going to be the head of a department. You may, indeed (as the cliché goes), be getting coffee for the boss on the first day out, even if you have a master's degree.

> ***It is the finesse and enthusiasm with which you do the rote (and often boring or unattractive) tasks involved in an entry-level position in just about any industry that will get you noticed by a person who may have the power to promote you.***

Scott used his local chamber of commerce to find a movie that had just started filming in his town. Since the chamber had the phone number of the production coordinator, he was able to call and get the name of the hiring manager—in this case, the art director.

The chamber of commerce has information about *all* of its corporate members, and most reputable businesspeople and companies from diverse industries join the chamber. You'll find information on everything from golf teachers to semiconductor manufacturers at the chamber, and its staff will be characteristically helpful about assisting you with your inquiries.

He used a technique called *direct contact* (which you'll learn how to master in Chapter 8) and called his way directly to the art director who was involved, at that very moment, on the set of the film. He then presented his phone script (an easy summation of your skills that you'll write in Chapter 8).

> Hello. My name is Scott R. I have a bachelor's degree in art. I am excellent with people, and I would be glad to show you my design portfolio. Last year, I built sets for two community theater productions, and I have excellent references from the directors. When can I come in for an interview?

"Do you have a truck?" was the only interview question asked by the art director. "As a matter of fact, I do," Scott said.

He was hired *on the phone* and asked to show up at 7:45 the next morning. Scott didn't just get lucky. He was able to effectively communicate his transferable skills to the employer, and he was willing to take the risk of just diving in, relying on his own ability to improvise, learn quickly, and adapt to new situations. He also accepted the fact that he'd have to initially work at entry level and learn everything he could through direct on-the-job experience.

Not everyone strikes gold on his or her first direct contact or gets hired over the phone, but it is certainly possible. Realistically, prepare yourself to make as many as a dozen or more calls to get an interview and then to proceed with the usual interviewing process.

Again, in Chapter 8 you'll become thoroughly acquainted with job seeking and interviewing tactics that will grab you that position you've dreamed about.

Let's review what Scott did to make this fearless career change:

1. Transferable talents	*Yes*	Had a bachelor's degree in art and a portfolio and some experience in building sets for theater.
2. On-the-job training	*Yes*	The film industry always uses on-the-job training.
3. Strategic education	No	
4. Short-term education	No	
5. Internship	No	
6. Volunteering	No	
7. Just Dive In!	*Yes*	A one-day career transition without any experience!
8. Entrepreneurship	No	

From Attorney to Dog Trainer in 12 Weeks with Short-Term Education

Name: Han

Former occupation: Attorney

New occupation: Dog trainer

Primary strategy: Short-term training

Other strategies: Internship, entrepreneurship

Length of time from career decision to a paid position: 12 weeks
Cost (if any) of transition: $1,900

It can be difficult, coming from a society in which money and status are deemed to be two of the most important or the *only* important goals, to imagine that someone might want to give up both for a little peace of mind.

Yet, there are those who reach a point in their lives where no dollar amount on a paycheck can compensate for a feeling that their work has no meaning and no joy for them anymore.

That was exactly the case for Han. At the early age of 39, she had already been successful in a corporate law firm and was easily commanding a salary of over $350,000 a year. She also suffered from conditions that are sometimes attributed to stress. Chronic migraines and insomnia, coupled with recurrent depression, kept her from fully enjoying her ample earnings and a life full of opportunities.

Han said that her job was so consuming that she didn't even have time to date. She felt unhappy and isolated.

She had thought about getting out of law before, but she felt apprehensive because she really didn't have another plan of action. This year, she'd come to a breaking point. Somehow, she knew she had to get out of law and do something new. Han spent a long time trying to figure out what that was. When she performed the career fingerprinting process that you did at the beginning of the section, she came upon a unique talent that was, ironically, the very talent that attorneys use to win cases—persuasiveness.

Salespeople, teachers, and marketing and advertising executives use persuasiveness in their careers, but those careers didn't interest her. Neither did other forms of law like estate planning, criminal defense, divorce law, or entertainment law. In fact, nothing from the list of job titles you explored earlier in the section caught her fancy.

I asked her to make a list of the last five times she could remember being really happy. Her response went like this:

1. Watching the sunset over the ocean
2. Walking alone in a eucalyptus forest
3. Reading a great novel and drinking wine alone in the hot tub

4. "Dog sitting" for a friend
5. Stopping to pet a dog while jogging

"I think I like dogs better than people," she joked. "They're completely without guile, totally authentic. Dogs are better than the best antidepressant in the world." Odd that none of her happiest moments included people, and two out of five included dogs.

"What would you think about a career with animals?" She thought for a while. "Like what?" "Well, there are several," I replied. "Veterinarian, veterinary assistant, dog groomer, dog walker, opening a trendy doggie day spa or doggie day-care center, working with a volunteer group for the welfare of animals, being a dog trainer." As soon as I mentioned dog trainer, she became very animated. "That's something I'd like to look into," she said.

She researched the title on the O*NET. It was clear that Han was not going to make anywhere near $350,000 annually for being a dog trainer. In fact, the top ninetieth percentile of trainers in the United States made about $45,000 a year, according to this resource. Was she ready to take that kind of pay cut?

She was. Remembering how much she adored her childhood fox terrier and recalling how she was always the first to offer to babysit others' pets, she realized that the love she extended to animals and received in return was worth thousands, even tens of thousands, more than the emptiness and blandness of her experience of practicing law.

Han said something to me that I often hear when people find their authentic calling. "I would not only be a dog trainer for free, I'd even pay someone else just to be allowed to do it!" The feeling of *inner wealth* when doing the work that you love is often more than enough to trade for a high-paying job that doesn't strike a chord with who you really are. Han trained at a 12-week program that cost $1,900 dollars. From day 1 she reported feeling "happier than I can remember." Later, she did an informal, unpaid internship with a more experienced trainer. They led canine obedience classes together. Though Han was not paid, she was free to accept business from any of the dog owner students in the class who wanted private training.

This was one of the fundamental ways that she built her private business in animal obedience. I'll point out other techniques that Han used to become a successful entrepreneur in Chapter 8. A year later, Han tells me she's never regretted making the change and that she's finally found something "natural and effortless" to her.

Let's review the strategies that made Han's new career possible:

1. Transferable talents	*Yes*	Persuasiveness.
2. On-the-job training	No	
3. Strategic education	No	
4. Short-term education	*Yes*	A 12-week dog-training course.
5. Internship	*Yes*	Cotaught canine obedience classes.
6. Volunteering	No	
7. Just Dive In!	*Yes*	She built her own clientele.
8. Entrepreneurship	No	

A Promotion from Job Developer to Vocational Rehabilitation Counselor in Three Weeks Using Strategic Education

Name: Rodrigo

Former occupation: Job developer

New occupation: Vocational rehabilitation counselor

Primary strategy: Strategic education

Other strategies: Transferable talents, on-the-job training

Length of time from career decision to a paid position: Three weeks

Cost (if any) of transition: $450.00

Rodrigo was first hired in the early 1990s by a vocational rehabilitation firm that helped workers who were injured on the job to change or modify their occupations and get back to work. He was brought onboard as a *job developer*, someone who assists clients in learning the job search skills—such as résumé writing and interviewing—to obtain employment. In some cases, the job developer makes contact with employers to get interviews for the client and/or to discuss how a client might engage in paid on-the-job training in an unfamiliar field.

Rodrigo wanted to take a step up to being a vocational rehabilitation counselor. Being a rehabilitation counselor would allow him to have more impact and influence on his clients' career decision-making process. He would be interfacing with the workers' doctors, lawyers, and training programs as well as being instrumental in helping them make choices about new career directions that would not aggravate their injuries.

Rodrigo knew that a master's degree in counseling or a related subject was necessary to move from a job developer to a full-fledged counselor. What he did not know was that the master's degree was a *preference*, not a *requirement*.

In other words, though a graduate degree was the industry standard, there was nothing ethically or legally stating that a person without that degree could not do the job.

It is very important that when you read the job requirements for a certain career or position, you understand the difference between preferred and required. A preferred requirement is usually one that may be overlooked if you have other attributes that interest the employer. A required qualification is something that is "hard and fast" because it is mandated by law. For example, a physician cannot practice medicine without first obtaining a medical degree and a license to practice, no matter what his or her intelligence or talents.

Of course, there are some fields wherein advanced degrees are required, especially in the medical field, law, and academia. But many, if not most, degree requirements in other fields may be waived in favor of a person's possessing a superior background, speaking more than one language, or having specialized knowledge and other factors.

If you have a BA and you see a job in the newspaper that asks for an MA, consider that requirement as part of a wish list.

Research the position carefully to see if a certain degree or certification is mandated by law or simply expected by the employer. There is a vast difference between the two, and if you're not aware of it, you may miss a good opportunity to get hired in a position for which you are *qualified by experience* and for which an advanced degree is merely a preference.

Even if you are competing with others who might have superior academic qualifications, it is your *ability to communicate* how well you can help the employer *make a profit* that will win over any academic degree.

In Chapter 8, we'll talk about ways to present yourself, using what I call *Q statements*, which will enable you to *prove to the employer* that you will make the competitive difference—not by having a degree, but by having the ability to draw on past successes, to demonstrate, without a doubt, that you can bring more to the company than others competing for the same position.

> ***If you have enough of a certain kind of experience, or if, like Rodrigo, you are simply enrolled in a more advanced degree program, you may very well get the job despite not yet having the degree.***

When Rodrigo became aware of this fact, he discussed his plan with his employer. The employer agreed to promote him if he were to enroll in an MEd program (master's in educational counseling) at a local university. Not only that, the employer agreed to pay a tuition reimbursement of 50 percent. About a month into his classes, Rodrigo was promoted, and he received a substantial raise. Rodrigo was yet another person for whom strategic education really paid off. Rodrigo's $450 investment in strategic education resulted immediately in a 56 percent raise.

As a result of showing his employer *where he was headed*, he ended up getting a promotion that he would not have been eligible for had he not enrolled in a master's program.

Here is a picture of how Rodrigo gained the leverage for his promotion:

1. Transferable talents	*Yes*	Communication and working with clients.
2. On-the-job training	*Yes*	Needed to acquire some new skills.
3. Strategic education	*Yes*	Enrolled in a graduate course.
4. Short-term education	No	
5. Internship	No	
6. Volunteering	No	
7. Just Dive In!	No	
8. Entrepreneurship	No	

From Administrative Assistant to Midwife Assistant in Four Weeks Using an Internship

Name: Caroline

Former occupation: Administrative assistant

New occupation: Midwife assistant

Primary strategy: Internship

Other strategies: On-the-job training, short-term education

Length of time from career decision to a paid position: Four weeks

Cost (if any) of transition: $300

Caroline told me that being laid off from her job as an administrative assistant was exactly the "wake-up call" she needed to let go of a position that she said she could "almost do in my sleep." Sometimes a layoff can bring a welcome relief if you didn't like your job anyway, especially when it is accompanied by a sizable severance package.

When she came in for career counseling, Caroline completed a career fingerprinting process in which she discovered that her principle and most cherished talent was "to nurture." She told me that, for years, she had wanted to be a midwife assistant, but like so many of us, she was so absorbed in "paying the bills" that she had little time to really think about how her authentic calling could come about.

Midwife assistants (also known as *doulas* or *labor assistants*) help fully certified midwives or doctors in prenatal, birthing, and postnatal care in either home, birth center, or hospital births.

Caroline knew what she wanted to do, and she decided to perform some research on just how to do it. She found out through her *labor market readiness research* that most birth centers and midwives (who were the most likely people to employ her) preferred a midwife certification program of study followed by an internship period with a reputable organization or licensed nurse midwife.

Four out of ten potential workplaces mentioned a school in Seattle, Washington, that had a good reputation for turning out competent and employable midwives. Caroline put her severance package to use to pay for the cost of training and the waiting period (if any) she might need before her new career began. Her research revealed that training programs required from three weekends to three months of classes and attendance, as an internship at anywhere from 3 to 15 births. Schools cost from $300 to $4,500.

Caroline chose a school in Seattle that cost $425 for a three-day weekend set of seminars. Based on her research, she chose the school that fit her time and budget as well as having an *excellent placement rate* and a good name with employers. Within three months of study in school and observation of 11 births, Caroline was up and running—a new and fulfilling career awaiting her!

Here's another look at Caroline's strategies:

1. Transferable talents	*Yes*	Interpersonal communication, nurturing.
2. On-the-job training	*Yes*	Needed to acquire some new skills.
3. Strategic education	No	
4. Short-term education	*Yes*	Completed a three-day seminar.
5. Internship	*Yes*	Observed and assisted in 11 live births.
6. Volunteering	No	
7. Just Dive In!	No	
8. Entrepreneurship	No	

From Vice President of Human Resources to Career Coach in Six Weeks Using Transferable Talents

Name: Tom

Former occupation: Vice president, human resources

New occupation: Outplacement consultant and career coach

Primary strategy: Transferable talents

Other strategies: Entrepreneurship, short-term education

Length of time from career decision to a paid position: Six weeks

Cost (if any) of transition: $0.00

At age 55, Tom thought he would be ready for an early retirement in a few years. In the fall of that year, though, there were talks of a merger in the multinational telecommunications company where Tom had worked for 17 years. He was afraid, despite his seniority as a vice president of human resources, that his job might be impacted if indeed the merger were to take place.

While still working, Tom took some time to do his homework and went to several interviews with other telecommunications corporations as a backup plan. Tom confided in me later that, despite his youthful enthusiasm, vast experience, and excellent health, he was convinced that no job offers were materializing *simply because of his age.*

It is disheartening to think that there would be traces of ageism, especially in the otherwise progressive high-tech industry, but many of my clients have reported similar observations to me, and it seems apparent that many people who are over 50 have a similarly unfair experience.

It can be frightening to even think about changing occupations in a job market that devalues your talents and experience because of an age bias, and this fear was something Tom had to face in his transition. Fortunately, it didn't stop him in his tracks. If this is a concern you have, don't let it stop you.

As it turns out, Tom's position *was* eliminated as the result of the merger several months later, and he found himself without an office, a title, or a paycheck. Tom had hoped to work at least a few years longer. This was too early, even for an early retirement.

Fortunately, he left with an excellent severance package (a severance package may include cash, extended benefits, or other perks) and the use of free outplacement services to help him find a new position. Outplacement companies employ career counselors who assist entry-level to executive employees in managing their careers, particularly after a downsizing. The company that carried out the layoff pays their fees, and there is no charge for the downsized employees who attend.

Tom decided to take full advantage of the outplacement services, which included workshops, seminars, and individual career coaching. At some point, Tom's coach posed the possibility that with Tom's background and transferable talents from human resources, he might be an excellent candidate for becoming an outplacement consultant himself.

Tom jumped on the idea because he liked the possibility of the freedom the position promised. He could work on call for an outplacement company teaching seminars and coaching other executives and build a business on the side as a career coach (very similar to an outplacement consultant) in an independent private practice. He was free at any time to turn down work with the outplacement company without negative consequences. He would have some control over his flow of private clients, and he could therefore take off for a vacation whenever he wished. He could have the best of retirement—freedom and leisure—and the best of the working world—a high hourly fee, stimulating colleagues, and a prestigious title with a good company.

He found that, unlike his other unpleasant experiences in interviewing, the outplacement industry actually seemed to value his know-how and maturity. He interviewed with three companies in Atlanta, Georgia, and he received two offers. He accepted the offer with the highest pay scale. The company had a short and straightforward paid training program that lasted only two days.

He then did a very short four-day internship wherein he observed other coaches teaching seminars, while he got some practice teaching in front of a live audience. He was then certified as a consultant for that company. He started work the next week. Tom has become an entrepreneur (self-employed) with what is some-times known as a *portfolio career* (a career having several avenues of income). He is an independent contractor for the outplacement company, he earns income from his private career coaching prac-tice, and he is sometimes paid to lead seminars for church, school, and professional organizations.

If you are planning on becoming a successful consultant like Tom, I suggest that you read *The Consultant's Guide to Publicity* by Reece Franklin.* It will show you how to become well known in your field with a minimum monetary investment.

If you want to "brand" yourself as a consultant with a national or worldwide reputation in your field, there is no better way than to write a book and/or get quoted as an expert in major newspapers and magazines.

Also, Dan Janal, who has a Web site at www.prleads.com, is a fantastic resource to get you started on getting quoted by the best newspapers and creating the *expert image* that is so important if you are to attract business and be a leader in your profession.

Here's a review of Tom's fearless career change strategies:

1. Transferable talents	*Yes*	HR concerns itself with mat-ters of jobs and employment
2. On-the-job training	No	
3. Strategic education	No	
4. Short-term education	*Yes*	He took a paid two-day in-house seminar.
5. Internship	*Yes*	He did a paid four-day intern-ship.
6. Volunteering	No	

---

*Reece Franklin, *The Consultants's Guide to Publicity, How to Make a Name for Yourself by Promoting Your Expertise*, Wiley, New York, 1996.

7. Just Dive In!	No	
8. Entrepreneurship	*Yes*	He opened his own career coaching private practice.

From Corporate Events Planner to CEO in 12 Weeks Using Entrepreneurship

Name: Alice

Former occupation: Events planner

New occupation: CEO, discount travel and entertainment company

Primary strategy: Entreprenership

Other strategies: Just Dive In!, transferable talents

Length of time from career decision to a paid position: Three months

Cost (if any) of transition: U.S. Small Business Administration and home-equity loans (explained below)

It would be hard for most of us to imagine a job that was more fun than Alice's. Alice had the good fortune of being an events planner for a well-known computer company in Texas. She scheduled corporate events like large-scale seminars, picnics, and fairs. In addition to planning internal events, she was in charge of booking travel, entertainment, and sporting events for executives and employees of the company.

Because her company was so large and so many people were interested in these events, Alice was sometimes able to negotiate discounts of up to 60 percent from vendors for theater, opera, sports, cruises, and a host of other goods and services. For most of us, this might have been a job to keep for life, but Alice had a special dream of starting her own discount travel and entertainment business where customers could buy tickets on the Internet, and she had a strong calling to be a philanthropist.

Right at the heart of Alice's plan was the idea that for every ticket sold, 30 percent of the profits would go to charities and nonprofit organizations. It was *absolutely essential* to Alice that she oversaw a company that was committed to giving back to the community. Her talent, as she saw it, was philanthropy. Owning her own company was only a vehicle for her to be able to give generously to her community.

Like many of the people we've talked about in this book, Alice's wake-up call came when her employer was downsizing due to its shifting of much of its computer manufacturing to factories outside the United States.

Alice sought advice about how to get her business up and running. She was referred to the Small Business Administration (www.sba.gov), a department of the U.S. government with offices in most cities.

The SBA assists entrepreneurs in starting and improving their businesses. They give free classes in starting a business, getting government and private loans for businesses, small-business bookkeeping and accounting, sales and marketing, and other topics of interest to people starting new companies.

Alice would be able to consult, for free, with a mentor (someone who had already started a successful business) through a government-funded program called SCORE (www.score.org). Establishing a working relationship with one or more of the expert counselors from SCORE is one of the first steps you should take if you wish to start an enduringly successful business. You might pay up to $500 an hour for this kind of consulting elsewhere, but at SCORE it will cost you nothing!

By attending classes at the SBA and working with her mentor from SCORE, Alice found the best way to fund her new business. She was somewhat concerned because her credit score was far from perfect, but she was able to receive a $15,000 microloan cosponsored by the Small Business Administration and a private bank.

It took only ten days from the day she filled out a simple form to the day her bank account was credited with the funding. In addition, because she owned a home, she was also able to borrow $70,000 against her equity in the home by refinancing her original mortgage.

Like almost every small-business owner, Alice wore many hats at the beginning of her enterprise: Web designer, owner, administrative assistant, bookkeeper, marketing director—and, well, you get the picture. Later she was able to assemble an executive staff and pay them a monthly stipend until the business was off and running.

Eventually, she hired a Web designer, a chief technical officer, a chief marketing officer, an executive vice president, and a chief financial officer. Alice is in the final phases of completing her Web site, but she already has a full house for several events—to Broadway plays, a trip to Las Vegas, and a 12-day Mediterranean cruise.

For all her hard work, Alice and three of her family members are traveling for free, but what satisfies her most is that *30 percent of the profits* from all these events will be going to adult literacy, AIDS prevention, and breast cancer research.

Alice's success can be attributed to the following strategies:

1. Transferable talents	*Yes*	Developed same skills as an employee.
2. On-the-job training	*Yes*	She had to learn how to run her own business.
3. Strategic education	No	
4. Short-term education	*Yes*	Free SBA classes.
5. Internship	No	
6. Volunteering	No	
7. Just Dive In!	*Yes*	From employee to CEO!
8. Entrepreneurship	*Yes*	She started her business from "scratch."

From Retirement to Jewelry Designer in Eight Weeks Using Transferable Talents

Name: Elsie

Former occupation: Retired

New occupation: Jewelry and crafts designer

Primary strategy: Transferable talents

Other strategies: Just Dive In!, entrepreneurship

Length of time from career decision to a paid position: Two months

Cost (if any) of transition: Up-front costs for materials

Elsie, at age 72, had been enjoying retirement on her late husband's military pension for over ten years. She was busy, healthy, and content for most of those years until her son, granddaughters, and daughter-in-law moved out of state. Without the support and warmth of her family, she suddenly experienced a void.

She came to career counseling saying that she wanted to return to part-time work but she wasn't sure she had the skills. In her active working years when Elsie was a secretary for a large insurance firm, she used a typewriter—not a computer—and she feared that going back to work as a secretary would mean learning to use computers. It was not an area into which she wanted to venture, and I could tell from her voice and body language that being a secretary was no longer of interest to her. She certainly wasn't desperate for money, and she wanted to do something meaningful and fun.

What we uncovered with the career fingerprinting process was that Elsie was an artist. For years she had been doing oil painting, making wooden toys for children, and designing and making jewelry in her spare time, but she *never thought she could make money at it.*

When she examined her fears about stepping out into the marketplace after so many years of retirement, she figured she had nothing to lose. She decided to give it a try. First, she began displaying her custom-made jewelry at local street fairs and charitable events. She was happily surprised that people were actually willing to pay up to $300 for her beautifully designed necklaces and bracelets.

After building her confidence for a few months by witnessing other people's excitement about her work, she began to approach retail stores and sell her items to them in bulk. Soon, she had more orders than she could handle and had to hire an apprentice.

Elsie, once unable to even balance her checkbook, was now taking Visa and MasterCard. She never, to my knowledge, learned how to handle a computer, but that was okay—her assistant did that for her. Elsie is as active as ever, and her jewelry seems to be giving joy to many people.

> ***Often, we find our true calling is a hobby like photography, planning weddings, fixing cars, doing historical research, electronics troubleshooting, cooking, sewing, writing, drama, or sports.***

Elsie is a great example of someone who took the transferable talents from her hobby and turned them into a profit-making enterprise.

Here's a brief capsule of how Elsie used her resources to make a fearless career change:

1. Transferable talents	*Yes*	She transformed her hobby into a business.
2. On-the-job training	No	
3. Strategic education	No	
4. Short-term education	No	
5. Internship	No	
6. Volunteering	*Yes*	At first, auctioned some work at charity events.
7. Just Dive In!	*Yes*	With no extra training, she just took the plunge!
8. Entrepreneurship	*Yes*	She started and ran her own business.

Key Strategies

You've just taken in a lot of information, so stop for a moment and think about the strategies you like—the ones that seem to best suit your own personality. Also, take some time to determine which of these strategies (or perhaps other strategies of your own) you'd like to use in your next career change.

Strategies I like:

1. _____

2. _____

3. _____

4. _____

5. _____

Other:

_____

_____

_____

_____

_____.

Most practical strategies for my next career change:

1. _____

2. _____

3. _____

4. _____

5. _____

Other:

_____

_____

_____

_____

_____.

In the next chapter, on goal setting, you'll use the strategies you've selected to devise a plan of action. Then you'll move on to the next phase—enacting your plan with accelerated job search techniques.

CHAPTER 7

Setting and Reaching Enticing Goals

How to set goals is one of the most important things you can learn in your life. It is a skill that can guide and transform every area of life from your health and finances to your social, spiritual, physical, and career pursuits.

> **Once you learn the goal-setting techniques in this chapter, you'll find that setting goals is a simple and straightforward process.**

As you begin to reap the rewards from regularly writing your objectives and making realistic plans to meet them, you may choose to make goal setting a lifelong tool.

Studies on Goal Setting

The two anecdotes I'm about to tell you are almost folklore in the fields of self-improvement and human motivation, but just in case you've never read them in a book before or heard them at a seminar,

I want to make sure you get these stories under your belt and really put the lessons in them to use.

The first story involves the graduating class of an Ivy League university in the 1950s. The researchers asked every member of the class, "Do you have clear, measurable goals?" As the story goes, only 10 percent of the class reported that they had clear, measurable goals.

This study was a *longitudinal study*, meaning that the behavior, attitudes, or conditions of a group or individual were examined first at one time and then again at a much later time. In the case of this first study, the graduating class was looked at first in one decade and again (that is, those who could be found and were still alive) in two more decades.

When the researchers contacted the surviving members of the class 20 years later, they found that the *10 percent of the class* who had stated that they had clear, measurable goals had, on average, an income *seven times higher* than that of the former students who did not report having goals.

Shortly afterward, another group of researchers from another prominent university saw this evidence published. The researchers wanted to try the same experiment with a bit of a "spin" on it. This time they took the graduating class of their own university and asked the question, "Which of you have clear, measurable, *written* goals?" *Only 3 percent* this time reported that they not only had clear, measurable goals but they also had committed their goals to writing.

When the surviving members of this second group of subjects were examined 20 years later, it was found that the minute 3 percent of men and woman who had clear, measurable *written* goals were worth, financially speaking, *10 times more* than the *entire* remaining 97 percent of the class combined.

You may or may not believe in the power of setting goals, but the studies recounted above strongly suggest that knowing how to set goals and, especially, writing them down are skills that are closely related to our performance and achievement.

> *Almost all truly great achievers have some sort*
> *of system of conceptualizing their future goals*
> *and using methods to bring their desired*
> *objectives about.*

Some may use a more formal system like the one you will learn. Others may think of their goals as mere "daydreams" and write them down, less formally, in a journal. Some people find it relaxing to make drawings and/or flowcharts of their intentions in a notebook.

I have known people who jot down all their goals on a piece of paper and place that paper in a special box or a special file and then review their progress once a month. Others only think clearly and intently about their goals or, perhaps, share their aims with just one trusted person, and, even though their goals are not written, their intensity of purpose and commitment to action brings about the result they planned on.

Setting Balanced Goals

To be sure, truly successful people conceive of goals for every part of their lives—not just career goals. This holistic approach to goal setting reminds you that happiness and success are the fruits of a balanced life that includes social, spiritual, recreational, financial, fitness, health, and other elements of existence.

Although there are many areas for which to fashion new and exciting goals, we're going to begin with focusing on your career goal since I assume you're reading this book because you're interested in making a quick and economical career change. However, once you learn to design and actualize your career goals, you will be able to use the same formula to achieve goals in other areas of your life.

Steps for Writing an Attainable Goal

Step 1. Write a Clear, Measurable Statement of Your Goal, Described in the Present Tense, Using an Exact Calendar Date for Its Attainment

An example of this sort of goal statement is, "I now have a wonderful career as a certified financial planner on June 17, 20xx."

Why do we write the goal in the present tense? Because if you say "I will" rather than "I am" your brain will subconsciously keep putting that goal off into the future.

It may also seem odd to write an exact calendar date for a goal whose attainment on a specific day cannot be precisely predicted.

In spite of the seemingly impossible task of predicting an exact date, the majority of people I have worked with who use this method actually end up attaining their goals within a week or two of the stated calendar date.

Again, your subconscious mind has a better chance of *keeping you on track* if you provide it with a *specific guideline* as to when the goal will be realized.

Step 2. Design Your Goal So That It's Both Believable and Attainable

It's one thing to think big and imagine great things for yourself. It's another to plan for something that is so outrageously unattainable that even you have a hard time believing it could really happen.

For example, it may not be at all unreasonable to write a goal saying "I now make $7,000 a month as a presales hardware engineer on September 9, 2006," but it is rather doubtful that you could make, let's say, a million dollars a month in that position.

Though I encourage you to dream, it's best when goal setting to commit to goals that are humanly attainable. Then when you reach your goal of making $7,000 a month, you can always set another goal for an incremental increase of your income.

Step 3. You Must Have a Workable Plan to Reach Your Goal

Your new career will probably not come about by sheer magic. It's important to consider the concrete steps you need to take to make your dream happen. Those steps may include raising or saving a certain amount of money and/or applying one or more of the fearless career change strategies discussed in detail in Chapters 8 and 9, such as working in an internship position or enrolling in a short-term education program, or taking the steps needed to implement your job search or to start your new business.

It is also important to note any obstacles *(inside or outside of you)* that might prevent you from reaching your goal. For almost everyone navigating a major career transition, fear is likely to rear its head. You're no different from most people if you feel some trepidation on the road to your dreams.

This takes us back to the very beginning of this book when you wrote down the fears that you associate with change. It may be that when setting your goal, you'll notice a bit of anxiety well up again. Refer back to the first chapter and review your record of dealing with fear and risks successfully in the past, and remember that if you did it then, you can also master your fear now.

Perhaps your obstacle is an external rather than an internal block. Maybe, for example, you are a single parent and your young child needs babysitting at night while you go to the evening seminars you need in order to make your move into your new vocation. Perhaps you don't have enough money to afford both the seminars and child care. This brings us to the last step in the goal-setting formula.

Step 4. Brainstorm Ways to Break Through or Get Around the Obstacles to Your Goal

Brainstorming means allotting a short time, perhaps two to ten minutes to write down every single thing you can think of that would solve the problem, no matter how remote or silly it might sound. Inviting friends or family for a group brainstorming session can also be quite effective.

In brainstorming by yourself or with others, you may come up with solutions like "trading" child care with a neighbor who also has children, winning the lottery, taking on an extra job, standing on the street with a sign saying "put me through school," or getting a loan to help defray your costs.

Of course, some of those solutions are ridiculous, but brainstorming helps your mind be more creative and uninhibited. Out of all the solutions you write, it's likely that one or two will be feasible.

You could ask the neighbors to watch your child for the time it takes to complete the seminars, and you can return the favor and watch their children at a later date. Or you can get on the phone to your mom in St. Louis and see if she wouldn't mind staying in the guest room for a few weeks and watching her "little angel." (You know she won't mind!)

If you simply cringe at the thought of living with Mom cleaning up after you and giving unsolicited advice, you might consider trimming one of your preferred activities or products as we did earlier in your "transition budget"—even if it means putting off buying that wide-screen TV for now or cutting back on the cell phone minutes so you can afford a sitter.

Whatever your obstacle, brainstorming—that is, writing down every single possibility you can think of within a given time limit—will almost surely present you with one or more workable alternatives to chip away at those barriers.

Let's look at the goal statement on the next page, which is one Miguel wrote preceding his new job as a financial planner.

Your Own Goal Worksheet

For this exercise, take the career that you determined earlier and elaborate on it in goal-oriented language. Fill out the goal template on page 458 with your own data, using the information in Miguel's goal worksheet as a guide. For now, if you aren't sure about a date or about the cost of something, do some research, if possible, and then write your best guess.

Your telephone is your most valuable tool in guessing about the price of something. Call a few stores or schools to get the prices for the things or classes you need. Take the price of three of the same things, add them up, and divide by three. That way you can at least anticipate the average amount of an item or educational program you'll need. You can always adjust the amount at a later time to be more accurate.

Great! Remember, you can use the work you've just done on your career goal for many of the other goals you set for yourself. I don't expect you to construct goals for every area of your life right now (unless you really want to). First, I recommend that you get some practice at focusing on and working toward one goal at a time. Later, you'll be more adept at the process and will be able to juggle multiple goals simultaneously. For now:

- Read your *career goal* once each morning and once each night.
- Begin taking the steps needed to reach your goal and implementing solutions to any perceived obstacles. *Check your progress at least once a week.* Are you following through on your plan of action? What measurable progress (like phone calls, purchases, sending letters, reading, research) have you made?
- *Mentally rehearse* your goal once or twice a day. (More on this idea later.)

Goal statement: "I now have a position as a financial advisor with Henley, Scott, and Thompson making $65,000 per year on October 22, 20xx."

Date: October 22, 20xx

Materials or things needed and cost
New briefcase, $90
Financial calculator, $60
Two new suits, $600
Four new ties, $80
Palm Pilot, $350

People and organizations to contact and cost
E-mail news of career change to friends, family, former associates (this will be a good source of referrals when building my client base), $0
International Association of Electrical Engineers (IEEE). Attending luncheons and other functions will also attract clients from my old profession. Consider possibility of being a speaker. Annual membership fee, $160

Knowledge and/or education needed and cost
Must pass 12-week basic training, $0
Must take and pass Series 63 Licensing Exam, exam fee, $220
Must take and pass Series 7 Licensing Exam, exam fee, $80
Learn how to manage a Microsoft Outlook calendar, contact database, and task list to keep myself organized. Cost of CD tutorial, $40

Potential obstacle(s)
I don't feel like I have a "sales" type of personality.

Ways to overcome the obstacle(s)
Join Toastmasters to learn public speaking.
Go to the library and check out books on sales.
Role-play sales situations with people I know.

Sample Goal Worksheet for Miguel

Goal statement:

_____

_____

Date: _____

Materials or things needed   **Cost**

_____   _____

_____   _____

_____   _____

_____   _____

_____   _____

People and organizations to contact   **Cost**

_____   _____

_____   _____

_____   _____

_____   _____

_____   _____

Knowledge and/or education needed   **Cost**

_____   _____

_____   _____

_____   _____

_____   _____

_____   _____

Potential obstacle(s)

_____

_____

Ways to overcome the obstacle(s)

_____

_____

_____

Your Sample Goal Worksheet

Goals are the places where dreams and actions meet. Pick out the kinds of goals that *motivate you* and give you pleasure to think about, and then make them materialize with your *sustained and persistent efforts.* Success requires action!

Mental Rehearsal

Extensive research in the fields of sports, psychology, peak performance, and medicine has proven that visualizing your goal (picturing it vividly in your imagination with your eyes closed) will help you get there that much faster and achieve it with a greater degree of precision. Sometimes visualization is called *mental rehearsal* because that's exactly what it is—a moving picture with sound, smell, temperature, faces, shapes, and actions all perceived from your own viewpoint. It is as if you are actually in the scene, a part of the picture, hearing the sounds, smelling the smells.

A visualization is something you design for yourself to help you "rehearse" the outcomes of your goals. For example, if you'd like to be very relaxed on your first day in your brand-new career, you might design a mental rehearsal session for yourself that placed you in your new office feeling very comfortable, at ease, and confident.

If you close your eyes, you can construct this office in an ideal way for yourself—see the furniture, windows, desk, and what's on your desk. You may notice that someone enters your office with a smile on her face, and all the while you are feeling very relaxed and confident. You might even imagine your boss saying "Good job!" at the end of the day or someone who looks interesting inviting you out for lunch.

You can create anything you wish in your ideal rehearsal, and the more detailed you are—the more you see vibrant colors, hear the qualities of people's voices talking, really imagine how you feel as you talk to a client or customer, and even sense the temperature of the room you're in—the more you are likely to feel the emotions you'd like to feel when the real day arrives.

Professional athletes have been using this technique for decades to make field goals, score baskets, win contests, and break records. Consider it for yourself, and have some fun with it!

If you don't want to make up your own rehearsal, you might buy an audiocassette tape or CD with a prerecorded generic mental rehearsal on it. Most of these recordings help you picture yourself in any situation you like and handling it at your very best, usually in a very relaxed, comfortable, competent way.

An excellent author of these recordings is Dr. Emmett Miller, a physician who has worked for over 20 years with top athletes and entertainers. He is considered to be at the forefront of the science of mental rehearsal. His audio recordings are available for purchase on his Web site (www.drmiller.com), and they are highly recommended.

Merely acting on impulse or putting one foot in front of the other without a clear compass delineating where you're headed will simply leave you in lost dreams and frustrations. That's why it's important to take the steps described in this chapter.

Goal setting is a serious business, but you may find yourself having fun as you realize that you really do have the power to bring your fantasies to fruition. I know you can set concrete goals and make plans to meet them. In Chapter 8 we're going to put those goals into purposeful action.

CHAPTER 8

The Accelerated Job Search

Now that you've identified your destination and you've planned a way to get there, the next step is to take action. In this chapter you'll learn how to apply the strategies for accelerated job searching. You'll also receive examples of résumés, cover letters, and special phone scripts to use as tools to help you land your dream job.

The Accelerated Job Search Process

Making your journey to the job you really want in the fastest way possible is the aim of this chapter, and there are six important skills to learn in the process:

1. Stacking the odds of getting an interview in your favor
2. Writing your own fearless career change résumé
3. Writing approach, cover, confirmation, and other relevant letters
4. Using direct-contact techniques to secure job interviews
5. Applying fearless career change interviewing techniques
6. Discerning when and how to follow up on phone calls, letters, and interviews

How to Beat the Competition by Interrupting the Hiring Cycle

In a common hiring cycle, a new job opening appears when *someone who has the power to hire you* perceives that there is a need for a new person in a project, department, office, or organization.

This idea to hire may have arisen for a number of reasons: someone quit, someone was fired, someone died or moved out of the area, or someone is out because of an extended period of illness and it's not clear if that person is going to return.

It also could mean that a higher head count is needed in the company because there is a new product or service that needs fresh ideas or because an executive or manager needs a second person in charge. There are a score of other reasons.

Four Phases of the Hiring Cycle

In the fearless career change methodology, we have a way of bypassing—even eliminating—the competition by *interrupting* what I call the *hiring cycle* before it reaches the final phase. It's important to understand each stage to know how to interrupt it at the advantageous moment.

Phase 1. While the hiring manager who sees the necessity of bringing on someone new first has the idea in his or her mind, only *one* person (namely, the person with the idea) knows that there is a possibility of a job opening. In most cases, this decision maker has to get permission from a *higher* decision maker.

Phase 2. While the decision maker and his or her superior are discussing the potential hire (which, in larger companies, can take up to a month or more), *only two or three* people know that there is a possibility of a job opening. If the senior person approves the hire, it will be submitted to the human resources department.

Phase 3. In the human resources department, a job description, in-house announcements, advertisements, a pay scale, and legal documents pertaining to the position are drawn up. This part of the process can take from three to nine months, depending on the size of the company. The opening may be announced internally, and up to 300 people may know of its existence. At this point, the competition is somewhat higher but not insurmountable.

Phase 4. The employment opening is announced to the general public via various media such as newspapers, the Internet, the radio, or trade journals. Experts estimate that at this phase your competition skyrockets to as many as 10,000 or more potential job applicants.

The Unadvertised Job Market

Remember, *no one* in the general public has yet to hear of the new posting until it reaches phase 4 of the hiring cycle. Because phases 1 through 3 are "hidden" from the outside world, they are also sometimes referred to as the *hidden job market* or the *unadvertised job market.*

> **The unadvertised job market is your window
> of opportunity.**

If you were somehow to hear of a potential opening at phase 2 or 3, you would have *only a handful* of other people competing for the opening.

If you had a way to directly reach the decision maker in phase 1 *when it was first conceived,* you would not have *any* competition. That's it. *Zero!*

Beating the Job Search Statistics

Let's take a look at what happens if you wait to see the opening in the classifieds of your local newspaper. As mentioned before, as many as *10,000 other people* may see that ad, take interest in it, and become your competition. The numbers go up astronomically when you think about the millions of people around the world who have access to a job opening when it's advertised on the Internet!

This is not to say that you should *never* open a newspaper again if you're looking for a job. Newspapers, networking, and the Internet are still viable means to get a job. Used along with direct-contact techniques aimed at the unadvertised job market, they are an important part of the job search. Just make sure that you don't spend too much of your valuable time focused on advertisements.

Now that you understand the difference between the advertised and the unadvertised job market, you can undoubtedly see why many career coaches are beginning to advocate the use of direct-contact techniques in the unadvertised job market. Finding an unadvertised job opening is somewhat of a numbers game. Studies show that anywhere from 1 in 12 direct-contact phone calls (in a healthy job market) will yield an opening and that the odds of finding an opportunity in a slower market are 1 in 20. Can you predict an opening in the unadvertised job market before placing a call or sending a letter of inquiry? It's difficult, but several guidelines can help you choose the kinds of companies that are more likely to present potential positions.

1. It's important to remember that very large companies in the process of massively downsizing may also be hiring at the same time. That's because layoffs usually take place by job function or departments rather than by arbitrary numbers. Hundreds, even thousands, can get laid off in the manufacturing department while scores of people are getting hired in sales or human resources. Similarly, sales could be waning while manufacturing is booming! A company may be skimming off upper-management positions while actively hiring for entry-level functions.

   Therefore, just because you read in the newspaper that there has been a huge layoff at a company does not mean that you should omit that company from your list of potential workplaces.

2. There is no way to make an absolute judgment about how many people might be hired at some point in the future, but there are ways to make educated guesses about the probability that an organization is increasing its head count. Two ways to make such a determination are with the help of the following resources:

   • Your local newspaper, the *Wall Street Journal, INC.* magazine, or *Forbes* magazine. Find stories that mention a local plant or corporation is opening new offices in your area. These offices and plants will need staffing and management even though the company may not be advertising the openings yet.

     The same thing applies to companies conspicuously reporting new projects or products. They may not need someone today, but when the project starts or the product is being manufactured and marketed, employees, managers, and sales teams will be needed to support those efforts.

- Use the Internet. One of my favorite sites for business information is www.hoovers.com. You can enter the name of several companies in the specialized Hoover's search engine and compare their one-year employee growth rates. At least relatively, you could determine lesser and better chances of openings arising in the near future. A 5.6 percent employee growth rate versus a rate of 21.7 percent can be found in two companies in the same industry that are practically next door to each other. Ironically, the company that seems more famous and successful may have a much lower growth rate than a lesser-known company.

  Hoover's also contains current news with clues about company expansion and implosion. You can find releases (things the company writes about itself, versus news, which is written by journalists and reporters). New-product releases and project initiations are often announced well ahead of the point that a company would normally hire people to staff these new ventures. Geographic data as well as companies' intentions to create new locations or new offices and factories are also reported in press releases. The classified ads in newspapers and on the Internet don't reflect these changes because they haven't happened yet. Again, if you uncover these clues, you'll be the first there with little or no competition for upcoming positions.

- Another useful site is vcbuzz.com. This site issues reports when start-up companies receive large infusions of venture capital (funding). Guess what happens after funding? You guessed it: hiring!

Beginning Your Direct-Contact Campaign

Advertised or unadvertised, you are most likely going to need a résumé to make your career transition and job search successful. There are three basic types of résumés: *chronological, functional,* and *hybrid,* which is a combination of the first two.

When making a career change, you should probably use a chronological format, which is contrary to the traditional advice given to job searchers. I recommend chronological because in my experience, employers strongly prefer a chronological format. Please refer to the sample résumé later in this chapter, and in section one, for an example.

How to Write Your Fearless Career Change Résumé

According to several surveys of hiring managers and human resources professionals in larger Fortune 500 companies, as many as *1,500 résumés* can pile up on one person's desk in as little time as a week.

> **These managers, department heads, and human resource professionals admit that they read only about the first five or six lines at the top of the résumé—about three to seven seconds' worth!**

That means that we *must* get the employer's attention within that crucial seven seconds of that first look. Here's how to do it.

Streamline Your Objective

The first step in preparing your résumé to grab the reader in the first few seconds is to streamline your job objective (see sample résumé). Several years ago, it was popular to write objectives that sounded something like this:

> Seeking a challenging position that will leverage my interpersonal skills, business savvy, and technical know-how to make a significant contribution to the company, with the potential for continuous growth and advancement.

How long did it take you to read that sentence? About two or three seconds? Well, once that time is over, so is your first chance at "hooking" the employer's attention.

A fearless career change résumé uses *only a job title* to express the objective. That way, the employer knows *immediately* what you want and can get to the "meat" of the next few lines of your résumé right away. Here are examples of a fearless career change objective statement:

- A position as an environmental planner
- Environmental planner
- Biotechnical sales manager
- Licensed clinical social worker
- A position as a systems analyst

If you *must* write a more general objective, try to at least specify the *industry* and the *level* of position you're aiming for:

- An entry-level position in the sports management industry
- A managerial position in the food services field
- An executive position with a telecommunications start-up firm

If you're writing your résumé to a company that already has a written or advertised description of the job, try to use the exact same title on your résumé as the one in the written description.

Compose a High-Impact Summary Statement

Your next tactic in swiftly capturing the reader's attention, while at the same time presenting almost all the information he or she needs to evaluate your readiness for an interview, is to pack the summary statement (which follows your objective) with an abundance of relevant, specific, and attention-getting information.

Your summary statement can be read in that *sensitive seven seconds*, and it provides the reader with a powerful first impression. Here are some sample summary statements to use as a guide:

Over ten years' experience as a landscaper and landscape designer as the owner of Big Bear Landscapes, specializing in native plants, low-maintenance gardens, and waterfall design. Responsible for landscaping a 12-acre property with low-maintenance native plants, coming in eight days under deadline and $1,300 under budget. BS biology, Yale University. Currently enrolled in a course of study leading to a master's degre in environmental planning at California State University a Burlingame. Flexible, dependable, adaptable to change

467

Over six years as an electrical engineer in a Fortune 500 company, specializing in wireless communications, project management, and testing. Won the Employee of the Year Award in 2000 and 2003. Master's in electrical engineering from the University of Georgia at Atlanta. Currently possess a series 65 and series 7 license and have passed a 12-week financial advisor training program at Henley, Scott, and Thomas, LLC. Trustworthy, proactive, detail oriented.

Over three years as a customer service representative for a nationally known health insurance carrier, specializing in customer satisfaction, troubleshooting, and training new employees. Handle over 200 customer inquiries daily, with only 3 percent escalation rate. Bachelor's degree in art from the University of California at Berkeley. Currently enrolled in courses leading to a certificate in video arts at the University of California, Santa Cruz. Reliable, creative, energetic.

Notice that these summary statements share a similar format. Each is three to five sentences long and no more. Every sentence has a very deliberate function. Let's take a look at what information each of them contains.

1. The first sentence states the number of years' experience in a given job title and industry and three areas of specialization. If you do your research on the O*NET, labor market readiness research, or by other means, you'll discover what "specializations" certain industries or employers demand. Since your résumé can and should change with every company to accommodate that company's preferences, your specializations can also change. For example, a human resources professional's résumé might say, "specializing in staffing, team building, and triaging" for one employer, but the wording might be altered for another organization to read "specializing in benefits, compensation, and sexual harassment issues." Same basic résumé—different companies, hence different specializations.

2. In the second sentence, pick out an accomplishment that will really dazzle the employer. Just because this accomplishment may have been achieved in a school, training, volunteer, hobby, or an intern situation does not mean that it's not relevant. Treat your achievement just as you would if you

had accomplished it at a paying job. For example, a computer networking professional just out of a certification class can still say, "Handled networking protocols for TCP/IP and wireless function on Linux and Solaris platforms." If you can, make your accomplishment into a Q statement (that is, an assertion that is quantified) like, "Built seven custom homes within a nine month period managing a crew of 12 construction workers."

3. Introduce your past educational background, if it applies to the job you're seeking, in the third sentence, and in the fourth, note your short-term education, strategic education, or other strategies. A great way to describe a training program that's not yet finished or just getting underway is "currently enrolled in a course of study leading to . . ." or "currently completing a degree in _____."

4. Last, you can list some of the personal strengths (not skills) that you bring to the table. Personal strengths are things like dependability, flexibility, and the ability to work well under pressure.

After reviewing the summary statements, write one for yourself using the following summary statement template. *Fill in the blanks on the template and leave out the italicized words.*

After you finish your statement, ask yourself (or maybe someone else!) these questions:

- Does my summary statement read like a "mini-résumé"?
- Does the summary grab the reader's attention and make a powerful impact?

Turn Your Accomplishments into Q Statements

Q statements (an abbreviation for *quantified statements*) use quantifiable terms—numbers, percentages, amounts of time or things, and, occasionally, rating scales—to present your accomplishments in concrete, measureable ways. Here are some examples of Q statements:

- Decreased waste by 20 percent, resulting in an overall savings of $1.2 million a year.

Over ____ years as a _____ in the
_____industry, specializing in
_____, _____, and
_____. *[See below for how
to write a Q statement and write one that most pertains to the
type of skills you'll be using in your next job.]*

_____
_____

_____

BA *(or AA, BS, MBA, Ph.D., etc.)* in _____
from the University of _____. Currently
enrolled in a course of study leading to a _____
in _____ at _____ College.
*[Write three personal traits that describe you and most closely match
qualities you'll need on your next job—for example, dependable, team
player, learns quickly* _____, _____, *and*
_____.

Résumé Summary Statement Template

- Attained gross annual sales of $193,000.
- Operated a multiline phone system and personally handled over 200 calls per day.
- Acted as a regional manager for 12 offices overseeing 147 salespeople throughout the Midwest.
- Initiated and developed a retraining program that improved employee satisfaction from 2.7 to 4.1 on a scale of 1 to 5.
- Decreased production time by six days a month, resulting in a savings of $360,000 quarterly.
- Maintained a caseload of 65 patients.
- Built a prototype that could tolerate 15 percent more stress than its predecessor.

- Introduced an on-site safety program that decreased workers' compensation claims by 18 percent in one year.
- Processed more than 250 customer requests daily.
- Won an award for decreasing materials costs from $6.41 per inch to $5.20 per inch.
- Instrumental in increasing customer satisfaction (on a scale of 1 to 10) from 3.0 to 7.5.

Once you start thinking of your job responsibilities as *measurable* accomplishments, Q statements will come easily to you and you can incorporate them into your résumé. It's not always possible to use a Q statement to describe what you did, but, no matter how small the accomplishment, there is usually a way to find a quantifiable value to include on your résumé. Take a look at how Q statements are incorporated into the sample résumé. Take a few moments now to write a first draft of your résumé using the sample résumé as your guide.

This résumé checklist will ensure that your résumé is sharp, powerful, and influential to the reader:

❑ The objective is crisp and concise. Just a job title if possible.
❑ Your summary presents a powerful picture, in just a few seconds, of what you can do.
❑ The bulleted statements are *quantified* wherever possible.
❑ The *years only* (and not the months) of employment are included.
❑ If you had more than one title at the same company, you place the *cumulative* years you were at the company at the top on the same line as the name of the company and the years you were in each *different* position next to the name of the job title in parentheses. (See sample résumé, "Anderson's Nursery").
❑ Going back into the job history more than ten years is avoided. (This is true except in cases wherein a job more than ten years ago has information that directly pertains to the job for which you're now applying.)
❑ Dates of college graduation are omitted. (In case the employer makes a judgment that you are too young or too old for the position.)

❑ It is all right to repeat items from your summary in the body of the résumé.

❑ There are no more than six and no fewer than two bullets under each job heading.

❑ You never refer to yourself in the first person. The words *I, me,* and *myself* are not part of the résumé.

❑ The résumé is written with *Times New Roman or Arial style font in 11- or 12-point* size. It should be printed on simple white, cream, or gray paper. No colors, pastels, or special textures other than résumé bond or plain copy paper should be used.

❑ The résumé is one to two pages, never more than two pages. (The exception to this is if you have a large number of scientific publications and/or patents. In that case, submit them as addendum on a separate sheet of paper, after asking whether or not the hiring authority wants to see them.)

Radical Career Changes

If you're making a drastic career change—say, from attorney to fashion designer—I recommend that you still use the same format as above, but you should make some important alterations in the summary statement section of your résumé.

Unless you are using the tactic of Just Dive In!, it is likely that to hasten your transition, you've enrolled in a strategic education course, have started or even completed a certification program in your new field, and/or had the benefit of an internship or volunteer position.

Since we already know that employers are likely to get only a three- to seven-second "snapshot" of the first few lines of your résumé, it's imperative that you build strategies like internship, short-term education, and strategic education right into the summary statement at the beginning of the résumé so that they will see that you're already a "player" in their game.

Things that place you on the same playing field are experience (even if it's only in an academic or volunteer setting); specific statements about some areas in which you have concrete, immediately usable skills; or personal qualities that would reflect favorably on

Marie L. Sanchez
757 North Elmwood Drive
Los Gatos, CA 95136
(408) 337-2481 Work   (408) 297-3373 Home
(831) 223-9798 Mobile
marie_s@techmail.com

Objective
A position as an environmental planner

Summary
Over 10 years' experience as a landscaper and landscape designer as the owner of Big Bear Landscapes, specializing in native plants, low-maintenance gardens, and waterfall design. Responsible for landscaping a 12-acre property with low-maintenance native plants, coming in eight days under deadline and $1,300 under budget. BS biology, Yale University. Currently enrolled in a course of study leading to a master's degree in environmental planning at California State University at Burlingame. Flexible, dependable, adaptable to change.

Employment History
Big Bear Landscapes, Saratoga, CA 1993–present
Owner

- Designed and implemented a plan for a 13-acre residential property in Los Altos, California, using low-maintenance native California plants which was photographed and printed in *Better Homes and Landscapes* magazine.

- Saved a total of $1,300 by completing work eight days before deadline on a commercial property in San Jose, California.

- Reduced water usage and water bills by an average of 35 percent on each of 23 residential properties.

Sample Résumé

- Invited to lecture 60 community college students on the topic of native plant maintenance for the horticulture department at Hillsdale Community College in Fremont, California.
- Expert in native plants and plant biology. Able to identify over 300 varieties of native plants and succulents of the coastal region of the western United States.
- Trained and supervised a crew of 17 employees.

Anderson's Nursery, Los Gatos, CA 1989–1993
Outdoor Products Manager (1991–1993)

- Sold approximately $450 worth of merchandise daily to up to 120 customers per week.
- Hired, trained, and managed 11 employees.
- Wrote a 28-page new employee orientation booklet.
- Recommended soil treatments, gardening methods, and gardening tools to customers.

Outdoor Gardening Associate 1989–1991

- Served up to 30 customers daily.
- Counseled customer on proper plant selection and garden care.
- Operated a cash register and credit card processor.
- Won Employee of the Month awards in January 1990 and September 1993.

Education

Currently enrolled in graduate studies in environmental planning, California State University at Burlingame
BS in biology, with honors, Yale University, New Haven, Connecticut

Sample Résumé (Continued)

you in your new profession (dependability, ability to work under pressure, friendliness, ability to meet deadlines, and so on).

Finally, it's always a great idea to join some sort of professional organization that represents your field. As a participant (even passively) in the organization, you will seem to be that much more a member of a new team of professionals.

The best way to find organizations to which your new colleagues belong is to either search for them online—try, for example, *financial association, finance professional organizations,* or *financial planning networks*—or go to the library and look through a copy of the *Encyclopedia of Associations.*

You may be surprised at how many professional organizations exist for just about every occupation that exists. These groups may charge annual or monthly dues starting at as little as $5 a month and running as high as $600 a year. You should consider joining one or several. It would be money well spent.

Remember: Half the battle in getting hired is not *what* you know but how the employer perceives what you know. "Packaging" yourself as part of a professional or trade association can add as much credibility to your presentation as could years of schooling and experience.

Summary Statements for Radical Career Changers

If you were making a radical career change from an engineer to a financial planner, it would do little good to lead your summary statement with "ten years as an engineer." Instead, it would be better (assuming you had completed some financial courses) to lead with something like this:

> Knowledge of state insurance practices and 401k and Keogh plans. Expertise in mathematics due to a master's degree in engineering and 10 years as an engineer. Effective interpersonal skills gained from 7 years managing over 18 people as a project manager. Professional, meticulous, responsible. Currently enrolled in a course of study leading to a certificate in financial planning at the University of Michigan extension. Member, Michigan Institute for the Development of Financial Advisement.

Similarly, one way our administrative assistant's summary statement could instantly downplay her years of serving as a secretary and highlight her midwifery training—however brief—could be something like this:

Experienced in midwifery assistance and prenatal and postnatal care. Excellent grasp of massage techniques, basic herbology, and interpersonal relations. Graduate of a certification course in midwifery assistance. Experienced in assisting in breach and other difficult birthing scenarios. Trustworthy, warm, empathetic. Member of Midwife Society of America.

How to Submit Your Résumé

The *ideal* way to submit your résumé is to place a "warm" or "cold" phone call to the decision maker (something we'll discuss in the section of this chapter called "How to Make Direct Contact with a Decision Maker"). Second best would be an in-person interview, at which you present your résumé directly to the employer at the time of the interview.

When neither of those routes is possible, I'd like you to *beat your competition* by using an alternative to the regular U.S. mail service.

Whether you are penetrating the unadvertised job market or responding to the advertised job market, sending your résumé by normal U.S. mail is the least effective way to get it noticed.

Hiring managers are flooded with e-mail, which means that although an e-mail message is fast—almost instantaneous—your résumé will not receive the attention it deserves if you are up against up to 300 other e-mails per day.

To sway the odds back in your favor, use one of these methods:

1. Send it via Federal Express (FedEx).
2. Send it through the U.S. Postal Service Priority Mail in a Priority Mail envelope.
3. Fax it.

There is no mail that is opened faster than an overnight FedEx package slated for arrival by 10 a.m. the next morning.

Both the color of the FedEx envelope and the urgency conveyed by overnight delivery create an almost *irresistible* urge for the receiver to see what's inside. FedEx can be a little expensive though. USPS Priority Mail, also because of its red and blue motif and its priority status, quickly captures the interest of its recipient.

Submitting a Résumé on the Internet

If you plan to submit a résumé using the Internet, *be careful* not to fall into the trap of clicking on the "apply here" or "apply now" button (usually located at the bottom of the page on your computer screen).

Because this is the easiest way to apply, hundreds and even thousands of others will be doing the same thing. Instead, we have found that faxing your résumé to the fax number on the online advertisement is the superior way to get it noticed. You also have the option of sending it by FedEx or USPS Priority Mail.

Cover Letter or No Cover Letter?

I've spoken to hundreds of people with the power to hire others. The vast majority of these people have so little time to even read your résumé that they consider a cover letter to be just so much more paper to "wade" through. I don't recommend that you write a cover letter unless it is *explicitly* asked for. If you happen to need a cover letter because you've spotted a written request for it, please see the following sample approach cover letter to use as your guide.

Q Letters

A *Q letter* (or *qualifications letter*) is a special kind of cover letter, and I highly recommend its use. It can be submitted *with or without* a résumé. Using the same type of quantifiable statements you created for your résumé, a Q letter gives the employer a swift and efficient glance at how your qualifications stack up to the requirements of the job.

Q letters have been amazingly effective for people who have used them. You will see in the following sample Q cover letter that they certainly meet our "seven-second first look" requirements.

They're an attention getter, they communicate relevant data in a concise format, and hiring managers report that they like them.

July 15, 20xx

Dr. Paul Robinson
125 Doctor Lane
Madison, WI 12345

Dear Dr. Robinson:

Hello. I am interested in the position of midwife assistant in your clinic, either at present or some time in the future. I possess the following qualifications:

- Graduate of the Doula program at West Denver Institute of Midwifery.
- Successful internship, which included assisting in 12 births at the Gentle Birth Center.
- Knowledge of prenatal, birthing, and postpartum procedures for labor assistants.
- Excellent interpersonal skills due to three years volunteering at Colorado Mountains Hospice Program.
- Three letters of recommendation.

Please expect a call from me within three business days, after you have had an opportunity to review my qualifications.

Sincerely,

Alice Livermore
(727) 333-6760
livermorea@cbc.net

Sample Approach Letter or Cover Letter

Ethan Jenner
1659 7th Avenue
Heraldtown, Vermont
(416) 555-5555
ejenner@emailaddress.com

February 22, 20xx

Ms. Deborah Scott
ABC Corporation
23 Broadway
Washington, DC 12345

Dear Ms. Scott:

In response to your advertisement for a chief financial officer in the Monday, February 21, 20xx, posting on www.monster.com, I would like to respectfully submit my qualifications.

Your Requirements	My Qualifications
1. Five to 10 years' experience as a CFO in a Fortune 500 company.	Over 10 years' experience as a CFO.
2. Oversees other accountants.	Supervised more than 12 accountants and high-level financial personnel.
3. CPA desired.	CPA since 1985.
4. BA required, MBA preferred.	BA in history. Currently enrolled in a course of study leading to an MBA from the University of Vermont.

Please call me at your earliest convenience for an interview. Thank you.

Sincerely,

Ethan Jenner

Sample Q Letter or Cover Letter

Compose Your Own Q Letter

The way to write a Q letter is to first determine the requirements of the job. You can do this by looking at a job description, looking at a general description in the O*NET, or by asking a person already in that profession what the typical requirements are.

Then, pick four or five requirements and write them on the left half of your page (see sample). On the right side of your page, for every requirement find a qualification you possess that is equal to or better than the requirement.

How to Make Direct Contact with a Decision Maker

Once you've sent your résumé and Q letter, it's time to make direct contact. So, just what does *direct contact* mean? Direct contact means placing a "warm" or "cold" telephone call to a key decision maker in a company for which you want to work. On the phone, you convince him or her to set up a face-to-face meeting with you.

By *warm call* I mean a call that is preceded by some sort of written communication—a letter, a résumé, or note of some kind. See the earlier samples of an approach letter and Q letter and the following warm-call pitch:

> Hello, Dr. Thomas. My name is Alice Livermore. I'm a midwife assistant graduate of West Denver Institute of Midwifery and an intern from the Gentle Birth Center. *You may have noticed from the FedEx I sent you* that I have excellent references and a good grasp of the birthing process. When can I come in for an interview?

A *cold call* is made directly to your contact, without any written introduction, such as the following example:

> Hello, Dr. Thomas. My name is Alice Livermore. I'm a midwife assistant graduate of West Denver Institute of Midwifery and an intern from the Gentle Birth Center. I have excellent references and a good grasp of the birthing process. When can I come in for an interview?

Both cold and warm calls work (although a cold call has the element of a "surprise attack" that can be quite effective). A cold call, we have found, can actually be more effective when placing a call to executives, upper managers, and business owners because the very methods you are using to place the call—aggressiveness, proactivity, courage, initiative—are sometimes the very qualities that brought the executive up "out of the ranks" and the very ones he or she will most admire in you. It's up to you which kind of calling best suits your personality and the particular situation.

Four Steps for Making Direct Contact

Remembering what you know now about the unadvertised job market, these four steps are the game plan for getting yourself an interview:

1. Choose up to 40 companies or businesses for which you'd like to work, regardless of whether or not they have an advertised job opening. You can generate your list from the business directory of the phone book, from hoovers.com on the Internet, or from *Rich's Guide, Standard & Poor's Directory, Reference USA,* or *Thomas Register,* which are available in hard copy (and sometimes online) at your local library.

2. Determine the *exact first and last name* of the person most likely to have the power to hire you. Most often, this is the person who is the boss of *your* next potential boss.

   So if you are a manager, rather than calling a senior manager, you would call the *director* or vice president. Similarly, if you were a director you would call the executive vice president or the chief operating officer. If you are calling a small company, ask for the owner or manager.

   You can find exact names of managers and executives on the Web site of the company or, in one of the *directories listed above in step 1.* Or you may have to use a direct approach.

   For a direct approach, call the receptionist of the business and say, "I'm going to send a FedEx to the *(vice president, manager, director)* of *(marketing, engineering, manufacturing, health services, production).* Can you give me the exact spelling of his or her name?" Three times out of five, you'll get the name.

3. Send a fax, USPS Priority Mail, or FedEx with your Q letter or approach letter (see sample on page 478). You may send the letter alone or with a résumé. The approach letter is a great way to strike up productive communication with someone

you've never met before. This, or a Q letter, sent with or without a résumé, is excellent for laying the groundwork for a warm call.

4. Place a call to the person one to three days after the expected arrival of the letter. See the next section for details on what to say during your call.

The procedure for a cold call is the same as the preceding four steps except that you do not precede the call with a letter or any form of written communication. In other words, skip step 3.

Your 30-Second Phone Pitch

The core of your cold or warm call is something that is sometimes referred to as a *30-second pitch*. You can compose your own pitch by using portions of the summary statement from your résumé. Let's take a moment to rehearse this technique so that you can get the feel of writing your own pitch. Take a look at the previous samples of both a warm- and a cold-call phone pitch. Use the following phone pitch template to construct your own pitch for a cold call or a warm call. You will have to make slight modifications in this pitch template to suit your own situation. Just keep in mind that your pitch has a very specific aim.

Hello, my name is _____. I have _____ years' experience as a _____, and I'm currently making a career change into the field of _____. I have an (AA, MA, etc.) degree in _____, and I just finished a certificate program in _____. (Optional) You may have noticed in my letter to you that _____. When can I come in for an interview?

Cold- or Warm-Call Pitch Template

The purpose of the pitch (for both a warm and a cold call) is to accomplish the following:

- Grab the listener's attention.
- Impress him or her with one or more of your qualifications.
- Target your statement to those qualifications you think the employer values most.
- If possible, mention a relevant fact you have learned to prove that you have researched the company.
- Ask for an interview. (An interview is *any* face-to-face contact with the employer.)

Handling Screening-Out Questions and Objections

It's rather unlikely that the decision maker is going to answer the phone initially. It's more likely that you'll get a receptionist, supervisor, or executive assistant whose job it is to screen out unwanted calls. In large companies there may even be more than one of these assistants.

The script in the section "Making the Phone Call" will show you exactly what those assistants are trained to say—and you may be pleasantly surprised that the dialogue shows you exactly how to counter their screening efforts and get past them to the hiring manager.

You'll also notice that it's unlikely (though not at all impossible) that the decision maker will agree to a meeting the first time you ask. The sample phone script shows you exactly what we've found to be the typical doubts (we call them *objections*) that the employer may have.

Again, it may surprise you when you actually start making calls that, indeed, these are exactly the objections you encounter. Fortunately, you'll be prepared. Before you make a call, be careful that you are comfortable with your pitch and know the tactics for getting past the assistants. Also, learn to anticipate the objections the employer will raise and become competent at dealing with them.

Making the Phone Call

When three business days have passed since you sent your letter to the decision maker, it's time for you to give him or her a phone call. At this juncture, it's a good idea to practice your phone script with a friend or family member several times before you go for the real thing. If you feel a bit jittery about ringing up your No. 1 favorite company, try a "dry run" with a few companies (even companies out of town) that you don't care too much about.

With a little practice you'll get into the rhythm of getting through the screening process with the receptionist and countering typical objections from the employer. With your phone script in hand, this should be a breeze! The following is a script of a typical warm call.

Phone rings

RECEPTIONIST: Hello, Ellen Robinson Childbirth Clinic.

JOB SEEKER: Alice Livermore for Dr. Robinson.

RECEPTIONIST: May I ask the nature of your call? *(Screening out—see below.)*

JOB SEEKER: It's business.

RECEPTIONIST: All right, I'll connect you.

DOCTOR'S ASSISTANT: Maya Rhodes speaking.

JOB SEEKER: Alice Livermore for Dr. Robinson.

DOCTOR'S ASSISTANT: This is Dr. Robinson's nurse. Can I help you? *(Screening out.)*

JOB SEEKER: No, but thank you. I'd prefer to speak to Dr. Robinson directly.

DOCTOR'S ASSISTANT: What is this regarding? *(Screening out.)*

JOB SEEKER: It's about a document I FedExed to her yesterday.

DOCTOR'S ASSISTANT: Is she expecting your call? *(Screening out.)*

JOB SEEKER: Yes. *(Remember, you faxed or sent something saying you would call.)*

DOCTOR'S ASSISTANT: All right, I'll connect you.

Sample Phone Script

HIRING MANAGER: Dr. Robinson.

JOB SEEKER: (*This paragraph is what is referred to as the pitch.*) Hello, Dr. Robinson. My name is Alice Livermore. I'm a midwife assistant graduate of West Denver Institute of Midwifery. I had a 30-day internship and participated in 12 births at the Gentle Birth Center. You may have noticed *from the FedEx I sent you* that I have excellent references and a good grasp of the birthing process. When can I come in for an interview?

HIRING MANAGER: Did I get your FedEx? Oh, yes, let me see . . . It's right here on my desk. Hmm . . . Yes, Alice it does look like you have some excellent skills. Unfortunately, we're not hiring right now. (*Objection.*)

JOB SEEKER: Oh, that's fine. I'm not interested in just *any* company, and I *don't need a job right away*. I'm looking for an organization that's a good match for my skills so that I can make a long-term commitment. (*Optional: I looked at your Web site, and I really like your clinic's philosophy on child bearing, especially the quote by Margaret Mead.*) I'm interested in talking to you about *future* or *unexpected* openings.

HIRING MANAGER: Can you send me your full résumé? (*This is an objection, a way to keep you at bay, not an invitation to an interview. It would be easy for the employer to simply toss your résumé into the "read-later" pile or even in the paper shredder. A living, breathing person with whom you're interacting face to face is much more of an investment than handling a piece of paper. You want the employer to* invest *in meeting you* in the flesh.)

JOB SEEKER: Of course, thank you, but I will be in your area of town next week. I'd love to schedule a very brief 15-minute talk and get your *personal opinion* on my qualifications.

HIRING MANAGER: Well, . . . I'd like to but I'm just jammed with patients next week. (*Objection.*)

JOB SEEKER: No problem at all. How about if we schedule something for the following week, say, Wednesday or Thursday? How would that work for you?

Sample Phone Script (Continued)

HIRING MANAGER: Actually, on that week, Friday the 22nd would probably be better.

JOB SEEKER: Morning or afternoon?

HIRING MANAGER: Let's see. My morning is booked.

JOB SEEKER: Would 2 p.m. or 3 p.m. work?

HIRING MANAGER: Yes, why don't I see you at 3. I'll transfer you back to the receptionist, and she'll make the appointment for you.

JOB SEEKER: Thanks so much, Dr. Robinson, I'm looking forward to it!

HIRING MANAGER: Goodbye.

JOB SEEKER: See you on the 22nd.

Sample Phone Script (Continued)

Perseverance Pays!

It's certainly *possible* that you will *not* have to deal at all with being screened or with the employer's having objections. I know someone who made a cold call to a medium-sized company on a holiday. Guess who answered? The president of the company. Who else would be there on a holiday? The president was so impressed with the bravado of the caller's phone pitch that *he offered her a job on the spot*—on the phone!

If you get the decision maker's voice mail, it is best not to leave a message. That puts the ball in his or her court. Try the phone call later.

Perseverance really pays off when it comes to warm and cold calling. One of my clients to whom I taught direct-contact techniques called me after the second call and said she couldn't do it. I urged her to continue. She called me after her eleventh call and said she'd absolutely had it.

After talking for a while, she decided to give it one more try. Her twelfth call, to Time Warner, yielded a talk with a vice president. He granted her an interview. She now has a job, earning over $100,000 a year.

Is an hour of making repeated phone calls, and possibly facing momentary rejection, worth that kind of money? You decide! Your goal is not to sound polished or even friendly. *Your goal is to get an interview.*

Once you get the interview, stand up and cheer! Then, send the hiring manager a brief note or e-mail confirming the date and time of the meeting and thanking him or her in advance for his or her time. (See the following sample confirmation letter.)

Preparing for the Interview

You made it! Now it's time to prepare for your interview. One of the very best ways to prepare is to know your talents and skills and be ready to tell anecdotes (examples) about how and when you used those talents. Preferably your specific examples should be in story form using quite *specific* details and *Q statements.*

Since you are a career changer and you don't yet have stories to tell about your new career, you may have to bring your *transferable talents* from former occupations, school, or even hobbies to bear in your interview.

Transferable Talents

Remember, transferable talents are things like analysis, management, and problem-solving and interpersonal skills that can transfer from one occupation to a completely different one. Here is a list of transferable talents, similar to the list we saw in Chapter 2. Check off each of these skills you have performed—you need not be an expert. You may need to rely on talents you haven't used since high school, but if you used them once, you can improve upon them and use them again!

❑ Advertising   ❑ Arranging

❑ Advising   ❑ Assessing performance

❑ Analyzing   ❑ Assessing progress

November 2, 20xx

Robert Coleman
XYZ Big Company
789 First Street
Kansas City, MO 12345

Dear Mr. Coleman:

Thank you for your time on the telephone earlier today. I'm very pleased that we could set up a time for a meeting.

I know from my research that your company is well regarded for giving generously to charitable causes, and with two new offices opening in West Virginia this year, you must be enjoying great success.

I'm eager to meet you and find out more about XYZ Big Company. I'll look forward to our meeting at 9:30 a.m. on Thursday, December 2.

Thank you again.

Regards,

Amy Levin
(222) 756-9123 home
(222) 333-3433 mobile
alevin@fastnet.com

Sample Letter of Confirmation

- Assessing quality
- Assisting
- Attention to detail
- Auditing
- Budgeting
- Building cooperation
- Building credibility
- Building relation-ships
- Building structures
- Calculating
- Classifying
- Client relations
- Coaching
- Communicating feelings
- Communicating ideas
- Communicating in writing
- Communicating instructions
- Communicating nonverbally
- Communicating verbally
- Computer literate
- Conceptualizing
- Consulting
- Correcting
- Corresponding
- Counseling
- Customer service
- Data analysis
- Data processing
- Decision making
- Decorating
- Delegating
- Developing designs
- Developing systems
- Developing talent
- Diagnosing
- Directing
- Drafting
- Drawing
- Driving
- Editing
- Educating
- Empathizing
- Enforcing
- Engineering
- Evaluating
- Filing
- Financial planning
- Forecasting
- Formulating
- Fund raising
- Healing
- Helping others
- Imagining
- Implementing
- Influencing
- Initiating
- Intervening
- Intuiting
- Inventing

- ❑ Investigating
- ❑ Leading people
- ❑ Lecturing
- ❑ Lifting
- ❑ Listening
- ❑ Managing tasks
- ❑ Marketing
- ❑ Marketing and communications
- ❑ Massaging
- ❑ Nurturing
- ❑ Observing
- ❑ Organizing
- ❑ Prescribing
- ❑ Program managing
- ❑ Programming computers
- ❑ Project managing
- ❑ Promoting
- ❑ Public speaking
- ❑ Reconstructing
- ❑ Recording
- ❑ Repairing
- ❑ Reporting
- ❑ Researching
- ❑ Sales and marketing programs
- ❑ Selling
- ❑ Servicing
- ❑ Servicing customers
- ❑ Supervising
- ❑ Surveying
- ❑ Team building
- ❑ Team leading
- ❑ Telephone skills
- ❑ Tending
- ❑ Tooling
- ❑ Training
- ❑ Troubleshooting
- ❑ Understanding
- ❑ Using of equipment
- ❑ Using of the Internet

Now that you've completed the exercise, I'd like you to pick six of the talents you checked that you think you will most need in your future career.

1. _____
2. _____
3. _____
4. _____
5. _____
6. _____

For each of the talents that you picked, please write three quick stories about how, where, and when you used them, including the positive *results* of your efforts. Your interviewer will want to hear these stories as proof that you can really do what you claim you can do. You will shine as someone who is thoroughly prepared and knows his or her strengths.

> ***In a national study conducted by an organization called JIST in Indianapolis, 4,000 employers, declared that 85 percent of job candidates do not clearly state their strengths. You'll be in the top 15 percent by clarifying your talents and strengths and providing information to back them up.***

Use Q statements wherever you can, and be as detailed and specific as possible without going over about 90 seconds. Please write your stories (or keywords that help you remember them) in the following section. It's a good idea to have at least two stories for each talent you've selected. The *more* anecdotes you can relate, though, the more prepared you will feel and the more convincing you will be.

1. _____

   a. _____

     _____

   b. _____

     _____

   c. _____

     _____

2. _____

   a. _____

     _____

   b. _____

     _____

c. _____

_____

3. _____

a. _____

_____

b. _____

_____

c. _____

_____

4. _____

a. _____

_____

b. _____

_____

c. _____

_____

5. _____

a. _____

_____

b. _____

_____

c. _____

_____

6. _____

a. _____

_____

b. _____

_____

c. _____

_____

Other _____

_____

The Career Change Question

As a career changer you will most definitely be asked the following question during your interview: Why did you quit your former career?

The most favorable answer to this question is one that is *not* negative and does *not* reflect badly on you. An answer that indicates you were bored, "burned out," hated your old profession, had trouble with your boss or coworkers, were fired, or that you are seeking out a new career "just for the money" may sound negative or even petty to the interviewer.

Better answers to this question would be the following:

1. My last career was not a perfect match for my interests and skills. After researching this (*the new*) profession, I think I'm very well matched and would be very happy to be part of it.

2. I have been researching the profession of _____ (*the new career*), and I find it fascinating. There are some trends and innovations that really interest me, such as _____, and I'd like to make a career of being a _____.

> **Notice that the better answers to this question focus less on the old job and much more on the new career.**

Other Typical Interview Questions

The following are some of the most common interview questions. Write your answer under each question, remembering to be specific and to not state anything bad about yourself, your former boss, or your former company. Emphasize your transferable skills with the specific *anecdotes* about your previous experiences you've just written.

Tell me about yourself.

_____

_____

What are some of your skills?

_____

_____

What are some of your most important accomplishments?

_____

_____

What are some of your personal strengths? Can you give me some examples?

_____

_____

What would your last boss (or coworkers) say about you?

_____

_____

What do you know about our company?

_____

_____

Why do you want to work with this company?

_____

_____

Why did you leave your last company?

_____

_____

Where do you see yourself in five years?

_____

_____

Are you better working independently or being part of a team?

_____

_____

What would you do if you found out one of your coworkers was stealing from the company?

_____

_____

How much were you making in your last job?

_____

What are your salary expectations at this company?

_____

_____

Why should I hire you?

_____

_____

Good! Now that you have at least two stories for each of your transferable talents, you can anticipate some of the most common questions, and you know how to answer the question "Why are you switching occupations?" then you're ready to shine during the interview. You can now go into the interview and be *fearless*.

Follow-Up Letters

A letter following an interview should always be sent within 24 hours—mail or e-mail is fine. I call a thank-you note a *focus letter* because in a thank-you note you can further influence the employer by showing that you heard and thought about some of the items discussed at the interview.

You can also illustrate how your talents can help solve some of the problems or meet some of the goals of the company that you learned about during the meeting, such as tidbits about the interviewer (a golfer, bowler, swimmer, tennis player, pianist, a rock and roll fan), new product launches, new projects, company milestones, the interviewer's career path to management, same alma mater, anything else in common? Whatever indicates that you were an attentive listener can be important to allude to in the focus letter. Additionally, you can tactfully add anything valuable about yourself that you might have forgotten at the interview. (See the sample letter below.)

July 29, 20xx

Ms. Bettina Simmons
Executive Vice President
Ionit, Incorporated
554½ Second Avenue, Suite 237A
New York, NY 103xx

Dear Ms. Simmons:

What a pleasure it was to meet you earlier today! I must say I was very flattered that you extended our meeting from the half-hour we had planned to almost 90 minutes. I certainly appreciate your generosity in sharing your ideas about the company and acquainting me with Bob Delts and the others on the team.

Something in our exchange rang a bell for me, and I just thought I'd share it with you. You mentioned that Ionit would be opening an office soon in Minneapolis and that a senior vice president would be needed there for a time to get the January product launch off to a roaring start.

Sample Letter to Follow an Interview

I didn't mention it at the interview, but I happen to have experience with the marketing of D-Trek 5001 type software. I planned and executed a similar launch in my prior position at 4Tell, and I ended up saving the company almost a quarter of a million dollars by incorporating a direct-mailing component into the project.

I believe that I have the wisdom gained from experience to be instrumental in the same kinds of substantial savings for Ionit, and, if hired, I plan to present several scenarios that I think would be beneficial for the Minneapolis effort. I also am free to relocate there until the product is off to a healthy introduction.

Again, thank you for your time in the interview. If you have any questions I can answer or if you would like to see a sample proposal for my idea on the Minneapolis project, I would be happy to oblige.

Regards,

Han Nguyen
(212) 883-xxxx
h_nguyenvp@juno.com

Sample Letter to Follow an Interview (Continued)

Every time you send a piece of written communication to a hiring manager, follow it up within one to three days of its expected arrival with a phone call. Conversely, *every* time you talk to a hiring manager by phone, follow it up with a quick letter or e-mail.

This letter-phone-letter approach has been proven to work (as long as you have permission from the hiring manager to keep checking back every several days). By keeping your application at the forefront of the decision maker's mind, you are the first one she or he thinks of when an opening occurs.

Those of you who are planning on becoming entrepreneurs will most likely not need a résumé *or* an interview. Instead, you'll be in charge! The next chapter will get you started on your path to starting your own business.

CHAPTER 9

For Entrepreneurial Spirits

Are You an Entrepreneur?

Although 80 percent of people in America say that they have thought about running their own business, thinking about it and actually doing it are two very different things. You may indeed have had some fears about choosing another profession and becoming part of a preexisting organization, but you may find that your uncertainties increase when you think about going out all on your own.

The best ways to fend off those kinds of fears are with facts—facts that you assess for yourself and objective data about the nature of being a business owner. Those facts are exactly the ones we'll examine in this chapter.

There are decidedly many good reasons to run your own business or become a consultant, but for every plus, there is also a minus. Anyone who owns his or her own business or consulting practice will tell you that there are both assets and liabilities in being your own boss.

The purpose of this chapter is not to tell you how to set up and run your own enterprise. That would be the subject of a whole book! Rather, it is to assist you in figuring out the important question of whether or not you want to take on the responsibilities of being an entrepreneur or independent consultant and to point out to you the best resources you can access for free to answer all the questions you have about starting your own company or consultancy.

Pros and Cons of Starting Your Own Business

If you feel strongly that owning your own business or being a consultant is your authentic calling, then *nothing else*—not a personality or an aptitude test, not a friend or family member, not a banker or financial advisor, not a career counselor, maybe not even your own spouse or significant other—will be able to stop you.

That's good because even if you have all the support the world can offer, *you will still be challenged repeatedly* to demonstrate a deep desire to succeed under just about any circumstance if your business is to survive and thrive.

> **Yes, there are pros and cons, but your own gut feeling—your own thoughtful analysis—is what must guide you in making this important choice.**

The lists below show some of the advantages and disadvantages of owning your own business. Read them carefully and begin to formulate your own ideas about your entrepreneurial fitness.

Possible Advantages

- You are in charge.

- You create your own schedule. When you're more established, you may be able to work fewer and/ or more flexible hours. You may even be able to work from home.

Possible Disadvantages

- You must assume 100% responsibility for both successes and failures. This does not necessarily mean *personal* legal responsibility if you choose a corporation as a business structure.

- You may work up to 100 hours per week getting started. You are basically "on call" all the time until you hire someone else to help you or you "automate" your business to run itself.

Possible Advantages	**Possible Disadvantages**
• Your income is limited only by your ability to make a profit for yourself.	• Your income may differ considerably from month to month and year to year.
• You can choose with whom you want to work.	• Employees and even business partners can present problems such as cheating, lack of motivation, or legal or disciplinary issues. (You can hire an on-call human resources consultant to help you with employee issues.)
• You have almost unlimited creativity.	• People with money to loan you may not agree with your creative ideas. You must persevere to find funding or fund your business yourself.
• You can choose the image you wish to portray to the public.	• Some advertising, marketing, and public relations efforts can be expensive. You may need to market yourself constantly to stay competitive.
• Most small businesses, consultants, and corporations enjoy considerable tax benefits.	• None.

Consider carefully whether the advantages are *attractive* enough for you to take some major risks along the way in order to achieve your desired result. Also note whether or not you think you can *persevere* in the face of some of the disadvantageous aspects of running your own enterprise or being a private consultant.

Self-Assessment

The following pages present a test, or *self-assessment,* to help you think about some of the skills and personality traits that might be beneficial to you while you face the ups and downs of entrepreneurship or consultancy.

> **The test results should be construed not as the
> final answer as to whether you should make
> the choice to own your own business, but
> rather as a tool to show you the strengths
> you already possess and the areas you may want
> to improve on. It's up to you to assess the
> results, and it's up to you to decide whether
> owning your own business is really right for you
> at this time in your life.**

Remember, both the self-assessment and the chart are not meant to be scientifically conclusive in any way but are instead tools for research and self-awareness. The assessment is best used if you put it into action.

For example, if you find that you have several areas that need improvement, you can learn them from a book, a correspondence course, an online class, or perhaps a night class. You can even hire an executive coach to get you up to par on your leadership abilities and required skills.

Before we go any further, let's see how you match up to some of the classic traits, tasks, and obstacles inherent in the process of running a business or a private consulting practice.

Please answer the following questions by putting a check in the box to the left of the statement if the statement is true for you. You cannot "fail" the test, so take a moment to reflect and answer each question as accurately as possible.

❑ I'm a risk taker.

❑ I am very independent minded.

❑ I am results oriented.

❑ I consistently demand the best from myself.

❑ I am comfortable researching or asking others about things I don't know.

❑ I trust action more than analysis.

❑ I can overcome failure and recommit my energies to success.

❏ I am sometimes impatient for results.

❏ I am good at managing money.

❏ I plan and use my time carefully.

❏ Sometimes I'm a bit of a perfectionist.

❏ I consider myself a very hard worker.

❏ I am ambitious.

❏ I have a vision of how I want things to be, and I follow through until my vision is realized.

❏ I am a leader.

❏ I will do almost anything if it's ethical to attain my goals.

❏ I dislike being supervised.

❏ I dislike routine tasks.

❏ I am determined to win.

❏ I dislike being on someone else's timetable.

❏ The goals I set for myself are higher than average.

❏ I am confident.

❏ I am able to make on-the-spot decisions.

❏ I like myself.

❏ I am competitive.

❏ I have integrity.

❏ I do not need a salary; I prefer my earnings to be unlimited.

❏ I am willing to work up to 80 or 100 hours a week to get my business off the ground.

❏ I realize that I may have to "wear many hats"—even some that I don't like such as bookkeeper, marketing director, secretary, CEO, or receptionist—when my business first gets started.

❏ I see failure as a learning experience.

❏ I am good at persuading people to see my way.

❏ I'm a creative problem solver.

❏ I am not afraid to seek expert advice from others.

❏ Sometimes other people think I am very opinionated.

❏ I am comfortable with periods of uncertainty, including financial uncertainty.

❏ I believe in myself.

If you checked at least 50 percent (about 16) of the items on the above assessment, you probably have what it takes to own your own business or be a consultant *if and only if* you are *willing to grow* and seek help for the areas that need improvement.

If you got a lower score, it doesn't mean you can't be an entrepreneur. You might interpret a lower score as feedback that you have a couple of areas that will require extra focus.

Now, analyze what you've checked off. What areas do you think are your best assets? Which ones might need some extra attention?

❑ Self-confidence

❑ Risk taking

❑ Leadership

❑ Tolerance for uncertainty

❑ Tolerance for an uneven income

❑ Seeking out new knowledge and expert advice

❑ Motivation and ambition

❑ High self-esteem

If you're going to turn a weakness into a strength, you've got to commit it to writing and make a plan, just as you would do with any other goal. Either fill in the blanks below as a reminder to yourself or use one of the goal templates from Chapter 6 to note your plans. Either way, *develop a plan* and stick to it. If you find you're off course, adjust and try a new tactic or ask others for their feedback.

The one chief area of improvement that I will attack in the next month:

_____

_____

Here is my plan of attack:

_____

_____

Perhaps the first thing to think about when your business is in the planning phase is deciding what kind of business you want and what structure you want the business to have. Before you write a formal business plan, take a moment and think about the answers to the following questions:

1. Will you sell a product or service or both?

   _____

   _____

2. What kind of products will you sell?

   _____

   _____

3. What kind of service will you sell?

   _____

   _____

4. Why will your product or service be more attractive to customers or clients than what your competitors may provide?

   _____

   _____

5. Who will be your customers or clients? Ages? Gender? Financial status? Geographic area? Educational background? Special interests? Marital status?

   _____

   _____

6. What "problem" will your product or service solve for individuals, families, communities, and the environment? The world?

   _____

   _____

7. Will you start a business from scratch, build a consulting practice, buy an existing business, or own and operate a franchise?

   _____

   _____

8. Where, ideally, would the home base of your business be located? Office? Factory? Laboratory? Warehouse? Outdoors? Your home? On the Internet?

_____

_____

These informal questions will get you started in thinking about some of the basic components of your business plan, which I recommend that you write with the assistance of a class or mentor from the Small Business Administration (SBA), a government organization that offers free assistance to entrepreneurs.

The U.S. Small Business Administration

Keeping all of these things in mind, your next step is to get in touch with the Small Business Administration (SBA) near you or go to its Web site, www.sba.gov, and begin to explore some of the state-of-the-art, *no-cost* offerings for entrepreneurs. Make an appointment with one of the mentors, and start writing a formal business plan.

> **The Small Business Administration is a nationwide network of U.S. government offices dedicated to helping budding entrepreneurs like you in all aspects of getting started in a successful venture.**

There are SBA offices, where you can have access to in-person classes and advisement, in most medium to large cities. If you would prefer to take advantage of online training via the Internet, that too is available. The SBA's information is absolutely invaluable, and it may be just as good as you would receive in a more expensive, privately run business program. The SBA also supplies easy access to small-business loans underwritten by the government and/or cooperating banks. Here are some of the seminars and services offered by the organization:

- Determining a legal structure for your business—sole proprietorship, partnership, limited liability corporation (LLC), S corporation, or C corporation.

- Buying an existing business or starting a franchise.

- All aspects of business funding—government funding, private-bank loans, credit considerations, angel investors, venture capital firms, self-generated funding, or equity funding.

- Financial management—bookkeeping for small businesses, financial forecasting, understanding financial statements, and accounting and taxation issues.

- Marketing and promotion—the latest, most efficient, and most cost-effective means to market, advertise, and promote your new business. In concert with the Small Business Development Centers www.sba.gov/sbdc/ (with links on the SBA Web site), they provide instruction on how to write a marketing plan for your business.

- Liaison to SCORE, a group of retired executives who have already had the experience of building and running one or more successful businesses (www.score.org). The SBA offers one-on-one mentorship to new entrepreneurs from people in the community who have already assembled successful companies.

A Practice Business Plan

If you'd like to practice formulating a business plan, there is an excellent template for doing so on *Microsoft PowerPoint*, which is part of the *Microsoft Office* computer program. You can also find business plan templates at a very reasonable price at most computer software or office supply stores. To get to the *Microsoft PowerPoint template*, which guides you with written prompts all the way through a business plan and marketing plan:

1. Open the *PowerPoint* program.
2. Click on the choice marked Design Template.
3. Click on the Presentations tab.

4. Click on the Business Plan icon.

5. Later, if you'd also like to write a separate marketing plan, click on the Marketing Plan icon.

All the transferable-skills exercises you've done in previous chapters can be put to use here. There are many skills you may have developed over a lifetime in both work- and non-work-related settings that can be of value in starting your own business. Even if you've never been a CEO, you may have been captain of the volleyball team! You'll need essentially the same abilities for planning strategies, communicating effectively, and being at the helm of the ship when you're in your new office as when you were on the courts. If you've never managed a business or budget before, just think about what it takes to run a household or maintain a car—budgeting, cleaning, maintenance.

Many of the things you presently just take for granted will be the recipe you'll need for success when you're running your own business. It may be a little scary at first, but there is an interesting paradox about the emotion we call fear. When we experience fear in our bodies, we feel an elevated heartbeat, increased rate of breathing, and a rush of blood to our extremities. The emotion of excitement causes exactly the same reaction in our bodies as does fear. Have you ever considered that your fear may *actually* be excitement? I challenge you to consider this conundrum! Remember your first date? Was that fear, or was it excitement? A little of both perhaps? Welcome to the world of running your own business!

Being your own boss can be one of the most rewarding choices that you can make in a lifetime. If you are willing to take the challenge along with the rewards, the sky's the limit!

CHAPTER 10

Loving Your New Career

Congratulations! You've applied the fearless career change strategies and you have started your new job or business. You've faced your fears and overcome them, or you've found a powerful motivation to move through them. You've set new goals, anticipated the obstacles, and made plans to get past them. You have some superfast methods for bringing mere fantasies to full fruition.

Work is no longer a domain dominated by fear; it is a playground on which to stretch your limbs, a blank slate on which to sketch a brand-new blueprint. Now that you're on your way, it's time to learn not just how to *keep* a job or get promotions but how to really *thrive* in your new position or profession.

> **When you are truly expressing your special talents and living your "authentic calling," a job is not just a job. It's a mission, designated to fulfill a "higher purpose."**

Indeed, answering your authentic calling becomes a *mission*, a bold adventure and a testing ground for newfound courage. Your task now is *not* just to perform job duties or to prevent yourself from being fired or going bankrupt (although preventing either of those eventualities is a good place to start).

If, then, you *are* on a mission, what is it? Well, it is certainly something that transcends just a job title or the name of your new business. There are lots of people out there merely doing job duties and trying not to get fired.

> *Living with the mantle of your authentic calling will mean that you transcend routine, prescribed "duties" and go beyond "playing it safe." It means thinking big.*

Why would you start your own business if you just hope to break even or make enough money to get by? Surely with the special talents you bring to your new career or business you can hope for and even *demand* much more.

Again, what is *your* mission? It could be making a million dollars or hundreds of millions of dollars. It's been done before, and someone, somewhere will do it again. Your mission could be to become the finest and the best-known practitioner in your field. It may be to produce the most modern, efficient technology of its kind. Your mission could well be to relieve the world of suffering by making it a safer, more beautiful, more prosperous and peaceful place to live.

In Chapter 4, I briefly mentioned a woman who started a group focused on women's financial issues who charged $10 per person for a six-week program. At the time, she didn't know that disseminating her ideas was her authentic calling, but look what happened: She *started small* and *followed a path that beckoned to her.* Now, she has multiple best-selling books, has appeared on national television, is enjoying a syndicated magazine column, and earns large profits from the seminars she teaches.

What started as a job in which she was essentially earning less than $1 per hour ultimately became her mission. Her special purpose was not seeking the approval of others, settling for security, or staying out of the line of fire. It was her mission to make the world a better place by helping women to control and maximize their financial lives.

Her mission put her work into a much *larger* context than that of just making another dollar (although, as a result of following her calling, she is now a wealthy woman).

Sample Mission Statement

In the seminars I teach, participants write their own mission statements. I'd like you to do the same, because no job is perfect all of the time. You are sure to have ups and downs in your career, but when you've committed to a mission—to something greater than any one of the individual tasks you perform daily—even unpleasant tasks seem worthwhile. You'll be reminded, by recalling your mission, that even the darkest of times cannot endure when your higher purpose is guiding your efforts.

> **Writing your mission statement may very well be the most important fearless career change exercise, one that will shape the long-term character of both your career and your life.**

Here are some examples of mission statements:

1. To provide exceptional quality ergonomic devices and training by maintaining the highest manufacturing standards and teaching methods so that people at work will experience less stress, more ease, greater efficiency, and better health and will live longer, more productive lives.

2. To give back to the community by creating a corporation that sells discount goods and services on the Internet and contributes 30 percent of all profits to charities and community concerns so that customers get items and services at fair prices and needy, sick, undereducated, and disadvantaged people can lead more happy and successful lives.

3. To lead my company to be the No. 1 manufacturer of routers in the world by practicing the highest of human ethics and morals in all of my personal and business affairs so that all of my employees will experience a safe, secure, equitable, and harmonious workplace, and the company will make profits of over $200 million annually.

Your Own Mission Statement

You may observe that the structure of the example mission statements is relatively similar. They all begin by answering the question, "What am I doing?" Then they move on to, "How am I doing it?" And, finally, they ask, "Why am I doing it?"

It takes serious thought, focused concentration, and honest reflection on the most important aspects of work and our *most essential purpose* in life to write a meaningful mission statement that will actually *serve to guide* our actions and emotions. Using the three examples of the mission statements above, I would like you, carefully and respectfully, to compose your own credo.

People (and companies) with a mission are motivated within by a strong desire to succeed. They maintain a commitment to morals and ethical values, and they are less subject to flap with the winds of public opinion or transitory fads. Your mission statement helps to solidify your new vocation, to brand it not just with things you are "good" at doing but with things that are deeply and intrinsically good.

Your statement does not have to reflect that you want to save the whole world, although if you feel that's your authentic calling, that *is* what you should write. Your mission statement is about *you* and your *relationship* to the career and life you want.

It need be only two or three sentences, but it must serve the purpose of inspiring you to the apex of your abilities and encouraging you through difficult or fearful times. The statement you write today may very well evolve into something else tomorrow or a year from now. That's fine. A mission statement is a "living" thing. That means that it grows and transforms with time. Please write your own mission statement for today on the lines below:

_____

_____

_____

_____

_____

_____

By overcoming your fears and creating a better career for yourself, you've crafted a better life. When your life aligns with its true purpose, you can't help but make the world a better place and set an example for everyone you meet. Your new vocation may not be glamorous or even heroic. It may be very ordinary. Like the man who repairs shoes.

Every time I go to my shoemaker and he hands me my finished shoes, I notice his unmistakable pride in the work he has done. It is as if, by simply shining shoes, replacing heels, and fixing insoles, he is performing a work of art. He looks very happy to me. He is a man with a mission, and though I don't pretend to know what it is, it is palpable. This man does his work with a kind of integrity that is possible only when answering to an authentic calling. When I leave his store, I'm not just carrying a bag of shoes. His happiness goes with me.

INDEX

ABOUT THE AUTHOR

 **Marky Stein** has been a career coach and public speaker for 20 years, working with professionals from more than 75 Fortune 500 companies. She currently runs a private career-coaching practice in Northern California. Stein is the online job-search, career, and interview expert at Monster.com and has written numerous articles for Careerjournal.com. Visit her at www.markystein.com.

Marky Stein is a career coach and the author of:

Fearless Interviewing:
How to Win the Job by Communicating With Confidence
(McGraw-Hill 2003)

Fearless Career Change:
The Fast Track to Success in a New Field
(McGraw-Hill 2005)

Fearless Résumés:
The Proven Method for Getting a Great Job Fast
(McGraw-Hill 2010)

She also owns and operates a
private career-coaching practice in California.
Visit her at www.markystein.com